Pra

3,000 Mile

MW01104955

"Two narrators, one voice. In fiction, it'd be a problem. In a true story, it's fascinating. In a true love story, it's perfect. No matter what they're saying, Duane and Selena speak the same language: warm, funny, candid, and familiar to readers as old friends—people we've known ourselves and been rooting for all along."

—Jennifer Quist, award-winning author of internationally acclaimed novel *Love Letters of the Angels of Death*

"*3,000 Miles to Eternity* is a creative read that will capture your heart. It's a tale of reality, faith, hope, and technology! Life is a journey. How wonderful it is when it's filled with people who love us for who we are and who inspire us to become better."

—Trina Boice, author of *Base Hits and Home Run Relationships* and *My Future's So Bright I Gotta Wear Shades*

"Successful relationships often come in different ways. Duane and Selena have given us a delightful, true account of one such unusual path. Love does find a way. I'd greatly recommend this to those who have begun to wonder if their heart will ever find a place. Ultimately, this is an account of hope and faith—learning to trust that sometimes the road less traveled may be the one most blessed. It's also a reminder to the romantic in all of us that a loving Heavenly Father has a plan for us that is often a much different and better plan than we could ever create for ourselves!"

—Kevin Hinckley, author of *The Husband Whisperer* and *Habits, Hurts, and Hangups: 12 Steps to Heal the Natural Man*

To Deborah Ida-Belle —
Thank you for
your support. Sure
hope you enjoy our
story — you'll have
fun guessing some
of the characters :-

Duane ♥'s Selena

3,000 MILES TO *Eternity*

{ A TRUE INTERNET *love story* }

DUANE & SELENA PANNELL

CFI
An Imprint of Cedar Fort, Inc.
Springville, Utah

Disclaimer: Though this is a true story, some names have been changed.

ISBN 13: 978-1-4621-1631-7

Published by CFI, an imprint of Cedar Fort, Inc.
2373 W. 700 S., Springville, UT 84663
Distributed by Cedar Fort, Inc., www.cedarfort.com

LIBRARY OF CONGRESS CATALOGING-IN-PUBLICATION DATA

Pannell, Duane, 1961- author.
3,000 miles to eternity / Duane and Selena Pannell.
    pages cm
Summary: The story of how Duane and Selena Pannell met via the Internet told through a selection of their diary entries and e-mail exchanges.
ISBN 978-1-4621-1631-7 (perfect bound : alk. paper)
1. Pannell, Duane, 1961- 2. Pannell, Selena, 1963- 3. Mormons--Biography. I. Pannell, Selena, 1963- author. II. Title.

BX8693.P36 2015
289.3092'2--dc23
[B]

                            2015018500

Cover design by Shawnda T. Craig
Cover design © 2015 Lyle Mortimer
Edited and typeset by Kevin Haws

Printed in the United States of America

10 9 8 7 6 5 4 3 2 1

Printed on acid-free paper

Dedication

To our friend Paige, without whom there would be no love story, and Mom Margaret, the best cheerleader and referee that two sweethearts ever had on their team.

Contents

{ Part 1 }

♥

Duane's Journal
January 17, 1992

I've been talking to Mormon missionaries for nearly a week now and I've learned some interesting things about them and their beliefs. I have asked them, like I have the others that I talk to, to give me the basics of their beliefs. The fundamentals. It seems that many of the things that they believe are not unusual to Christians, but some are. Interestingly, though, they've suggested something that none of the other representatives from other churches have ever advised. One of the young men told me in the beginning of our conversations to ask God if what they are teaching me is true, to ask with a real desire to know and understand. That's good stuff, and I am doing just that.

It occurs to me today that I have learned two things about their beliefs that have left impressions on me, things I can't stop thinking about. I didn't find it necessary to pray and ask about them because the moment I heard these things I felt certain that they were true. The moment I heard them, I felt warm and happy, as if I had discovered something as certain as gravity.

The first is one I've never heard in any Christian belief. Mormons believe that our spirits and our bodies were not born at the same time. They believe that we lived as literal spirit children of God before we came here. Hearing this bit of doctrine instantly answered questions that I have had all my life. Why am I so different than the rest of my family? Why does God love us? What is the purpose of our lives? I think that believing and understanding this will help me in so many aspects of my life, and I'll be pondering it for a long time to come.

The second thing they taught was something that I have only heard people say as wishful thinking or illustrative of a deep commitment that they feel for their spouse, as in, "I will love you for eternity." But nowhere have I heard it expressed as church doctrine. Mormons believe that a husband and wife relationship does not have to end at death, that they can be married for both time and eternity. The moment I heard this doctrine, I knew it to be true and I knew it to be something that I want in my life.

Marie and I did not go into marriage with the right understanding or circumstances. We had lived together for three years before we married, and when we did marry it was with the understanding that when it wasn't working for us anymore, we would just divorce. We have not treated each other very well, and our lack of commitment to one another has been apparent in the problems that we have had. Now that I have completely given up drugs and alcohol and I'm getting my life together, I'm seeing the world a little different. It started with this feeling that I'm being called to the ministry, but there is so much more that I want for my life and my family. I want a real marriage like the "new and everlasting covenant" that the missionaries described. I think that Marie and I could have that if we both want it enough to work for it.

I have wandered through life with no real direction. I have always known the creature comfort things that I wanted out of life, but I've never really thought about my part as a husband and father and what it should look like if I'm actually doing it right. This is an exciting time for me. I've learned a lot from the Mormon missionaries and all the others who have come to teach about their religion, but just these two beliefs alone are golden, and I think that they are going to take me a long way in realizing the goals that I am setting for myself. I could build an entire ministry out of eternal marriage and premortal life!

Selena's Journal
March 15, 1992

"Marriage is perhaps the most vital of all the decisions and has the most far-reaching effects, for it has to do not only with immediate happiness, but also with eternal joys. It affects not only the two people involved, but also their families and particularly their children and their children's children down through the many generations" (Spencer W. Kimball, "Oneness in Marriage," *Ensign*, March 1977).

The truth is that you marry those you date. I remember being taught this in Mutual. I never thought about it much, though the prospect of marrying a worthy young man in the Church was not a reality. At least not where I lived, and more importantly not in my mind. I couldn't even imagine such a future.

In our high school of six hundred kids, five of us were members, all of whom were girls. Traveling to stake dances an hour away increased the odds mathematically, but it turned out the people dancing generally knew each other. I did a lot of sitting at stake dances. Back then I was too shy and insecure to put myself "out there." This would be to my detriment.

High school was painful. I didn't smoke, drink, or make out. I had one date in high school, an experience that couldn't have ended soon enough. My date made me carry the cake (that his mom made) into a football party! So that definitely did not help my reputation. But like most people, I survived, graduated, and got a job fresh out of high school. It was a time for new beginnings.

I was naïve and inexperienced, so when an older, more experienced and handsome young man started paying me attention, I was flattered, and we began dating. He was not a member of the Church. So today, as I sit and ponder these things, I am reminded again of the words of a prophet: "In selecting a companion for life and for eternity, certainly the most careful planning and thinking and praying and fasting should be done to be sure that of all the decisions, this one must not be wrong" (Spencer W. Kimball, "Oneness in Marriage," Ensign, March 1977).

I deliberately did not pray. I didn't want to know the answer. And I certainly couldn't imagine the future I was choosing. You marry those you date.

Duane's Journal
November 21, 1995

For the past three years, I've gone to Bishop Larsen (and now Bishop Cloe), ready and eager to go to the temple. Three times now I have been told not yet. Both bishops and President Meldrum have told me that it would be better if my wife and I could go to the temple together and that I should just wait a little longer. I don't know how to convey to them that it just isn't going to happen. Marie was sincere in her conversion, and we were baptized together, but she fell away after a few months. She started smoking pot again and now has no interest at all in the Church, or any church.

This week, Marie disappeared for a couple of days. I know that she was on a drug binge of some kind. I did as I usually do and tried to keep things as normal as possible for the kids, but this time I didn't get angry. I prayed about what I should do, I thought about it, and I prayed some more. As I was looking at things on the Internet, I discovered something that I didn't know. If members of the Church have nonmember or inactive spouses, they can still go to the temple if their spouses will give approval in writing. I checked with the bishop and he confirmed this to be true.

When Marie finally came home, she was a wreck, but she was ready for a fight, though. Imagine her surprise when I didn't give her one. I had prepared a letter that simply said she understood my desire to go to the temple and would support me in my decision to go and receive my endowments. I asked her to read it, and if she agreed, to sign it. She did and went to bed. I am amazed at how good I feel about things, considering the past few days. I'm going to the temple!

Selena's Journal
August 21, 1997

Being married to someone who doesn't believe as I do isn't so bad. He loves to watch sports on television and drives a lot for work. He has his interests and I have mine, which mostly center on being a mom. I do things with the kids, including travel without him, because he really doesn't want to have to drive more on his time off. I understand that, but it can be difficult and lonely to do everything by myself when I have a perfectly good husband at home.

And it gets a little crazy packing up all five kids and taking them to Church half an hour away every Sunday by myself. Talks and lessons about eternal marriage are still a little tender, but I am the first one to point out to anyone who is wondering that I knew I was marrying a nonmember and, while church is not his "thing," he doesn't stand in the way of me participating with the kids. I would rather have him be honest about his disinterest than go for the wrong reasons. I have settled into a routine that has become my "normal."

Today at a stake function, my former Mutual president told me that the Church has just changed its guidelines and, as a temple-worthy adult, even though I am married to a nonmember, I can attend the temple!

This is good news, but it means having to receive Steven's written permission. And once I go to the temple, I will be making covenants that will affect the clothing that I wear, bringing a new standard of modesty to my dress—not to mention the unmentionables. I'm stressing about asking him and am a little anxious about what it will mean for me too.

Duane's Journal
June 5, 1998

I have suffered from depression my whole life. Even as a child, I had periodic episodes where I retreated into myself, like going into a cave. My memories of those times are like gloomy black-and-white movies. As I got older, I found ways of avoiding the painful feelings associated with depression by medicating myself with drugs and alcohol. Of course, this led to worse and more complicated problems.

For nearly seven years now, I've been clean and sober. I have not had a bout with depression for well over five years. Until now, I was convinced that I was cured. I have been sure that my conversion to the Church, my born-again experience, had washed me clean and cured me. In my earliest memories, I had never gone more than a few months without that dark cloud, and it has now been years. Apparently, I'm not cured. For whatever reason, I've had a nice, long break from depression, but it's now back and as bad as I ever remember it being.

I don't want to be around people. I don't want to read, watch television, or listen to the radio. Everything seems hopeless. I don't eat or sleep. I'm miserable, but I can't turn it all off like I used to. I have three children who need me to be a dad, and I can't get away from that.

I love Dan, Renee, and Harry Dutton and my dear friend Noah McDaniel. We've worked together for a couple of years now, and they have all expressed concern for my obvious problem. Renee said to me the other day, "You know, Duane, we don't just consider you an employee; you're our friend, and we care about you." She hugged me and I cried. I didn't know what to say—I just cried. I'm on salary, and they can ill-afford too many extra expenses in their small business, but they gave me a couple of days off to work some things out. In the way of friends, I am a rich man.

Selena's Journal
September 9, 1997

When Mom and I drove over the last hill into Cardston and I saw the temple glowing in the dusk, I started to cry. It felt like I was coming home! I hadn't expected to feel such overwhelming emotion at just the prospect of finally being able to participate in the sacred ordinances of the temple. For so long, I had told myself I was fine without this blessing in my life.

I finally worked up the courage to approach the subject with Steven. He was not interested in writing me a letter giving his approval, so I wrote it for him and, thankfully, he signed it. So here I am! I was able to go through the temple with my little sister last night. It was our first time and we were treated like princesses by the angelic temple matrons. It was a beautiful and peaceful experience.

So "Uncle Louie" (as Mom calls the adversary) must not have been too happy with my decision and tormented me in my dreams all night. We stayed overnight with friends, so I asked for and received a priesthood blessing this morning from Brother Lybbert. He was the first member of the Church our family knew and his good example made a lasting impression on my mom. It was comforting to feel peace flood back into my heart.

I went back to the temple this morning. This time I went on behalf of Grandma, who died when I was a few months old. It made sense to share this wonderful experience with her.

And later, Arlene and Walter were sealed to each other and their beautiful children. I was so happy for their family and grateful to be there with them. I didn't expect the comments made to me afterward, though. Some people came up to me and said it must be so hard for me to be there because I didn't have an eternal marriage of my own. They gave me little pep talks, reminding me that I just need to remain faithful and Heavenly Father will bless me. I'm still baffled because it honestly didn't occur to me to feel sorry for myself.

Duane's Journal

June 6, 1998

I think I know why I've allowed myself to spiral down and out of control. I have thought for years now that Marie and I are heading toward divorce. We're going in two different directions, with different values and different goals. Things that are happening in our home are not good for our kids, and I believe that it would be better for all of us if Marie and I parted ways.

A little over a month ago, Marie disappeared for about four days. When she finally returned home, I was ready to make my stand. I told her we were done and I wanted her to pack her things and leave. She cried and begged, and I was a stone. I had made up my mind and I was not going to change it. I was ripping the Band-Aid off.

Marie did leave. She went into drug rehab. She actually went into the same program that I went into back in 1990. I filed for divorce and planned that she would not come back here when she finished her program, but all that has changed and she has returned home.

The day before Marie was to finish her rehab, Bishop Cloe called and asked me what was going on with her after this. After I told him of our plans, he asked me a question that I didn't expect. He asked, "Have you considered bringing her home, forgiving her, and giving her another chance? After all, she is making a sincere effort to change. I'm not saying as your bishop that you have to do this, but have you considered it?"

I was quick to tell him that I wasn't going to change my mind but I said I would think about it. Thinking about it turned into praying about it all night, and by morning I knew I would be changing my plans.

Marie has been doing mostly well. She's doing all the right things, and we are getting along okay. Maybe I feel guilty. I was ready to begin my new life without her and now I'm disappointed that it's not going to happen. A lot of really bad stuff was going on before she stopped using drugs. What if I can't get over that? Another thought that I can't get past is the understanding that God has forgiven me for a lot of things, especially when I was beginning my recovery from addiction—how could I do any less for my wife?

Bishop Cloe arranged a meeting for me with Dr. Dennison. He's a member of our stake presidency and a psychologist. He's a good man. I like him a lot. I am hoping for the best because I can't stay in this constant state of depression. I need some relief.

Duane's Journal
June 8, 1998

I hate the way I feel. I'm sure that the experience that I had today was important and significant, but my mind is so depressed that I can't appreciate it. I went to see Dr. Dennison over in Radford. The visit was just like I thought it would be. He's a kind and smart man. His teddy bear–like features not only put me at ease, but also made me feel safe. I really needed a talk like this. He wants me to take an antidepressant. I'm reluctant to do so, but he's convinced me it won't hurt me—as a person prone to addiction—and this has gone on so long that I really must do something.

Dr. Dennison told me that the Church did not expect people to stay in bad or abusive marriages, and, all things considered, if I decided to go through with the divorce, it would not be an issue as far as the Church was concerned.

I told him about my experience after talking to Bishop Cloe, how I prayed all night and felt that forgiving her and bringing her home was what I was supposed to do.

He asked me if I thought that this decision had anything to do with my depression, and I had to admit that it did. Saying out loud that I had been looking forward to moving on with my life without her and that I was disappointed it wasn't going to happen, made me feel even guiltier than just thinking it. Again, though, Dr. Dennison put me at ease, and I'm glad that I finally said it.

He asked, "So you're forgiving your wife and working on repairing your marriage?"

I said, "Yes."

He then said, "Forgiving your wife means that you will put the past behind you. *Truly* forgiving her means that you never bring up the bad stuff—like in the heat of an argument."

I nodded and said, "Yes, I know."

He said, "You know, she may go to Church with you for a while, but it may not last, and she may never decide to go with you to the temple. Are you going to be okay with that?"

I nodded again and said, "Yes, I understand. I'm not taking this lightly and I fully intend to do my best to forgive her and try to make everything work."

Dr. Dennison was just a couple of feet away from me in a rolling desk chair. He reached out, grabbed my chair, and pulled himself in close to me. He was face-to-face with me when he said something that had all the looks and feel of a prophecy: "Duane, I believe that you're sincere. I believe that you understand forgiveness and are willing to extend it to your wife to help her get through this and repair your marriage."

He was staring into my eyes. I felt like looking away but I listened. "I promise if you will do this, remain true to your word, and really forgive her that if it doesn't work out, one day you will stand with the Lord and you will look out over a multitude of worthy sisters. You will interview them one by one and find that one who will go with you and be sealed to you as your wife in the temple of God."

I don't know what this means. He was so intense, and it leads me to more guilty feelings. Immediately after he said that, I could only think, *Oh, great. Finally on the other side of the veil, after I'm dead and gone, I'll finally have the experience of a real marriage.* Because it did sound like a direct message from God, I feel ungrateful and unworthy, and maybe even a little more depressed.

Selena's Journal

February 23, 2000

Well, I did it. I left. I grabbed a laundry basket, threw in some clothes, and I left. I drove around some, and then parked in the garage and slept in the car for the rest of the night. Things have gotten progressively worse in my marriage, especially since my miscarriage and subsequent depression.

Depression is a weird beast because it's all too real, but nobody else can see it. I remember what I used to be like and what was important to me, but now it's like I'm two separate people. I can see the other me far off in the distance across the Grand Canyon. I can see her, but I can't get to her and I'm not sure it even matters. I don't remember what it was like to be her. We aren't connected anymore.

The only positive thing I've done during this surreal experience is hike a lot. I've been hiking five or six miles a day, so I look good, probably better than I have in years. The problem with that is Steven doesn't know I haven't shed a tear in two years or that I feel indifferent about anything that should be important to me. He doesn't know I don't really care whether I live or die. And so he accused me, again, of being selfish and faking this depression.

That wasn't what made me leave. This was yet another argument among many in our marriage. It was when he brought the older children downstairs to witness our pathetic inability to communicate at this most critical time in our relationship. Something in me snapped. I knew then and there that they must not ever be subjected to this toxic drama again. I can't do much for them these days, but I can protect them from this.

So I left. But not before Cody said tearfully, "Mom, if you love us, you won't leave." I remember saying to my son (almost a man now), "It's because I love you that I have to leave." His emotion and those words are haunting me, "Mom, if you love us, you won't leave."

Funny thing, I met his dad on this day twenty years ago.

Duane's Journal

June 29, 2000

I am way offtrack. When Marie relapsed and began using drugs again, I was ready with a plan. It was hard, but all things considered, the divorce is as painless as something like this can be. JR, Mallory, and

Emily all seem to be getting along well, and the peace in our home is a great contrast to what we had before. I feel like we mostly do the right things: go to Church, participate in activities, spend quality time together, and so on, but I'm not feeling the way I know that I can feel.

I was at one of Jr.'s baseball games the other day, and Bishop Cloe came up to me and we chatted for a few minutes. He noticed that I wasn't wearing my garments and he asked me about it. I told him that I wasn't really feeling worthy to wear them. He told me to come and see him on Sunday and we would talk, but to put the garments back on for now.

I have one foot in and one foot out. I do know that the Church is true and right, but there's something wrong with me. I actually have feelings of resentment when I listen to talks about eternal marriage and forever families. It just hurts. The only reason that I am participating in the gospel is because I don't want my children to suffer because of my temporary struggles. They need to know that I have a testimony, but how good is it when they see me get up and go to the bathroom to avoid listening to a talk on marriage?

Duane's Journal
July 17, 2000

I've made a grand discovery. My struggles are of my own doing and I've known this for quite some time. I don't pay much attention to what I am doing, so often I make choices that are in direct opposition to my stated goals. This is not the "grand discovery"—I'll get to that in a moment—but it has led me to that discovery.

It occurred to me yesterday that I have not been practicing what I preach. I've been telling my children that they should make it a goal to marry in the temple and do what they must to make that a reality. I'm not a stupid man and I know what I believe, but somehow I failed to realize what I'm doing in my own life. I sincerely believe that people should try to marry someone of their same faith and that they should have more in common than just physical attraction. I have the perfect opportunity to set an example and it's getting away from me.

I was content for a while to not date and just spend time with my kids and their friends. I seem to have gotten over that long spell of depression and I've been really enjoying life, but several months ago,

I started feeling lonely. Even though there are at least half a dozen teenagers around here at any given time, I've felt a bit alone. I needed some adult conversation and company, so I started dating.

There have been several women I have gone out with and, up until recently, that has worked out. I try not to be a jerk, but I have made it clear that I don't want anyone whom I date to meet my kids. I don't want to parade a series of women through my household and complicate my children's lives. If the day comes that I feel there is a future with someone, then I'll be happy to introduce them.

One woman has daughters who go to school with my kids, and that secret lasted about a minute. One woman kicked me to the curb because she believed that I "couldn't possibly be ready for a serious relationship" unless she was able to meet the offspring. The best of all is what happened yesterday. A woman I haven't even had a first date with called me to tell me what nice kids I have. She assured me that she was honoring my wishes because when she met my kids at their school, "They have no idea that we're dating!"

That did it. That got my attention. I haven't been much of a praying man lately, but that moved me to my knees. I cannot teach or expect my children to do the right thing if I'm not willing to do it too. This is what it took to lead me to the "grand discovery."

When I interrupted my dumb behavior with thoughtful prayer, I had some interesting thoughts: What is it about doing the right thing that has made me avoid it? That's easy. I have not been able to picture myself with an LDS woman. There are several examples of women around me who are wonderful; the problem is I can't see any of them married to me. I haven't even thought about what my perfect bride would be like. Does such a woman exist? I am not your average LDS bachelor. Would the kind of woman that I want even want me?

As I pondered these things, I made my way to the computer. I sat looking at it for a few minutes, thinking how there is something that I should do. I wasn't really thinking anything when I typed the words *LDS Singles* in the search thingy.

To my surprise, I got some hits! There are three main sites, and the one with the most members is actually called "LDS Singles." I signed up for that one and spent a little bit of time tonight looking it over. I like this idea.

I have learned over the last few years that part of the secret to getting what you want out of life is to become willing to do what's right. I think that if you show the Lord you want to do the right thing, He will guide you there. I think He's guiding me there.

Selena's Journal
October 11, 2000

I think I'm cracking up . . . again. I don't really want anybody else to know it, because I have weaned myself off antidepressants and the doctor I've seen a couple of times is harder to get in to see than Fort Knox. But today, I appeared to have it altogether as I was imparting wise and positive platitudes to Arlene in light of the bleakness that is currently invading each of our lives. It's strange to have both marriages circling the drain at the same time.

I came home to do a few simple tasks and found I was having to talk myself through them. I'm actually reassuring myself as a tender mother would a tiny, frightened child. I feel like I'm ready to cry, if only I had the energy to do so. I want to curl up in a little ball, become invisible, and just retreat from all the opposition I am facing.

Last night, Steven called, unhappily mentioning that I had bought new clothes. Imagine my nerve, buying a few clothes when I claim to be concerned about my ability to pay my bills and rent. His call was unwelcome and upsetting. Part of me feels guilty about buying the clothes while the other part is reminding me that I take as many extra shifts at the hospital as are offered to me. My walking around looking like a hobo won't do either of us any good. And his parting comment that I'm so happy now is almost laughable.

Because, you see, I'm slowly cracking up. I want to deny this and show that I'm stronger and fully capable of reversing this slide back into the pit. I want to pretend that the pit doesn't exist and that I've never been there before. But I don't have the energy to fool myself, even if I manage to fool others.

I have to do better. I have to feed my body better and my soul. I did get up early this morning (okay, so a nightmare woke me—the last words I heard from a little girl in my nightmare: "Are you homeless?"), so I did some yoga. I hope that helped. I need help. I look so darn fine on the outside, don't I? Looks are deceiving.

Selena's Journal

October 15, 2000

So today I drove to Calgary, met with a high-priced lawyer, and filed for divorce. After eight months of living six houses away from Steven and making too many unsuccessful attempts at reconciliation, I know now that there is no hope for our marriage and somebody has to pull the plug. He will never do it, so it's up to me. The lawyer said she'd do the initial filing but politely told me I can't afford her services and recommended a lawyer she knows in Red Deer. I should have known from her fancy office.

Afterward, I treated myself to a nice dinner in the city and, because I have a few days off from work, I will head to Cardston to stay with Paige, a good friend of mine. We used to go to the same ward a million years ago, but I don't think it will matter that I don't go to Church anymore. She's the kind of friend where we can go for years without seeing each other and pick up right where we left off. And she's fun. Seeing her and her wonderful family will be like a treat after the trauma. I could use a break.

I wonder what Steven will think when he gets the papers. There may be fireworks (and not the happy kind).

Duane's Journal

October 25, 2000

I had breakfast this morning with one of the guys from the bottling plant. We see each other a couple of times a day for a few minutes as I make my way back and forth to my warehouse and we have become friends. Mark is a big man and really opinionated. He probably knows a lot about some things, but I don't think I'm going to take relationship advice from him.

I told him that I had been on the Internet for the past few months looking for a potential wife. He thought that was outrageous. "You know women lie. You're liable to end up with some crazy chick that'll strangle you in your sleep, or . . . or worse, take all your money and leave you with a bunch of kids that don't even belong to you."

I asked, "Well, Mark, how do you suggest I meet a good woman?"

"I met all three of my ex-wives in a bar," he said. "See, that's the best place to look for a woman because when they have a few drinks, they can't keep a secret—they got anything bad, it's comin' out!"

I think I'm just going to stick with my current plan.

Noah is working at Pepsi now too and I see him periodically. I told him about what I've been doing, and he doesn't seem to think that it's such a bad idea.

To me, the advantage of "dating" online is the number of potential women I can meet. I could go to a bar—no scratch that. I'm not ever going to go to bars. I could go to social events where there are more LDS singles to meet or move to Utah so I'm nearer to more of the kind of women I want to meet, but this method is introducing me to hundreds of women in the comfort of my own home. Granted, I have not met anyone yet, but I think my chances are better this way than going to bars. (I wonder why Mark's been divorced three times?)

I could meet a lot of women and spend time going on real dates only to find out why we're not compatible. This way we can screen each other without obligation or an investment of significant time. A great example—and this may sound shallow to some—is that there are women who prefer tall men. I'm 5'6" and a woman who cares about that doesn't even have to bother contacting me. For me, if I'm looking at the photos that a woman has posted of herself that are revealing or skimpy, I have to think that she's probably not the girl for me. I can't think of a better way for people to find compatible dates.

I sound like a commercial for ldssingles.com, but I haven't met anyone yet. I haven't even met anyone I've wanted to go to the next level with—meeting face-to-face. Every night before bed, I sit by myself at the computer, say a prayer, and then go to my homepage. I check for messages and see who's new. I have had a few brief friendships, but no sparks. Part of me is tired of looking and not finding, but another part of me, a stronger part, is just sure that the right girl is out there.

Selena's Journal
October 16, 2000

It's been such a relief having this time with Paige. Lots of laughter and time to talk about everything under the sun. Though when the conversation came around to Church, like I knew it eventually would, she sat facing me on the couch and just couldn't believe I haven't been going "because [my] testimony was always so strong." It made it all the more strange when her friend Donna called out of the blue to tell her that after twenty years of not going to Church (mainly because of anti-Mormon pressure from her family) she was back in. I tried to explain that I still know Heavenly Father lives and I know He's out there, but that He's not talking to me at the moment and when He's ready, He knows where to find me.

It bothered me at first during this depression that I couldn't feel the Spirit, and reading the scriptures left an emptiness because I somehow felt disconnected. Not sure how to describe it exactly. I've had friends tell me I'm not praying hard enough or that I've been the one to close the door on Him. In essence, that I must be doing something wrong.

I'm not so sure I buy this idea. Joseph Smith felt all alone in Liberty Jail. Even the Savior (whom I am not comparing myself to for obvious reasons) cried out, "My God, my God, why hast thou forsaken me?" (Matthew 27:46). If these two valiant spirits, one being the Son of God Himself, could feel *abandoned*—for lack of a better word—then why not me? "Art thou greater than He?" I think not. So on that basis, I take comfort in knowing that Heavenly Father knows what He's doing, even if I feel pretty darn alone right now.

But I digress. Having a weekend away has been a needed break for me. Kristine, another of Paige's friends, came over and all our talking and laughing took a decidedly unexpected turn. Paige was telling her about Donna's news and apparently during the phone call between them, she had also told Paige about being on a single's website. She said she saw Paige's sister Jacqueline on the same site. Paige, with her little "tee-hees," thought it would be great fun to sneak into single's world and have a look at her sister's profile. We tried to do that, but the way the site is set up didn't allow random people to just come on in and gawk. Someone had to sign up.

Well, guess who got this dubious honor? My dear friend Paige said, "Selena, you're almost divorced. You do it." Almost divorced? Are you kidding me? I only filed two days ago! But I was a good sport (sort of) and did the deed. While those two giggled among themselves, I zipped through the "sign up free for seven days" registration. I couldn't help but mutter under my breath at how ridiculous this whole thing was, all these silly people shopping for love. It seemed kind of pathetic and made me want to gag. As I was grumbling, Paige and Kristine were having great laughs at my expense and my obvious discomfort with the whole crazy idea.

And so we entered the forbidden zone, wandering around singles' world and peeking here and there. Satisfied that we'd stealthily invaded Jacquie's privacy and seen all there was to see, we signed off. This little adventure, however, has not changed my mind.

I've decided I will never marry again, ever, under any circumstances. And I will definitely not be wearing a ring, the symbol of bondage. I know it sounds harsh, but the truth is, I honestly don't believe a man is capable of cherishing a woman, not even the one he has chosen to be by his side through thick and thin. I have no frame of reference for that kind of loyalty, what with Dad's serial infidelity and similar attitudes of the few key men in my life. And when my uncle left my aunt after more than twenty years of marriage, well, that shook my world. She was the perfect wife as far as I could tell. What chance does an imperfect girl like me have if someone like her is unceremoniously discarded after almost three decades?

I confess I have wondered secretly about the point of me being so faithful all these years, hauling five children by myself to Church thirty miles away every single Sunday. I've been as active and participating as someone in a part-member home can be. Did Heavenly Father even notice any of that?

But I'm not going to think about that now. Tomorrow is my last day here. We're going to have a picnic after they get home from Church. I wonder how my little chicks are doing. It's so good to get away, but I can't wait to see their sweet faces when I get home!

Selena's Journal
October 17, 2000

I woke up this morning from a deep sleep with tears streaming down my face. I'd been dreaming about Steven's mom. She was screaming at me for leaving her son.

Selena's Journal
October 19, 2000

Tonight, I was struck by a horrifying thought. I was so busy enjoying myself when I was at Paige's that it didn't occur to me until after I got home. It startled me really, because it just hit me out of the blue: I am on a singles' dating website. I AM ON A SINGLES' WEBSITE! NOOOOOOOO! People (okay, to be more honest—men) out there now know that I exist. That is definitely not what I had in mind when I signed up on a lark.

I've been a closet "man-hater" for a while now, painting them all with the same extra-large brush and being pretty okay with that. They're all pigs, plain and simple. And while I was sitting here, thinking about all the pigs who would now be looking at my sparse profile, thinking their pig thoughts, I was interrupted by a little voice of reason. I say that because I don't know how else to describe this thought (more like a whisper, really) that said, "Selena, you never have to get married again, but you can't indulge in being a man-hater. You have two sons."

It hit me like a ton of bricks that just maybe this attitude of mine really was indulgent. Now, my mind is filled with all these new and opposing thoughts that it's making my head hurt. Are all men really the same? Is it possible that LDS men, with whom I have no personal experience, are any different?

It's crazy, because this calm came over me; it's like I have detached from this overwhelming concept. I decided on the spur of the moment to pay the $12.95 for one month and sign up with LDS Singles Online and turn it into my own personal anthropological study. Obviously, I'll be honest and upfront with anybody who steps into my world as to why I am there, but maybe this will help me heal a little from the hurts of the past and perhaps even restore my faith in mankind—literally. This should be interesting. Or not. I may live to regret this. Fools rush in where angels fear to tread.

Duane's Journal
October 26, 2000

I think my priesthood is at half-mast. I've thought this for a long time, but today I had a bit of inspirational thought about it. Emily was feeling a bit under the weather and I gave her a blessing before school. I had these thoughts after she left and I pondered on them all day. They weren't bad feelings; they were actually happy feelings, almost like when Christmas is coming and you're anxious for the festivities to begin.

When I joined the Church, it was not a decision that I took lightly. I had my name on several church's rolls in the past, but I knew this was different. Being a Latter-day Saint wasn't just being counted among a group of people in a congregation; it was going to be a real life change. I wasn't just joining a church. I was joining a culture. I committed to learn all that I could about the people and the history. I read many of the classic works of the Church that first year. I studied how the Saints lived and applied the Restoration and truths that were being revealed to them, and I studied the priesthood.

What I love most about the priesthood is that a man can use the power of God right in his own home to bless his family. But the more knowledge that I gained of this power, both in my reading and in my experience, the more that it magnified my heartbreaking deficit. The family is designed to have a father and a mother. While the priesthood is administered by the man, the sustaining support of the woman makes it whole. This bit of revelation has shown me the bigger picture of our world. It isn't just good advice for a young man or young woman to thoroughly vet a potential marriage partner; it's imperative for the strength of the Church and the power of the priesthood. To carry out the mission of the Church, the Lord's people need to be obedient and try to live within the family design. I know that the Lord does not cut me off because I am without a wife, but I also know that if I can manage to do this in the proper way, I will be more useful to Him and happier for my obedience.

For many months now, I have been preoccupied with the idea of getting remarried. Much of my motivation has simply been the desire for companionship, but if I do this properly and prayerfully, I will realize my potential as a priesthood holder. Could it be that I have become conscious of this blessing because the right woman is just on the horizon? If it is true, that would go a long way in explaining my anxious, happy feeling.

Selena's Journal

October 21, 2000

Now when I come home for my supper break or after one of my shifts and, if the girls are at their dad's, I head for the computer instead of turning on the TV. I hate to say it, but going online and scrolling through a few profiles is pretty decent entertainment, and sometimes even enlightening.

It's interesting to me that men who are inactive would even come to this place, looking for women with LDS values. Why do they want someone with beliefs that they're clearly not prepared to support? And I find it equally curious that men who claim to be active are posting shirtless photos of themselves. What's that all about?!

You wouldn't believe how I can amp up the interest from men who are clearly commitment-phobes when I'm upfront and let them know I'm not looking for a relationship. I'm exactly the girl they're looking for, apparently. And so, send them packing, I must. It turns out they aren't interested in committing to be part of my study either. Not that I'm surprised.

And then there are those who seem sincere in their search for love. The ones who have contacted me have been kindly rejected and redirected. I do hope they find what they are looking for, but it's not me, I tell them. Trust me, I tell them, you wouldn't want me. Oh, and good luck on that whole finding-your-eternal-companion-on-the-Internet idea. I hate to break it to you, but Internet romances absolutely never work out.

Sometimes I just have to laugh and shake my head. Occasionally, a man will pique my curiosity enough with a clever or thoughtfully expressed profile that I will delve further into his mystique by looking through his photo album. I saw one tonight where the guy was pretty funny, and his unusual sense of humor was underscored with a picture of him holding a white mouse up in the air, with his mouth open as if he was going to eat it. Not sure what kind of woman he's going to attract with a picture like that, but may the Force be with him. It reminded me of the TV show *V*. I wonder if he's an alien or just impersonating one? Seemed like a fun guy, but I'm not looking, so scroll on, Selena. Scroll on.

At least this has given me cheap entertainment. I know that sounds bad because it comes at the expense of real people who are here legitimately while I'm just an infiltrator. I still reserve the right to maintain my inner skeptic, but I am finding myself more open-minded because I can say that I have seen some (who appear to be, anyway) sincere and decent men being honest about wanting to find someone they can love. Maybe this is cheap therapy rather than cheap entertainment?

Duane's Journal
October 27, 2000

Okay, here's something. When I started with LDS Singles, along with my profile I chose an option that asked for personal preferences. I wrote that I didn't want my search to include anyone more than three hundred miles away and no more than three kids (I figure I have three kids, so I'll allow her three kids). A profile showed up the other night that interested me. I thought about sending her a message, but I noticed that she was from Alberta, Canada! That's got to be about ten times further away than my preference. In addition to that, she's got five kids.

I went on with my normal routine and decided not to send her a message, but as I was winding up for the night, I went back and looked at her profile again. She's funny and there's a story there behind that profile. That's two things I can't resist. So I went ahead and sent her a message. She has responded in a fun way—she's asking me questions. It's like she's doing a social experiment. I'm playing along for now (after all, I have no good prospects), but I have to question my own motives to spend time with a woman that I will never meet and who is apparently not interested in marriage. Maybe I'm not sincere in my stated goal to marry an LDS woman and I'm dragging my feet?

{ Part 2 }

♥

Profile: Moongoddess

Alberta, Canada

No picture- Thirty-seven years old

No picture- Divorced

No picture- Has five children, lives with two

No picture- Occasionally attends Church

No picture- High school diploma

No picture- 5'4" tall

No picture- Blonde hair, green eyes

No picture- Average build

No picture- Email address is private

Greeting: I'm not here looking for a soul mate/husband like every-one else. I really only wanted to take a peek, but apparently one can't go window shopping in single's world without buying the whole window. I don't expect to be here long, so there will be no need for lengthy details. I have eighteen years of marriage experience to one nonmember and have raised our children in the Church.

Education: I'm not going to count my single college course as "some post-secondary education."

Church & Community Services: Yes.

Hobbies & Interests: Creative and earthy. True but lacking specifics, I know. Not big on revealing my "self" to the general public.

Sender: Papabear38
Recipient: Moongoddess
Date: 10/24/2000
Subject: Hi there—from Papabear

Dearest Moongoddess,

I do wish you lived closer to me—I've never met anyone funny from Canada before, except maybe my former stake president, but he doesn't mean to be. I'm also a pushover for a pretty, down-to-earth blonde who doesn't reveal herself to the general public.

Best wishes,
Duane, alias Papabear38

Sender: Moongoddess
Recipient: Papabear38
Date: 10/25/2000
Subject: From the funny Canadian . . .

What a fun note! I've got to be honest. I'm only here by default and not looking for a husband. So in that respect, you can breathe a sigh of relief because I'm not going to want to look in your mouth and see if you've got good, sound teeth or ask for a financial statement from your accountant.

However, if you feel so inclined, I decided to stay here for a while so I could maybe learn more about the LDS male. I was married to a nonmember, so I have zero knowledge of what the LDS man is looking for in a mate, what's important to him, or what he's thinking and how that matches (or not) men in general. Are LDS men and other men inherently similar, or does the gospel bring about great changes, something akin to the Incredible Hulk when he gets stressed out? (The startling metamorphosis, I mean.)

One other thing, what is the one thing women should know about men (this is a general, non-denominational question ☺)?

Thanks for taking the time to say hi. Your profile is good, and I think it reflects a great sense of humor and sincerity.

Selena/Moongoddess

Sender: Papabear38
Recipient: Moongoddess
Date: 10/25/2000
Subject: Free Wisdom
Dear Selena,

You certainly know how to put a man at ease. I hate it when I'm trying to carry on a conversation and women are looking in my mouth. As for my accountant, he's asked me to "stop wasting" his time—our relationship has been strained ever since.

I must say that I only speak for this LDS male, but I'm sure that once they all hear what I have to say, they'll all rally to make me their spokesman.

First, I would like for my hands to meet when I embrace my ideal woman. If she grows some over the years because she is such a good cook and we are required to eat a lot, if pregnancy causes her weight gain, or she puts on pounds out of sympathy for me for doing the same—that's fine, but we must start off believing that our ideal mate is out there somewhere and it is only respectful to take care of ourselves for one another. (At least until that contract is signed.)

Second, now that I've revealed myself as being completely shallow in my first expectation, I must now recover by offering up something a little more complex. I think that the ideal woman sets the moral compass for the whole family. While the man holds the priesthood, the woman makes it complete. Let's face it . . . men are idiots. There's just no denying this. The ideal woman inspires a man to be his best, sometimes without him even knowing it. He magnifies his callings; sets a good example for the kids; and is a great lover, listener, and leader in his home. One day, he wakes up in the celestial kingdom and wonders how he got there. (Okay, maybe he's not totally baffled, but I bet he doesn't know all the details.)

I guess I'll have to tell you *the secret*. Though don't tell any men that I told you. All right, here it is: Most men feel like women have a little more on the ball than we do anyway, so the worst thing a woman can do is remind us that she is smarter or more worthy—we already suspect these things. The ideal woman shows her adoration for her man and makes him look good.

Third, this thing is like the second—loyalty. I personally desire to be the most important person in my eternal companion's life. When I go out of the confines of our home and into the real world, and the opportunity to do something real stupid and embarrassing arises, I want to know that I still have at least one person who will love me anyway.

While this isn't a complete list (the complete list got washed in my other pants), it's certainly some of the important stuff.

So what should women know about men? Women should know that men are only a step away from being bears. In fact, if bears wore clothes and mowed grass, they would be men. We can be sensitive and talk about our feelings, cry, and watch Oprah, but these things are not our natural inclination (think of a bear riding a unicycle and smoking a cigar at the circus—the bear *can do it*, but you're going to have to lure him into it). By nature, we are problem solvers, hunters, and warriors. While mushy on the inside, there is a hard-candy shell. Break that shell, Selena, and you shall find your mushy little man! Or a bear mowing grass . . . or something. I don't know; it was a spontaneous analogy and seems to fall apart at the end.

Anyway, I hope that I have helped you in your study.

Duane, alias Papabear38

Sender: Moongoddess
Recipient: Papabear38
Date: 10/25/2000
Subject: You made me laugh . . .

Thanks, I definitely needed that today. Yes, you did indeed help me see a little more clearly, but I'm afraid I might need a little more input. Are you game?

I must say, you've got a great sense of humor, and your honesty is appreciated. Thanks for a great message. ☺

Selena

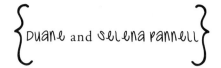
Sender: Papabear38
Recipient: Moongoddess
Date: 10/26/2000
Subject: My, but you are a Moongoddess . . .

Am I game? Are you kidding? You're what, three thousand miles away in an igloo someplace? You are the safest woman I've ever talked to, so of course I'm game!

One rule, however, I can't divulge just any secret of male-dom—if I get kicked out of the Man Club, there are relatively few other options available to me. Otherwise, anything goes (that's just an expression). Hit me with your best shot (once again, an expression). I'm your indispensable source of information (not an expression; I apparently do show signs of being something of a blabbermouth).

Duane

Sender: Moongoddess
Recipient: Papabear38
Date: 10/26/2000
Subject: Ok, first tough question . . .

I have been told that men have this penchant for acquiring things. One of the things they like to acquire is the woman of their current desires. It's like adding a trophy to the case (not my expression—this came from a man). The main problem with this is that once they have gotten this woman, they think, *Gee, if I can get this one, I'll bet I could have that one.* Thus comes the idea of "trading up." And so goes the endless quest to fill up their trophy case. Again, these ideas are not mine. They've come from men. I'm curious. What's your take on this theory?

Selena

Sender: Papabear38
Recipient: Moongoddess
Date: 10/26/2000
Subject: Wow! You can trade up?!

Okay, humility. You're forcing me to do some introspection that is somewhat painful. I too am guilty of "collecting" on some level (not the same level as your Neanderthal, socially inept friend, but a level nonetheless).

I would like to think that I have matured way beyond this sort of thing, but if you were to visit my little office and see some of the pictures on my desk and wall, you would think that maybe I'm a Mormon from the "old school" (if you know what I mean). I have pictures of many pretty women who are friends I have dated or have been close to. There are also pictures of my beautiful daughters and ex-wife. I guess it gives my ego a bit of a boost when truck drivers and warehouse workers admire those photos and ask my "secret" (the secret: film, 35mm film). It's my way of collecting, I guess. It's childish, but sometimes so am I.

With that said, however, I must say in my own defense that I don't "collect" real women—just photos of real women. I am fully prepared to give myself totally to the woman who goes to the temple with me to be sealed. I will be going into my next marriage with the idea that no other woman exists in the world. There is no trade-up option when you're at the top.

I'll also offer you some insight on this particular phenomenon: This sort of behavior is usually indicative of a low self-image and self-esteem, poor confidence, and so on. The irony is that when a man is operating in this mode, he is setting himself up for failure. You see, when he does win the object of his current desire, he begins to think that there must be something wrong with her. After all, if she were really such a great catch, he wonders, *What's she doing with a guy like me?*

I don't know how to explain it other than to say that a full trophy case is not really as fulfilling as you might imagine; it can actually be a really empty feeling.

PS: I'm sorry your friend is a socially inept Neanderthal. . . . No, that's wrong. I meant to say that I'm sorry that I *called* your friend a

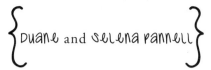

socially inept Neanderthal. I'm sure that he tries very hard to be a loyal, non-woman-collecting grown-up.

Duane

Sender: Moongoddess
Recipient: Papabear38
Date: 10/28/2000
Subject: In a serious vein . . .

Your collection seems harmless enough at first glance. My question then is whether you'd be secure enough for your eternal mate to have a similar collection—perhaps on a bulletin board in the laundry room? No, that wouldn't be the best place because women don't often congregate in the laundry room to visit and admire said collection. How about the kitchen?

Do you see what I'm getting at?

Honestly, I'm not trying to be difficult. I just want to understand. If it's okay for one spouse, shouldn't it be okay for the other? And if not, why not?

Selena

Sender: Papabear38
Recipient: Moongoddess
Date: 10/28/2000
Subject: Oh, nice try—but the question is MOOT.

Dearest Selena,

I think you underestimate my sincerity. I would no longer have the pictures of other women (with the exception of my dear daughters) when I make my commitment to my eternal companion (I will take them down when I know that she's the one—I won't bother waiting for the actual trip to the temple). I'll even destroy the photos upon discovery of the eternal mate. These women are a passing fancy, sort of like my long hair and pictures of Clint Eastwood and John Wayne on my bedroom wall. I don't expect to be a bachelor forever, and these are things that I consider harmless enough until the right woman comes along.

I'm starting to get a vibe from you. Could it be that you would still like to know if I would be accepting of my mate collecting photos? I don't have a problem with my spouse noticing that there are men out there who are blessed with superior looks—but there is a courtesy that I would extend to her that I would expect in return. If I'm sitting on the sofa watching television and Jennifer Anniston's towel falls off, I promise to look away and not comment. My eternal love will never be compared to any other woman, the theory being that once you have reached the top rung, you cease looking.

I know that you would like to catch me swimming around in the cesspool of double standards, but I don't go there—I'm just too darn loyal.

Duane

♥

Sender: Moongoddess
Recipient: Papabear38
Date: 11/01/2000
Subject: Cesspool . . .

Not a word that you typically find on a dating website (just guessing). That said, I don't underestimate your sincerity, nor did I hope to find you swimming in the cesspool of double standards (you can swim, can't you?) when I posed my question to you.

Of course, we all tend to gravitate our questions to those spots that are important to us, and I think that's what I was doing before. You see, particularly after I'd gone through the temple, I never really felt good enough in the eyes of my nonmember spouse, albeit an excellent man in many respects, because of subtle comments and other not-so-subtle actions.

So there is this broken part of me that can't imagine a man ever thinking one woman (the one he has) is all he ever wants and needs. Does this make sense? If it seems too heavy a topic, I do apologize, but

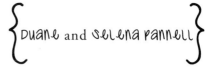

I beg your indulgence. You seem like a great guy. I love your sense of humor and sincerity and I feel you might be approachable regarding matters of great import. Still game?

Selena

Duane's Journal
November 2, 2000

I have believed for a long time that everything has a purpose; that there are no coincidence or chance meetings. That everything is designed for us and our experience on this planet. I don't know how it works, but we are placed in these experiences and yet are still afforded our agency to choose.

I don't know if the Moongoddess is the woman I was meant to be with, but I do know the purpose that she serves in my life right this minute. It may be because I believe that I'll never meet her face-to-face that I have been completely candid with her. She has engaged me in a different sort of conversation than other women that I have met on the singles website. She seems less interested in my history, activities, and assets and more interested in my beliefs and philosophy of life. This has forced me to examine what I really believe and desire for myself, to really look at where I'm at and what I want out of life. For that, I am grateful. I now feel like this isn't a wasteful indulgence until the right one comes along, but in fact may be a necessary engagement to prepare me for when the right one comes along.

An interesting sidebar: When I first contacted the Moongoddess, I signed my real name. When she wrote back, she wrote her "real name." Maybe she felt obligated because I was revealing something personal about me to make the same gesture. I don't want to be one of those kind of guys who is suspicious about everything a woman does, but the name she gave is one of those beautiful, maybe exotic kind of names that is probably not on her birth certificate. Selena. Doesn't that sound like a name that a woman might give herself as an alias?

Sender: Papabear38
Recipient: Moongoddess
Date: 11/02/2000
Subject: Among the approachable, the game . . .
Dear Selena,

It is difficult to be light-hearted about some things. I too had my heart crushed by someone I dearly loved. Even with all that I know about human nature and what can happen to the mental and spiritual health of a person who chooses a certain path, I found it easy to accept that there was something wrong with me that caused the breakup of my marriage. Luckily, time does heal all wounds (even the ones caused by banging your head against the wall). I have come to appreciate that I am considered among the top eligible bachelors in my community— too bad my community is made up of mostly Gentiles. The point being that I once had tunnel vision. It was easy to have the perception of myself that I did. What my ex-wife gave me was all I had to go by, but a little bit of time and exposure to other women proved to me that you're not all bad. In fact, I think some of you are quite lovely in your devotion. I suppose the problem of trust is not gender specific, but when you've had your heart mangled . . .

I have only been in the Church for eight years (Rookie of the Year 1992), but my life has changed significantly in regards to what I want for myself and my family. First off, that I even include my children (let alone that I put their wants and needs ahead of my own) is a marked improvement over the old me. I once fancied myself to be quite, um—I don't know—*cool*. That's not really the word, but it'll do. Anyway, I was so hip and carefree that there were no boundaries. I had no fear, not even reasonable, healthy fear. Now, though, I'm finding things are quite different.

I have been dating this woman who is really attractive. She is not a member of the Church, she sometimes dresses less than modestly, and she's not exactly "mother of the year'" to her daughter; other than that, she's perfect. Being with her and around some of her friends is sort of stomach-turning. I don't want to hide in a closet, but I want my most intimate relationship to be with someone who's a refuge from that world.

It's the same thing at work—I'm friendly with lots of people there, but all the cussing, vulgarity, lies, and backstabbing; it's revolting, and

I hate that it exists within my sphere. I'm also weary of the behaviors and circumstances that my children are exposed to in their circles of friends. I'm no goody-goody, but I want my home to be a sanctuary that provides a celestial reprieve from the outside world.

Now you might say, "But, Duane, what has this got to do with the husband and wife trust issue?" Well, I don't know. I've been rambling on for so long that I forgot my point.

Oh yeah! I guess the point is that two people can realistically expect to give and receive total devotion to one another without fear of being deceived or manipulated. I didn't used to believe it, but so many good LDS people in my stake have shown me that what the scriptures describe about the marriage relationship is attainable. I believe it's true. Eternal marriage is true.

Now, one last thing. I decided the moment that I was taught the principle that I wanted to be sealed in the temple to my family. While my ex did get baptized with me (in fact, she was the reason that I took a hard look at the Church to begin with), she fell away after a few months—it clashed with her lifestyle. I didn't give up on her and tried for five years to be a good husband and example, to make the Church as attractive and inviting to her as possible. The kids and I attended our meetings almost every Sunday for years without her (not trying to sound like a martyr; just trying to paint the picture). On several occasions when I was at the Washington D.C. Temple, I became emotional (okay, I cried, but just a little and never in direct sunlight). I would see couples getting married, doing work together, or walking hand-in-hand on the grounds and it would make me feel so sorry for myself, jealous and angry—and a whole lot of other feelings that I didn't want to admit were in me. It just didn't seem fair.

I believe I have sufficiently repented for my thoughts concerning those times, but they were necessary. I am now certain that I will not marry outside of the Church and I will not settle for less than a temple marriage. Everything that I have told you comes from the most sincere corner of my heart. I am confident that it can and does happen for people with the right stuff, just like Heavenly Father promises. And I promise you that there are men out there who are capable of making a commitment to you and never looking any further than you for the fulfillment of their dreams.

I hope I haven't run too deep. Something about writing at three in the morning makes me sort of mushy.

PS I saw my former stake president's wife this past Sunday. I told her that I finally found a Canadian whom I can get along with—she suggested that there may even be two or three people right here in the states that could tolerate me as well. See, you are the only funny Canadian.

Duane

Sender: Moongoddess
Recipient: Papabear38
Date: 11/03/2000
Subject: Hi in the middle of the night . . .

Okay, it's 1:37 here and I can't sleep, so I thought if you can write at three a.m. and get "mushy," I may as well risk it too.

I really do appreciate your candor. You've taken the time to write important stuff to me, a total stranger, and I thank you. I also want you to know that I don't take lightly those serious things that you've talked to me about. They are safe with me.

So tell me, how long have you been on LDSSO, and what's the experience been like for you? Ever feel like it's open hunting season and you're Bambi?

I should probably go back to bed and try to get more rest. I have to be at work at 7:45 and have to be on my A game to get my little chicks, Savannah (nine) and Auriana (eight in three weeks) up and ready and over to their dad's before I have to be at the hospital. I work part-time in Admitting & Reception there and enjoy my job immensely. You never know what you're going to get in a hospital, and I especially like the unpredictability.

Anyway, as you may have noticed, I made a concerted effort to keep things lighter with this note. But don't go getting complacent. I may bring out the big guns next time. ☺

Selena

Sender: Papabear38
Recipient: Moongoddess
Date: 11/04/2000
Subject: Are you toying with me?

If you go easy on me, I become vulnerable. Is that your game? I'm at my best when I'm on the ropes, so take your best shot.

All seriousness aside, I appreciate your being easy on me—all that soapy stuff in my last note took a toll on me. I'll soon find myself with a box of tissues, watching *Sleepless in Seattle* or some other chick-flick, and crying my eyes out.

You really are a great candidate for exploring some baggage with. I mean, we're not likely to meet face-to-face or anything, and I really do need a good filter. I need to make these adjustments before I mess around and actually meet a potential mate. If I were to gain that kind of extraordinary courage in the near future, would *you* be game?

So I have been on LDSSO for a few months. I've interacted with dozens of women, but I've only really spent any time talking to a few. It's been pretty light in nature overall. I would have to say that my discussions with you have had more depth than any other correspondence I've had online. I believe it's because you appeal to the intellectual and humorous side of my feeble brain, and that is a comfortable place for me. I have enjoyed it because it's not the chore that getting to know some people can be. Well, there's that and the fact that there are a lot of flakes out there.

I've talked regularly with four teachers who are nice and seem like really sweet and faithful members of the Church, but they can't spell! It may sound dumb or nitpicky, but that is a pet peeve of mine. I may not be the perfect word jockey, but I do manage to spell most of my words correctly—and I'm not a teacher. The experience for the most part has not been that productive as far as finding a bride is concerned. Maybe I'm expecting too much. I guess if it were to happen as I did expect, I'd be worrying that things were moving too fast and I'm not developing the friendship factor.

Well, I've promised my kids that I'd go to the movies with them. Of all the things that I tell them, they NEVER forget the things that I say that I'll do for them! I'll write to you later.
Duane

PS Your profile is less than forthcoming when it comes to photographic documentation—maybe you could cough up some pics?

Sender: Moongoddess
Recipient: Papabear38
Date: 11/04/2000
Subject: Am I game?
Dear Duane,

My first thought is sure, why not? I have nothing to lose here. You are the one bearing your soul in mushy, *Sleepless in Seattle* ways. (My own baggage is safely crammed inside of a stale locker at an undisclosed Greyhound bus depot, collecting cobwebs.)

But I have to wonder what makes me a "great candidate to explore some baggage with"? Makes me sound like I live in a convent and am a seasoned and safe eighty-five-year-old crone. But that aside, picking through your baggage sounds a lot more appealing at this point than having to pick through my own.

So my question is this: What do you really want or need from me once I've got the gloves on and sifting and sorting has commenced? Do you want to know what to say or what not to say to a potential mate? You're going to have to be a little more specific and help me help you go through your baggage. (And just how much of this stuff is there, anyway?)

As for pictures of me, I have always been the photographer, so any photographic evidence of my existence is pretty sparse. I did have some professional pics taken a few years ago, but it's kind of pitiful to offer up the photo-enhanced version of my glory days. I don't even look like me.

So are you ready to tackle this so-called baggage? Let the exploration begin!
Selena

Sender: Papabear38
Recipient: Moongoddess
Date: 11/05/2000
Subject: Charlie's Angels owe me money . . .
Dear Selena,

Unless you're unable to find a window to throw your money out of, or you just really like theater popcorn, you can wait for this one to come out on video. It's action-packed, but you have to be able to ignore certain laws of physics to enjoy that action. I possess not this talent. I'm actually a fan of Drew Barrymore. I think she's adorable—that's why I think it's a shame that they try to dress her skimpy. Her appeal is mostly her cuteness. I give it 2.5 stars and a moon. This has been "At the Movies" with Duane E. Siskell.

You ready to be a filter? Okay then, let's dispense with any silliness right now and get down to some serious whining. I will start off slow, and when you feel like you're going to gag, you can back me off a little bit.

First of all, some background: As I told you before, I'm not a "lifer." I joined the Church when I was thirty years old, and life has never been the same. I mean that in a good way. Even with all that has happened to me with my ex-wife, I can still say that I have never been happier than I have been these past eight years.

I met my wife when I was eighteen years old. I was something of a tramp, moving from one relationship to the next. I had been dating older girls—girls with their own places, because my relationship with my parents was strained and I found it to be the cheapest way to live without having much money. She was twenty-six with a four-year-old daughter. I moved in, and we lived together for three years before we finally got married.

We had one particular thing in common: we both really liked doing drugs. As for me, I liked my drugs with a little (and by a little, I mean a lot) of alcohol. I also smoked a couple of packs of cigarettes a day.

Everything was going along just fine until around 1990, when I began to lose my mind. I don't mean literally. I did actually have some idea where it was; mostly it was just that it wasn't operating quite right.

I was worried about the way I was feeling and having some delusions and occasional hallucinations. I began losing the ability to read and write and carry on conversation. I convinced myself that I had a brain tumor and that I was dying. It didn't occur to me that it might be because of the beer and two pints of liquor a day. Or all those pills, or possibly the cocaine—nope, "I'm quite certain it's some sort of cancer, doctor. The chemicals are just my way of medicating myself through the pain."

Long story short, I went to a psychiatrist. I needed a professional to confirm my diagnosis—and possibly prescribe a little something to help alleviate my, uh, discomfort. The good doctor was familiar with my illness, and he convinced me that I needed to be in a controlled setting to cleanse my body of all the toxins so that I could begin treatment. So he checked me into a local hospital in-patient program. I was there for two months.

As I began to sober up and things started to become clearer, I started thinking about my relationship with my wife, and then it dawned on me: my wife wasn't being faithful. I had let the relationship deteriorate and I wasn't even aware of it. I confronted her, and she confirmed my worst fear. She had been carrying on an affair with a guy she worked with and didn't mind telling me that she didn't love me anymore. Wow, I was devastated. In my own sick little way, I loved her with all of my being and I had always taken for granted that she felt the same way as me.

I'd cheated on her too. Different times over our ten years together, I had been involved in cheap flings with several women and I couldn't say a thing. It was all coming home to roost. I was getting everything that I deserved for my childish, selfish, stupid behavior, and I was hurting. The drug trade breeds some trashy relationships, and I was among my own when I was there. Though the pain seemed more than I could bear at times, I was determined not to go back to that life. I was sure that I would die if I ever did another drug or drank liquor again. So I had to suck it up and accept the fact that my marriage was over and that I was going to have a long hard road to overcome a dirty lifestyle. Oh, but I loved her.

Dear Selena, you can feel free to stop me here if you like. I would understand. You can write me back and comment on what you know so far or just disappear into cyberspace forever—whichever you feel motivated to do.

Duane

PS Ever sense I brot up the speling thing, I have been kursed. I've never been so self-conshess abowt my smelling.

PPS Yes, any picture of you—glory days are some of my own best photos.

Sender: Papabear38
Recipient: Moongoddess
Date: 11/05/2000
Subject: If you're ready for more . . .
My Life Part II or, "Duane's Wretched Life Takes a Turn"
Well, before I start, I did in fact relapse. I was out of the treatment center for about two weeks and had a terrible relapse. I was mostly blacked out for about ten days and I don't remember most of it. I do know that it involved being taken before a judge and deemed a danger to myself and others. This was based on information provided by a doctor I don't believe I had ever seen and the testimony of my wife. I was released to the care of someone (details are a little bit fuzzy), but somehow I ended up in jail after being arrested for sleeping in my car in a nearby town. After I was released, I went on a "death-binge." I wanted to be done, and I wanted to be really drunk when it happened. It didn't work out, though. I woke up in the same hospital that I'd been discharged from a couple weeks earlier, feeling worse than I'd ever felt in my whole life.

I believe that the relapse was due partly to a relationship with a much younger girl (that I was trying to keep up with), but I also believe that it was actually wisdom from above. The experience taught me that I needed to respect my addiction and not be complacent in my recovery. I have never forgotten just how easy it was to go right back and I never want to do that again.

My wife and I separated for a little over a year. I went to a halfway house for a short time, and that was really not for me. I came back home and my wife wanted me to stay with her (rather than be out on the streets), so I stayed there for a little while, but it was too hard. I was still in love with her and she had a boyfriend, and the whole situation was just a challenge to my delicate sobriety.

During my short time there, I came to see how I was failing my children. They were essentially fatherless. I didn't have a real relationship with them. I didn't even feel like I knew them. I felt bad for them, but it wasn't even like I felt bad for *my* kids; it was like I was feeling bad for some faraway orphans on a TV Christmas special. I knew that I needed to be their dad, but I also knew that I was not yet prepared to take on the responsibility.

I had to get out of that house, so I took a job driving a truck for a year. I traveled all over the country delivering ammunition and explosive materials for the government. It relaxed me. I read the whole King James Bible from cover to cover that summer. Then late one night, I was in Texas and felt an urge to call home. My wife and I talked for a long time and she said that she wanted to try reconciliation and for me to come home. So I did.

After a month or so at home, she decided that she didn't really like my truck-driving job and my being away so much. She had a really good job and suggested that I stay home with the kids and go to school, and we would live on her income for a while.

It was the greatest five years of my life. I became a genuine father to my kids and really got to know them. I did all the meals and all the cleaning. I bathed them and did their hair. I taught them and got to know them like a lot of fathers could only dream of doing. I went to school while they were in school and I stayed home with them when they were on holidays. Life was becoming great. I literally replaced a life of abuse with a life devoted to family.

I enjoyed going to school, but I never got a degree in anything. I was too scattered. I moved from one interest to another (maybe we have that in common?), never settling on any one thing. I still don't consider it a waste of time, but now that I'm working again, it would be nice to have some letters after my name. ☺

This is when I decided to become a minister. I started studying all the great religions of the world. I was pretty sure I was Christian, so I studied the vast array of Protestant beliefs. I also studied Far East religions, Judaism, New Age, and Islam. I had studied Catholicism for a number of years earlier when I found out that they could drink alcohol and smoke—though turned out it was only allowed in moderation, so I abandoned that conversion in mid-catechism. I figured that with my training in theater and experience in stand-up comedy, I could become a famous TV evangelist, make tons of money, and serve the Lord, all at the same time. Could there be a more honorable calling? My study brought me to a belief that there was no true religion on earth, and I had an idea to take the best of all the religions of the world and create the perfect church.

Many things happened during this time. I quit smoking cigarettes. Oddly, I found that drinking coffee made me crave tobacco, so I quit my two-pots-a-day habit. I stopped cussing. I had a horrible temper during my youth and an ugly mouth to match, so I decided to surrender them both. I also quit gambling. I wasn't a real bad gambler, but I did buy a lot of lottery tickets and one day I just decided to cut my losses for life and never gamble again. I also did something that I had never done before: I made a promise to the Lord that I would be totally committed to my wife. I would be completely loyal to her the rest of my life. Little did I know that I was preparing myself for what would come in just a few short months.

In my search for doctrinal Legos, I stumbled upon the LDS Church. I figured that while I was studying all of these other religions, I might as well find out what the Mormons were up to. I had heard many things about them over the years and was curious. I'd been to Utah a few times and seen the commercials for the Church, and it seemed to me that all the anti-Mormon rhetoric and the observation didn't quite match. I called an eight hundred number that I saw on a commercial and ordered a video called *Heavenly Father's Plan*. The lady who took my order asked if I'd mind if missionaries from the Church delivered the video. That was perfect for me. I was interviewing every religious leader in the tri-county area and I loved talking to people about their beliefs. Turns out that the missionaries lived in an apartment behind a house just eight doors down! They showed up at my house the next day. They were ready to teach and I was ready to learn, so those nice young missionaries and I set out to either confirm or dispel the myths surrounding their religion.

I approached the LDS Church the way I did with all the others. I wasn't intending to join or be "converted," and I was not interested in having my ministry swallowed up in someone else's church, all of which I told them. I didn't want to have to pay any dues or share my proceeds with some franchise church. I was scientific in my approach and I had specific things that I hoped to glean from my interviews. I was building *The Church of Duane*, and I needed attractive doctrine to draw in believers.

These young guys were impressive to me. Though they did seem rather young, I could see right away that they could hold their own with any theologian I had interviewed in my studies. We had great discussions, and I loved the way I felt when they visited me. I would often try to get a rise out of them and engage them in a heated debate, but they just wouldn't bite. I wanted a battle, but they used scriptures, logic, and testimony in a peaceful, polite way that I felt invited a sweet feeling into my home.

After two weeks of meeting with these LDS missionaries, I had a lot of good stuff for *The Church of Duane*. Up to that point, my wife had never sat in on one of my discussions with anybody. She wasn't interested and regarded my religious investigation to just be part of my addiction recovery—like a phase that would pass. One day, though, as I was talking to the missionaries, she came into the room and sat down beside me and listened to what one of the elders was saying. I looked over at her at one point and I noticed that she had begun to cry. All of a sudden it hit me that there must be something to this religion.

I wasn't aware at the time, but that day was the anniversary of the passing of her mother. We were talking about the afterlife, and it was the right discussion at the exact right moment. She wanted to know more, so I started the discussions with the missionaries all over from the beginning, but this time with my wife. She actually committed to baptism before I did. On her birthday—March 15, 1992—we were baptized together.

Dear Selena, I am going to take a shower and get ready for Church. Read, ponder, and comment, and I'll write the real juicy stuff when I get back.

Duane

Sender: Moongoddess
Recipient: Papabear38
Date: 11/05/2000
Subject: You don't scare me . . .
Dear Duane,

I'm not sure whether you were subconsciously trying to push me away with the startling revelations about your life, but if this is the case, it did not work. I see your honesty as a need to come clean with someone, and, hey, who better than some chick a million miles away, or at least three thousand whom you're never going to meet?

On a more serious note, I accept your disclosure as something of a gift. You were brave enough to bring all your "stuff" to me on a silver platter (actually, probably more than one because there was a lot of said stuff), and most people wouldn't have the courage to do that. So, I accept your stuff and will respect and protect it as my own—and you know I'm good at that. I'll put yours with mine in the aforementioned undisclosed Greyhound locker. So yeah, I realize it's more a symbolic gesture, because who am I going to tell, really, but I do hope you get my sincerity.

I'm actually pretty impressed at your evolution from the epitome of the natural man to the humble, teachable family man you seem to have become. Who knows? Maybe the day will come when I haul my own stuff out into the light of day, let it get some air, and see what can be made of it. For now, though, I'm quite enjoying your story. Please continue.

Selena

Sender: Papabear38
Recipient: Moongoddess
Date: 11/05/2000
Subject: I should take a time out and fix you!

That is my next project. I have to finish my story, though, or I'll forget where I'm supposed to be tomorrow. Okay. As I said. we were happy for a few months after we were baptized (or at least I was). We were learning and growing in the Church as a family.

We decided to take a vacation down to Florida that summer. The first night that we were there, my wife smoked some pot with a family member. She became immediately inactive in the Church and never returned. I was devastated as I started to see my goal of being sealed in marriage to her begin to crumble like a whole lot of cheap potato chips.

Over the next few years, I caught her smoking crack in the basement in the middle of the night, as well as in several money lies. She would disappear for a day or two and not tell me where she'd been. She did not go just a little astray, and I didn't know what to do. What I did know was that I was falling out of love with her.

Then nearly two years ago, she disappeared for three days. When she finally came home, I told her that I wanted her to pack her stuff and leave. She was (understandably) upset and began crying, apologizing and begging me to let her stay. She started confessing things, really bad things, and then promising that she would never do them again. I didn't give in. She ended up checking herself into a hospital rehab, and I filed for divorce.

I had planned the divorce and was preparing to start my life anew, but on the day before she was discharged from the hospital, my bishop called to see how things were going. He told me that I should think about forgiving her and allow her to come back home. He didn't advise me to forgive her, but he did say that I should consider her efforts to get clean. He also reminded me of how generous the Lord had been toward me when I came seeking forgiveness. I told him right away that I didn't think that I could do that, but I said I would think about it. Thinking about it is all I did for an entire night. I thought and I prayed and by morning I knew what my Heavenly Father expected of me. I picked her up at the hospital and I brought her back home.

This was all stressful and resulted in an episode of depression that I thought was going to destroy me. I helped my wife all that I could— I actually have a rather good education in addiction recovery—and tried to be upbeat about everything. But on the inside, though, I was a mess. I went to see a psychologist that works for the Church Education System here in our stake at the recommendation of my bishop. He's an awesome man, and I feel like I'm whole again thanks to him.

After about five months, my wife began acting strange again and I had her investigated. I knew that I was going to divorce her and I needed all the information that I could get to guarantee that I would retain custody of my kids. When I was ready, I confronted her with all the information that I had and asked her to leave once again. She swore undying love for me and promised never to do it again, and so on and so on . . .

When I was done being a heartless jerk by putting her out (I actually gave her the newer of our vehicles, which is a real nice conversion van that a homeless person might consider a castle), I helped her get situated into a home of her own and get some furnishings. I wanted to make sure that she was comfortable—and I didn't want her to bounce back to my house. I wasn't totally confident in my own resolve to end the marriage and I wanted to make things as permanent as possible. She's been gone for over a year now. I rarely see her or talk to her. She sees the kids a couple of times a week, and I think that their relationship with her is much better now.

How's that for baggage, missy?! I'm a former drug and alcohol user, "washed in the blood," but worthy of critical scrutiny by any woman worth her salt. It's also apparent that I have some residual hurts that come with my experience, namely a speck of trust issues.

I know the drug culture and the moral decay that accompanies drug use. I know better than to take my ex-wife's transgressions against me personally. I suffered over her actions, but they were not personal shots at me. I know because I did the same thing to her when I was using; her feelings were never even a part of the equation. I know, and yet I still have to deal with the feelings.

While my intellectual mind says, "This had nothing to do with you," my emotions say, "You're not worthy of being loved" (sounds silly) or, "I feel like I'm not attractive" (looks silly) or, "If I had been a better person, I could have prevented this whole thing from happening." The fact is, my intellect can say whatever it wants because my heart is still a Doubting Thomas (my heart's name is Thomas).

I don't want to be one of those people who only feels good about himself or herself if someone is constantly pumping them up. It bothers me that I even think this way. Does any of this make sense? I have not shared these feelings and thoughts—and certainly not the entirety of these events—with anyone else before. I am embarrassed this even happened to me.

One last thing: I want my next relationship to be totally healthy, according to the precepts of the Church. I'm just not sure what that would mean. Given what you've learned about me, do you think that this experience has made me a stronger person or do you think I would be an emotional burden on a good woman? I feel normal now, but do I have some dormant emotional puke just waiting for the right time to spew forth and ruin things?

Please be gentle. I am anxiously awaiting your reply. I'm somewhat concerned about how you feel about me now, so don't wait too long to reply, even if you only send a short note.

Duane

Sender: Moongoddess
Recipient: Papabear38
Date: 11/05/2000
Subject: Stuff still safe
Dear Duane,

I'm distracted by the fact that you made sure that your ex-wife had a vehicle, home, and furnishings when you split up. Are you for real?! I've got to take a timeout here to give my head a shake. I so can't relate. Okay, all better now. Rest assured, your stuff is still safe with me. It's hard for me to imagine how all this has affected you, but I don't think your experiences make you a liability, considering you have overcome great obstacles to get where you are today.

I do think, however, that your self-esteem has taken some pretty big hits over the years. It's human nature to want to trust one's spouse with the most vulnerable parts of one's being. And to discover this was never a safe place is a shock to the system and can leave a person somewhat broken.

A friend once told me—after hearing some of my tales of woe—that I reminded him of a girl in some Tim Burton movie. He said she had to jump from a window to save herself or something and, in doing so, tore off her arm. But she just sewed it back on and kept going. It sounds like something I might do. I have felt broken for quite a while now, but I don't have the luxury of staying broken because I'm a mom, you know?

I don't think you have that luxury either. Distasteful as it may seem, you might have to look at the whole self-esteem issue because you're not only a dad, but it sounds like you want to have a healthy, whole relationship with a woman, and I can't see that working out all too well if you're still broken. You might not think so, but because of your mostly successful efforts to improve your life, you deserve to feel whole and good about yourself. That can't help but positively affect a new relationship.

Anyway, that's my amateur psychologist coming out uninvited. Let me know if you think I overstepped my bounds, okay?

Selena

Sender: Papabear38
Recipient: Moongoddess
Date: 11/06/2013
Subject: Wow! You're not just another pretty face . . .

You pinpointed my main problem. Low self-esteem is an interesting diagnosis. So I feel bad about myself? I get used to it, right? Of course, I learn to live with it, but (and there's always a big butt) the problem with a poor self-image is that it isn't internal—it oozes out all over the place and makes a mess.

I've recently found myself settling for less than I should in dating. Not that there is anything wrong with these women—it's just that I cannot reach my ultimate goal with any of them and I know it. I've made a terrible mistake in the case of one lady I have been spending time with lately. She's beautiful and all that other stuff that I shouldn't focus on. She's a great ego-builder, talking about me like I'm . . . well, sometimes I wonder who it is she's talking about. It's addicting, you know, when someone thinks really good things about you and tells all her friends about you and looks at you like you're Brad Pitt. (Did you know that I have never seen a Brad Pitt movie? I have nothing against the guy, but I realized it a while back, and now it would seem like a real shame to break my record. I'm a little ADHD, in case you haven't noticed.) Part of me believes that I should have her on my payroll or something, but (and there's always a big butt) this can't be good for me—or her. Oh man, I know she's not the one. I know it in my heart and I have known for quite some time, but (and there's always a big *however*) I can't seem to do the deed. I need to break it off, and between being a chicken and her whispering sweet nothings in my ear, I just can't bring myself to do the right thing.

I'm glad that you're really far away. This seems like the sort of thing a guy would tell a woman friend and she gives him a real violent slap to get his attention before she dispenses the advice. But (you know) you are far away, and I like your perceptions.

Write me,

Duane

Sender: Moongoddess
Recipient: Papabear38
Date: 11/06/2000
Subject: Poor Brad Pitt
Dear Duane,

He probably loses sleep at night because of people like you.

As for your dating dilemma, you sound like a normal male—or female. I hasten to add, in case you think I am questioning your masculinity, that any guy or girl is a sucker for positive feedback, especially when it's directed at them with a fire hose. It gets tricky though when only one person is getting wet and the other dries up and blows away. Sorry, my train of thought just derailed.

Selena

Sender: Papabear38
Recipient: Moongoddess
Date: 11/07/2000
Subject: More help, dear. I'm not very bright . . .
Dear Moongoddess,

Prove your moongoddliness and give me some suggestions. I have never found it too difficult to break up casual relationships, but (and I believe mine has been verbally abused) this woman is really nice, pretty (ugly women are easier to break up with, I'm assuming), and she's been so good to me. If all women thought of me the way she does, I'd be wealthy and quite famous. In other words, I think she may be more serious than I was thinking. And, mind you, I'm not one of those guys who is afraid of commitment; when I find the right one, she will have the most loyal, thoughtful, loving man who ever loved a woman. I just know that this one isn't her. What would you want to hear that wouldn't be hurtful but would be effective? Is there anything? Help me out here and I'll owe you big.

  Signed,
  Desperate

Sender: Moongoddess
Recipient: Papabear38
Date: 11/07/2000
Subject: My ultimate test . . .
Dear Desperate,
Who knew my moongoddliness would ever be put on the line?

My answer: I don't know that you need to punt her. She's positively affecting your life in ways you need right now, and that's not a bad thing. I think you do need to do something for her and yourself in order to be true to those feelings that you're having that she is not "the one," however.

I think you need to be straight with her and tell her the importance of an eventual eternal companion in your life. Of course, if she runs out and gets herself baptized, you're toasty-o's with that particular argument. Honestly, I don't know how you say to others without hurting them in some way that you like being with them and think they're great, but would rather be shot and hung by your toenails than be with them for eternity. There won't be an easy way to do it, and continuing on in the same flight pattern isn't going to help matters either. You need to have a heart-to-heart with her ASAP. With any luck, she'll still want to hang out with you and adore you in the same vein just for the sake of the company. But she does deserve to know that she's not "the one" sooner than later, don't you think?

Sincerely,
Moongoddess

Sender: Papabear38
Recipient: Moongoddess
Date: 11/07/2000
Subject: I bow to your goddessness
Dear Moongoddess,

You're very wise. I shall indeed have a heart-to-heart with the female in question, taking into consideration that I could very well be, as you say, "toasty-o's."

Though I don't know that even a series of dunkings can correct some of the impressions that I have had. But (and mine has been kicked verbally), you're right that she doesn't deserve to be left in the dark. Okay, I want to say, without being mushy, that I appreciate your honesty and gentle handling of my feelings, and—though you're a female—I trust you. I'm going to take your advice and do something about the doo-doo I got myself into. If there's some crown above that of moongoddess, you certainly have my vote.

Duane

Sender: Moongoddess
Recipient: Papabear38
Date: 11/08/2000
Subject: And now I'm blushing!

Your praise is too generous. I'm glad if I was helpful, in an impartial observer kind of way. Your comment about trusting me even though I'm a female made me smile. I take it you have trust issues where women are concerned? Also—and forgive me for not being able to resist the devil's advocate position I'm about to take—you thought that several dunkings might not be able to correct some of the impressions you've had about your lady friend, and yet you're living proof of a miraculous change. Just something to think about.

Selena

Sender: Papabear38
Recipient: Moongoddess
Date: 11/08/2000
Subject: Touché
Dear Selena,

First, there's no doubt in my mind that my lady friend is capable of redemption of miraculous proportions, but (and she has a nice one) I don't think that I'm a good enough person to forget some of what I know—first impressions are *really* important.

Second, trust issues? Oh, I have no trust issues. I'm just . . . cautious. I actually have people in my life whom I trust to the highest degree. I desire to one day share a trusting relationship with my eternal companion. I've only had a couple of romances in my life that I could say had an element of trust, but of course that was years ago when I was the one who didn't put enough value in trust.

Third, the tables are about to turn on you, dear lady; you need to give up some personal info—to balance the scales.

I'm curious as to why you make it such a point to advertise that you are not interested in pursuing a serious relationship? Is that some sort of defense mechanism, or is it part of some diabolical screening process? Or perhaps *you* are the cynical type who believes that you are far better off without the lesser gender? In which case, this would be a weird place to be expressing that.

I might remind you that you're currently in a trust-building mode and all comments must be selected with the utmost care.

I think I like this role.

Sincerely,

Duane

♥

Sender: Moongoddess

Recipient: Papabear38

Date: 11/08/2000

Subject: Dang! I hate when the tables are turned!

You ask difficult questions. I think there are a few reasons why I make a point of saying that stuff in my profile.

One of the reasons is that many of the men who messaged me are looking for a wife—pronto. Why waste their time?

My new message now is attracting those who have commitment issues, and they seem to think I'm perfect because I don't want them to commit.

Another reason is that the corpse that is my marriage isn't yet cold in the grave and it wouldn't be prudent or respectful to go hunting.

There is no *lesser* gender, but I admit that the men in my life (father, husband, brother-in-law, uncles, even to some extent, men I know in the Church) have hurt me and let me down in various ways, and I am like any other person who would go to the ends of the earth to avoid being hurt again.

Diabolical screening process? As I mentioned before, I've now gone from those who are mate hunting to those who want the perks but none of the commitment. I'm not sure which is worse.

The truth is, I shouldn't even be on here. But I don't want to distrust men. I really want to believe that there are some out there who aren't ruled their baser natures and desires.

Okay, so I have issues with men and the Church and I'm reluctant to throw either baby out with the bathwater. (I do so love babies!)

I'd love to feel the Spirit again and be reassured with respect to all the doubts and disbelief I now have developed. And I'd love to have a best friend to love and be loved back without reservation. But if protecting myself from future hurt can only be accomplished by building walls, pass me the bricks and mortar, please. So what do you think? Hopeless case?

Selena

♥

Sender: Papabear38
Recipient: Moongoddess
Date: 11/09/2000
Subject: Dear Hopeless Case,

That was funny. I want you to know it's 65 degrees outside and has been raining all day. The wind is also blowing a nice warm breeze and there are leaves everywhere—all stuck to everything.

As for you, I'm here to try and spread a little sunshine, and possibly some Bravo Sierra.

It was over two years ago now that I thought the pain was going to be a permanent part of my life. I had been made a fool (by letting it go on and hoping for the best). I was cheated on, lied to, exposed to whatever creepy-crawlies (wasn't that a pretty cute way to put it?), and made to feel like I was unworthy of true love and devotion. Probably worst of all, I was really harboring some serious resentment toward Heavenly Father.

I don't remember what day it was, but I do remember riding down the beltway in Washington, D.C., not far from the temple. I looked down at the car beside me and I couldn't see the people, but what I did see meant so much. It was two little wrinkled hands resting on the car's console. The smaller hand was resting gently on top of the bigger one, his hand gripping two of her fingers. I felt a lump grow in my throat and my eyes welled up with tears. It was as if the Savior himself were there with His arm around my shoulder, offering me a promise and comfort.

I am not going to give up on true love. I am certain—a testimony, if you will, from me to you—that a man and a woman can (and they do) make vows to one another and not break them; that we as children of our Heavenly Father are capable of living eternal principles right now; that I will find someone to tell all my secrets to and be vulnerable with without fear. I'm sure of it and I intend to keep that in my heart forever. I have only been to one temple marriage, and what I saw that day is etched in my mind. I want that for myself and that special someone.

My need to treasure, hold close, and love a woman is greater than my fear of being hurt again. I feel that my bad experience is the direct result of bad choices that I once made and a natural consequence of that kind of lifestyle.

I don't want to convince you that there is no chance of getting hurt again. That's all I really need: some wild-eyed Canadian chick shooting at me from a tower somewhere because of bad relationship advice. I just want you to know that I believe in love. It sounds kind of corny when I read it back, but it's true. I believe in true, honest, forever love. I don't want to know that you're too cynical for that kind of belief—it takes some of the magic away. Like when you're all wrapped up in the joy of Christmas and some snot-nosed kid is trying to tell you the "truth" about Santa. I'm feeling the Spirit here—don't harsh my buzz, man!

By the way, I'm not too privy to the Spirit myself lately. I know that He's a breath away because He brushes by me on occasion (like a moment ago when I told the story of the wrinkled hands). That's something that I really regret about my response to all that I was going through; it was wrong of me to assume that I had been forsaken, when indeed the Lord had been quite faithful to me (as I count my many blessings now). It's coming back a little at a time. Heavenly Father wants me to have it. I just have to be more obedient and I'll have that companionship back.

Lastly, please don't put up any new walls—you don't have to take down what you've got up (a small fortress might be just the thing for now), but please halt construction on all new high-rise projects. Those things are hard to take down once they are up, and one day you will want to venture beyond the safe zone. It'd be a shame to find yourself locked hopelessly inside. My own experience of putting walls around my heart has taught me something—the wall doesn't discriminate. You may shield off the bad stuff, but you will also drive away the good. We are meant to feel.

You need to hear this from someone, so it might as well be me. Best wishes and a good night from the southland. Your eternal friend,

Duane

Sender: Moongoddess
Recipient: Papabear38
Date: 11/09/2000
Subject: Okay, okay . . . point taken
I'd never be the one to take away the idea of a true love, especially for you. You are restoring my faith in the male persuasion teeny bits at a time, and, as I suspected, maybe all men aren't ruled by . . . well, you know. You also offer pearls of wisdom, and I thank you. (Want to borrow my crown?) Good advice about not building the walls too high in case I can't get out someday.

I like hearing about your daughters (they're beautiful girls, by the way). Thought I would send you a pic of my little chicks. Auriana is in braids on the left and Savannah is wearing the yellow shirt.

Selena

Sender: Papabear38
Recipient: Moongoddess
Date: 11/10/2000
Subject: Quick Note
Your daughters are gorgeous!
I'm glad that my gushing letter from last night hit the mark. I tend to get sentimental late at night, sincere but more sentimental than is good for me. Since you're so far away, it probably gives me the courage to be a little more vulnerable. Anyway, thanks for appreciating my words—you're smart and I love that in a woman, but that can be a double-edged sword when you put yourself out there.

Just to let you know, I don't think you'll go long in this life before your confidence in love will be renewed. Look into the eyes of those beautiful girls of yours. Now there's the place where true love lives. You have to know that it's not exclusive to the mom-daughter relationship; it would be such a cruel joke to the Lord's children.

Have a great day!

Duane

PS Do you have eyes like that? Did they get that look from you? How will I ever know without a picture for reference? If I can post a picture of me eating a live mouse, you can share a picture of you that features your eyes!

Sender: Papabear38
Recipient: Moongoddess
Date: 11/11/2000
Subject: Baby, I'm goin' to call you American Express . . .
'Cause you're everywhere I want to be!

I'm sorry, but I've been waiting to use that line for two years and there's never been a good time. Lucky you, huh?

Thank you for the pictures. You and your girls are really pretty.

I'm going to respond to your last question as soon as I can be in this room alone for a while. We've been having an exciting weekend, so things are a little chaotic.

Duane

♥

Sender: Moongoddess
Recipient: Papabear38
Date: 11/11/2000
Subject: Suffering "sender's" remorse

Keep in mind, since the photo on the rock a year ago, the hump on my back has become enormous and I've grown a third eye.

'Night,

Selena

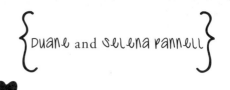

From: Duane
To: Selena
Subject: Last night and the pageant
Date: Sunday, November 12, 2000, 1:55 a.m.

We had a good time. Do these kids look too good to belong to a guy like me or what? Don't let their good looks fool you; they're quite rotten. I have promised them that because of their evil ways, I'll marry a wicked stepmother. You don't know any wicked, single women I could hook up with that happen to be LDS, do ya?

You shouldn't have told me about the hump and extra eye. I simply cannot fall in love with you from this distance. You couldn't possibly know, but since I was a small boy I have always said that one day I will marry me a gal like the one that married dear old dad. She's old now, and her eyes are all looking in different directions, which makes it hard to figure out who she's talking to, but that hump—oh, that beautiful hump is still perfect. Her doctor says she has the hump of a woman half her age.

You're going to have to try harder than that,
Duane

From: Selena
To: Duane
Subject: Change of pace
Date: Sunday, November 12, 2000, 7:28 p.m.

Sooo . . .

Want to hear a story? It all begins with a girl who's baptized when she's eleven along with her mom, dad, and little sister. She always took her faith seriously and was glad it gave her a reason to avoid the pitfalls other growing adolescents succumbed to. She even gained a reputation for being super straight and had only one date in high school.

After high school, she blossomed somewhat, catching the eye of an older, more experienced young man, who pursued her in part because she presented a challenge. He'd never gone out with a Mormon girl before. She'd never had any LDS boys show interest, so she was flattered and liked the attention from the nonmember boy. She'd always been rather judgmental of girls who got into trouble because she couldn't understand why they weren't strong enough. The humbling experience was just beginning.

She became pregnant within mere months of graduating and, with pressure being exerted on both sides by both sets of parents, she and the young man married, giving their son a family. Now these two young people didn't really know each other and didn't even have all that much in common, but they made pretty good parents for the five children they eventually had together. It was never particularly easy, but they managed to do okay.

She became used to doing things alone. She took the children to Church every Sunday and even went to those wacky Church evenings for couples by herself. She was dedicated. He didn't like to travel, so she also took the children on road trips alone, as far as eighteen hours away from home. She missed the companionship and sometimes found herself scared to be doing what she was doing, but she was stubbornly independent and determined that the kids would have good experiences to remember.

During the six years she taught their children school at home, the father came on only one of dozens of field trips—to the waterslide. She had taken the kids to museums, science centers, aquariums, forts, heritage farms, orchards, fish hatcheries, ballets, plays, symphonies, temple open houses, and so on. His excuses ranged from being bored by the stuff, not liking to travel, or to not wanting to go where all those "damn Mormons" live.

Through the years, it became apparent to her that she wasn't what he wanted. Her hair wasn't blonde enough, or short enough. Her nails weren't long enough, or red enough. All the evidence pointed to the fact that she was just not "enough."

After a couple really bad choices, sincere repentance, and a rededication to things of an eternal nature, she made it to the temple. She had to get her husband's signature, and this was accomplished by her writing the note of permission and him grudgingly signing. There is one part of the temple session that is voluntary and she never participated in this, because she wanted there to be a part of the temple ceremony that would be done for the first time by she and her husband. She wasn't perfect by any means, but she wanted to save something sacred for the two of them to share, even though she'd gone to the temple before him.

Hmmm . . . let me know if this story is remotely interesting to you and I will finish another time. For now, I'll let you rest your eyes.

Selena

♥

From: Duane
To: Selena
Date: Sunday, November 12, 2000, 8:23 p.m.
Subject: I can't wait a week for the next episode!
Dearest Selena,

What are you, some kind of professional writer or something? I hate/love cliffhangers.

I too wrote my permission note to go to the temple! My ex needed a "forgive and forget," and I said, "Sign here, please."

I too saved a temple ordinance for the time that I could participate with my wife.

I too took my children to Church, socials, and other special events for years by myself. People at Church are so sweet. They say that I'm a good father, but I would trade all the compliments to be a couple with someone who cared about these things as much as I do. I never thought I would be the one to hold a family together—busting one apart maybe, but holding one together never seemed likely, what with my treasured Brando persona. Now being a rebel means letting my dog poop in someone else's yard (though, after a certain amount of time has elapsed, I do go and clean it up—rebel or no, it's just the civic thing to do).

Please continue. I'm on the edge of my chair. This sort of reminds me of when Fonzie jumped his motorcycle over the garbage cans on *Happy Days*; when somebody shot JR on *Dallas*; when somebody shot Mr. Burns on *The Simpsons*; or any number of *Batman* episodes.

Duane

♥

From: Selena
To: Duane
Subject: Okay, more of the soap opera
Date: Sunday, November 12, 2000, 9:54 p.m.

She'd always had faith and hope to get her through the tough times. Going to the temple was a great step and she believed her entire family was blessed by her having gone. And for a time, everything seemed to be going well. After all the years of being married to this man, she'd finally come to a place where she loved him unconditionally, as he was, physically, spiritually, mentally, and emotionally. She was truly happy.

. . . And completely unaware that he wasn't. She doesn't know when things started to change between them, but he started wanting to do "new" things in their intimate life and once in anger told her how much he didn't like her wearing the temple garments. It got so that she didn't want to dress in front of him because his revulsion was so apparent. She didn't know what to do.

One day, she was cleaning up files on their computer and found more than she bargained for. She knew now where all the "creativity" was coming from and knew she couldn't compete with the airbrushed models. She had, after all, carried his five children in her now-less-than-perfect frame. The pressure to give up the temple garments was constant and, with no one to talk to about something so intimate, she stopped wearing them. She chose her husband over God.

In retrospect, she sees that that decision could only end in disaster and it merely prolonged the process. When she gave up that privilege, that hope she'd always had quickly disappeared. She felt she'd chosen to give up her own salvation. She started having trouble sleeping at night and would often be awake from late at night until early in the morning. During those months, she tired of all the infomercials and discovered the Internet. She began chatting with people from around the world—though mostly men because women didn't seem to want to talk to other women. She didn't realize it at the time, but she was on the brink of a serious depression. Then she found out she was pregnant.

This news was a shock. Things were less than rosy in the marriage, and her youngest was finally old enough to be in school. Among her first thoughts was one that held Heavenly Father responsible for trapping her once again (the marriage had been on the brink of breakdown when she'd gotten pregnant with the last child). She was devastated and told her sister, who talked her down from the ledge, reminding her that this was *good* news. Nobody had cancer or was in an accident. A baby was coming! This helped her and within twenty-four hours, her own natural love of being a mother kicked in and she embraced the idea of having another baby.

Of course, she had to tell her husband and—as with all the other pregnancies—the news was not happily received. However, there was no other choice but to accept it. And because she'd had troubles with the other pregnancies, it was decided that nobody would be told for a time. A couple of weeks later, the announcement was made, with mixed reactions from their other children. The oldest son (sixteen) was markedly embarrassed, no doubt because his mom was pregnant and that was uncomfortable proof that his parents were still intimate. All in all though, it went well. She even went out and bought a new playpen and portable highchair.

Her husband was becoming increasingly jealous over her conversations with "Internet friends." The tension between them increased, even though he refused to read what she was writing to them, despite her begging him to.

Then one day, she began to spot. She went to the hospital and was told that nature would take its course, one way or the other, and to go home. This was during his holidays, and he stayed at the lake with the kids in his parents' motorhome. For three days, the pain was constant as though in labor, and she sat (alone as always) through another milestone in her life. The actual miscarriage was and is today a horror. She believes this moment tipped her over the edge.

For the first time in her life, she felt anger such as she'd never even imagined and a complete loss of hope and faith in Heavenly Father. It was as though a switch inside her had been flicked off and it would be almost three years before she could physically cry. She was completely empty and devoid of emotion, though the anger lingered like a new best friend. Naturally, this was not an appealing trait for a wife to have, and the husband was confused and upset by her lack of responsiveness to him in any capacity.

For two more years, they limped along in a crippled marriage. She finally recognized the nature of the illness that had beset her, while he was unable to believe it was real because she was looking better than she had in years and was making a good show of "functioning." He would accuse her of not being depressed and of just being selfish and wanting to be independent. Meanwhile, she struggled with darkness that often threatened to overwhelm her if she didn't keep fighting it.

Okay, this is starting to bore me. I don't know about you, but this is really getting tedious. So what's the weather like where you live? By the way, the last picture of your children is wonderful! Again, you are a lucky man and you've done a great job from what I can see.

Selena

♥

From: Duane
To: Selena
Subject: THE WEATHER?
Date: November 13, 2000, 7:19 a.m.
Dear Selena,

Everybody talks about it, but nobody ever does anything about it. That's the weather! Forecast for tonight is dark, followed by widely scattered light in the morning. That's the weather! I think my heater came on during the night, but I'm not sure—now that's boring!

Selena, darling, maybe you have told the story a couple of times, or maybe you've gone over it in your head a couple of million times. But let me assure you that it's hardly boring. I'm starting to get a real feel for where some of that biting humor comes from. Don't leave me hangin'; reel me in. I'm an audience like you've only read about in the funny papers.

I have been near the place that you described. If it weren't for the miracle of modern pharmacology, I don't know where I'd be today. I am rather wary of taking any drug, but possibly the greatest decision I ever made was to take Paxil. If there is one thing I know, it's depression.

I was accused as a child of being self-indulgent and spoiled. As an adult, I self-medicated and had untold problems with relationships. I wasn't continually depressed. It ran in cycles, but when I went into that little dark cave—sometimes I didn't think I would ever have the will to come back.

Please talk! Tell me more! I will be anxiously awaiting your next installment.

Your friend,
Duane

From: Selena
To: Duane
Subject: Can you hear the violins yet?
Date: Tuesday, November 14, 2000, 1:24 p.m.

Honestly, I think you're right. This seems so old and boring to me because, yes, I've gone through it in my head millions of times. Okay, we're back for round three, and this should finish things up. (You'll notice this took me two days to write. It was really hard to finish.)

Yes, this is my sordid story, so I guess I should own up to it in the first person. I was on a downward spiral but hanging on for dear life, even though many things had now changed for me. (I see now that those were part of the symptoms). I talked to my bishop and told him how bad things had gotten; it was like I was only half alive while I was talking. He told me that I was displaying the typical signs of a battered wife (in this case, emotional) and in the next breath commended me on my resigning myself to stay another ten years for the children. I was determined that I would do anything for the children, but the truth was that my spirit was withering away with each passing day.

Speaking of spirit, I'd also lost the Spirit. It seems the numbness that overcame me also wouldn't let the Spirit penetrate the darkness. Some of my LDS friends told me I wasn't reading enough scriptures or praying hard enough. They told me I wasn't letting the Lord help me. The truth as I see it is that I was doing everything I was capable of doing. I believed Heavenly Father knew my situation, and He was going to have to get to me somehow because I simply wasn't capable of one more thing. I still haven't felt the Spirit and it's been almost three years now. I've stopped taking the sacrament because I don't want to be a hypocrite. I can sit in meetings where people are bawling their eyes out and it doesn't even phase me. I can hear good and logical talks, but I can only appreciate them for their scholarly merit. There is no Spirit to testify of truth for me now.

Someone told me once that as long as I was on meds, I wouldn't feel the Spirit. So I stayed on for the minimum six months and weaned myself off. Nothing. Oh well. Life was getting pretty okay in some respects, and I figured that Heavenly Father knew where I was, and whenever He wanted to get a message to me, I'd be there. Meanwhile, I didn't care about where I'd go after this life (heck, barnyard duty with the animals for eternity would be good). I'm glad that I wasn't married for eternity to someone I couldn't even envision growing old with. It sounded to me like the Church was saying that my ultimate salvation was dependent on my having a man to get me there, and I resent that (this would be where my rebelliousness comes in ☺).

What I realized as I began talking to other people in the chat format was that I was starving for human feedback. Just to be able to converse and share ideas and learn new things was like finding water in a desert. I felt as though I could speak again after being mute for so long—my husband and I rarely had any conversation. I also took the opportunity to try to figure out the male animal. You see, the Church makes it kind of difficult for members of the opposite sex to be friends (avoid the appearance of evil). And yet, how could someone with my pitifully limited experience with the opposite sex possibly learn about them in order to understand, and maybe even figure out the man I was married to? I found it a safe way to ask sometimes personal questions (like why men dig porn—that sort of thing). I began to understand a few things about men, but it didn't help my feelings of worthlessness. I didn't feel like somebody special in my marriage. I felt like a body that was there just to be used.

Meanwhile, one of the people I chatted with has since then become a wonderful friend. When I met Tracy, it was like meeting a kindred spirit, like we've always known each other. Steven was resentful of my friendship with her. I think maybe he was frustrated by his inability to connect with me the way others could. Sadness all the way around.

So increasing tension coupled with decreased understanding led to a less-than-positive atmosphere in the household for the whole family. I think he and I both knew divorce was imminent, but when we talked about it, he refused to leave. After one particularly bad night, I grabbed a laundry basket, determined my kids would never have to endure another time like that, and I left. A few days later, I found a place to live, just six houses away.

I've lived in this place for five months with a honey pail that could have doubled as a chair if I really wanted to sit down (I never sat on it). I took nothing and required nothing. For the first time in over two years, I was able to sleep. My instincts had been telling me for months that something this drastic needed to be done, but I listened to family, I listened to people at Church, I listened to my husband, I listened to everybody except my intuition—and it turns out my instincts were right on. I began to get better.

Now, if you think that's all there is, brace yourself. My divorce isn't final yet. So in essence, I'm on the LDSSO thing under false pretenses. Remember how my friend's sister was on there (her name is Jacqueline, if you want to check her out—Jacqueline is very pretty and eligible, I might add) and the only way my friend Paige and I could peek at her profile was by signing up? Well, Paige is happily married, so the "honor" fell upon me, and when I had to put my marital status down there were no options other than never married, divorced, or widowed. Soooo . . . I put divorced.

Okay, if you have any questions, now would be a good time.
Still friends?
Selena

From: Duane
To: Selena
Subject: That's a lot to digest
Date: Tuesday, November 14, 2000, 6:39 p.m.
Dear Selena,

It is not my intention to try to outdo your story, but it may sound that way. ("Oh yeah? Check this out . . .")

In Virginia, when a couple with children get a divorce, they have to wait a full year before it is finalized. Because I forgave my wife after the first filing, I have had to wait nearly two years. My divorce isn't final for four more weeks. Our original vow was never taken seriously and was broken by both of us many times over the years. We were both addicts and our marriage was a joke. I keep saying that I am going to do it right this time, but I'm not doing so hot so far, if you include my failure to wait for my divorce to be final.

I too have not been taking the sacrament for the exact same reasons. I don't want to be a hypocrite. For two years now, I have been alienated from the Spirit. I pray, but I don't feel worthy to pray. I don't believe that God has abandoned me, but rather that He is letting me work my way through this. I'm convinced that the answer is inside of me. I love the Church and I refuse to blame my shortcomings on it, or the Lord.

I used to be so touched by the testimonies I would hear in sacrament meeting sometimes. I loved any story that would extract a tear. I can really identify with you on this one item. I miss it and I'm so aware that it is missing. I did have a touching moment this past Sunday when both my daughters sang in our meeting. Emily sang a beautiful solo and all the girls sang "As I Have Loved You," with Mallory projecting her voice directly into my heart. I would hold out hope that maybe I'm softening up, but I know that the reason I had tears was because I could see how spiritual they are compared to me. Understand?

I need to go fix dinner for my rotten little kids. I have more to say, but feel free to respond to what I've written so far.

Too much self-disclosure?

Duane

♥

From: Selena
To: Duane
Subject: *Whew*
Date: Tuesday, November 14, 2000, 8:33 p.m.
Hi Duane,
Sounds like we've got at least a mutual understanding going on here. The cool part is that we both have different perspectives simply

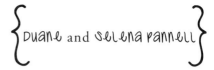

by virtue of our gender. I think I can learn some important things from you. Maybe I can help you with some things too. At the very least, I have felt comfortable talking to you about big stuff, and I appreciate that. If you don't forget to put the toilet seat down, I'll call you a prince among men. ☺

Okay, it sounded like you had some other things to say, so it's your turn.

Selena

From: Duane
To: Selena
Subject: A little more input
Date: Tuesday, November 14, 2000, 9:15 p.m.

Well, well, well, there you were trying to pass yourself off as Rebecca of Sunnybrook Farm. I can't believe that I almost booked a flight to Alberta to meet the girl of my dreams. I suppose my faith in the opposite sex is once again proving to be unjustified. You're all out to get me, it turns out.

Just kidding. I really am just kidding. That's what happens to me when things get too serious.

You know, you are healing as you should. In the coming months and years, you're going to look back on all this and understand why it all came about and how it all fell into place. It could be that you and I are having the same experience concerning the estrangement from the Holy Spirit.

Think of this: I believe my divorce is the closing of a chapter. Once upon a time, I made a conscious decision, in rebellion to my parents, to marry the wrong one. That was not my only poor choice, nor was it entirely wrong (I got three great kids out of the experience), but it was in defiance of what I knew was right. I have repented and worked toward making things right, but that doesn't excuse me from the consequences of what I have done. The Lord promised, "I will remember your sins no more," but He doesn't promise that I won't remember. My remembering is vital to my eternal progression.

I have come to believe that this "separation" that I'm experiencing is temporary. In my heart of hearts, I believe in the Church and I love the Church. I love the Lord's prophets. I love the Father, the Son, and the Holy Ghost. I have a testimony of these things, even though I'm not feeling it right this minute. Could this be part of the process? Perhaps this "separation" happens whenever we gain a monumental conviction of heart, which we were sent here to gain?

Selena, I enjoy reading what you write to me. I need a relationship like this right now, and I think you are right; maybe we can help each other. You are intelligent, and pardon me, but I find that to be a really attractive quality in a woman.

Oh, and you asked about pornography earlier. Oh no! You did ask about it, didn't you?! How embarrassing!

See how I do when things get serious? Okay, here it is, the good, the bad, and the ugly: Generally speaking, most women do not understand its appeal to men. As it turns out, men and women are different. Surprise! Women are primarily more emotionally driven, and from their perspective, it's hard to understand that a man looking at pornography is not actually an emotionally charged event. But for men, it's not emotionally involved—it's all mechanical. Pornography can, and does, become an addiction, like taking a drug. In fact, it really is a drug in a way. Looking at pornography releases neurotransmitters that excite the pleasure centers of the brain, and that can become incredibly addictive.

Some psychologists think that as long as it doesn't become a major problem, some indulgence in pornography may even help a marriage relationship. Of course, as you well know, some psychologists are full of crap.

An important aspect of addiction is that it's progressive. Just like an alcoholic who starts off drinking a beer once a week, someday he may find himself getting little satisfaction from drinking a six-pack a day. The alcoholic builds up a tolerance to the alcohol and it takes more and more to get the same results. It's the same with the porn addict; he may be satisfied in the beginning looking at girls in swimsuits, but as time goes on, his appetite grows toward more graphic pornography. It's actually not unusual for this obsession to become so bad that it leads to incarceration.

You can probably see this in your experiences with your husband. Sometimes men get involved in porn in a matter-of-fact, take-it-or-leave-it sort of way and later on find themselves sucked into it over time. In the beginning, perhaps it adds spice to a couple's intimacy. It may enhance his performance and he thinks, *How can this be a bad thing? I've made positive steps to improve our intimacy!* (Note: men equate sex with intimacy). But because it's progressive, it does become a bad thing. It's like being desensitized to violence; after repeated exposure, sex is totally separated from love and the ability to experience feelings like compassion and empathy become difficult, if not impossible, for the porn addict.

The most important thing for you to know, Selena, is this: Your husband's indulgence in pornography had nothing to do with you or your worth. This is your husband's problem. He may never stop—like any other addiction, he has to admit that it is a problem that he has no control over. These days, pornography has become accepted as normal, and those of us who stay away from it (I have my own personal reasons) are considered the abnormal ones.

I hope that this has been of help to you, even if only a little. There is no reason to allow someone else's addiction keep you in chains. My ex-wife had four wonderful children, and it would be disrespectful of me to think of her body as "the less-than-perfect frame" that it once was. I appreciate what she has done in bringing our children into the world. Hah! Bet she's missing me now! Oh sorry, I got a little carried away. Anyway, have a good night.

I'll be thinking of you,

Duane

From: Selena

To: Duane

Subject: Re: A little more input

Date: Tuesday, November 14, 2000, 10:36 p.m.

I have to tell you, I got really hung up on that last sentence. If you were joking, it still smacks of pain and anger. Am I close? I think you should have to tell me—purge and get the poison out. Though I don't mind if you decide not to.

The rest of what you wrote was really good stuff. So tell me, what are your personal reasons for not indulging in pornography?

Your friend,

Selena

♥

From: Duane

To: Selena

Subject: What, me? Angry?

Date: Wednesday, November 15, 2000, 7:22 p.m.

Dear Selena,

Okay, I am not angry—not like walking around, submachine-gun-in-hand angry anyway. I think that I've worked through this fairly well. I do have bitter feelings when I think of the extra fifteen months of my life that feel wasted (giving her another chance). But I'm on my way to new adventures, right? How can I be bitter when this could be the most exciting time of my life?

"No Porn." I have that tattooed somewhere on me. I have indulged in porn previously. I stand guilty. When I was about five or six years old, I remember seeing my first pin-up girls. It was appealing to me. My dad had calendars and magazines in his office, and I would go in there when no one was around and look at all the girls. When I was about eleven, a friend and I found a porn movie in his dad's closet and we watched it over and over again. I became obsessed with sex at a young age, and I believe it had a great deal of influence on my behavior. It's difficult enough just being an adolescent without complicating the experience with drugs, sex, and alcohol.

The combination of these things resulted in an inability to have a healthy relationship with any woman. I was so emotionally immature that I brought nothing of value to a relationship; I had nothing to offer a woman with healthy self-esteem and emotional stability, so I usually attracted girls that were no better off than me. That's probably why my wife and I stayed together for so many years—we were two drowning swimmers clinging to each other.

And when I began taking the missionary discussions, something happened to me. I began to think about all the girls that I had known over the years. I began to have some incredibly personal, deep feelings concerning these individual girls and women. The Spirit whispered to me. Many of the girls I'd known were abused. Though I had not been physically abusive to them myself, I had contributed to their problems, and they were experiencing pain to this very day that I had added to. I could see that some had shared thoughtfully with me and I had taken without even a small thought of who they were as a human being, let alone as daughters of the Most High God. I felt anguish over this, and it was a large part of my repentance process before I was baptized.

During that time, pornography was shown to me for what it is— poison. I know that I don't want those images in my head when I'm at the altar with my eternal sweetheart. When I look into her eyes, I only want to see her. I want my marriage to be healthy and whole, and I never want her to feel like less than the most important person in my life, now and forever.

I hope this answers some of your question. Have a wonderful day.
Your friend,
Duane

From: Selena
To: Duane
Subject: I'm learning . . .
Date: Wednesday, November 15, 2000, 8:59 p.m.

Thanks to you, I'm learning a little bit more each day. And because I'm being so darn benevolent at the moment, I'm not going to toss you another hardball. Tell me what you think women should know about men. And while you're at it, maybe you could enlighten me with what men want from women. Sorry that this is such a short note, but write soon anyway, okay?
Selena

From: Duane
To: Selena
Subject: Something important happened . . .
Date: Thursday, November 16, 2000, 6:41 a.m.

I owe you. When I wrote that note last night, I was really focused. I know that it is important to you and I wanted to do a good job of explaining what I know. I started it a couple of times—I would look at what I wrote and not be satisfied, and then start again. But then it occurred to me that I should pray and ask for the ability to organize my thoughts and receive inspiration. By the time I was done, I was feeling quite pleased that I was able to convey the message exactly as I had hoped. So I sent it off to you and went on about my evening routine. But that feeling didn't leave me. I was feeling *good*. I picked up my scriptures and read (randomly) in Doctrine and Covenants where it talks about gifts. One verse stood out to me: "To some it is given by the Holy Ghost to know that Jesus Christ is the Son of God, and that he was crucified for the sins of the world" (D&C 46:13).

It was highlighted, and I know that I've read it many times before, but this time I felt like it applied to me. I may have had some rough times lately, but I believe in Christ. I don't know what I'm lacking now that makes me feel this separation, but I believe it's temporary and I know it's because of me and not the Lord or His Church. Anyway, you should know that I had a rare experience to feel the Spirit of God last night, and I blame you—or credit you.

So, another question. What does a man want and what should a woman know? Almost the same question.

Keeping in mind that most people, not just men, often act in direct opposition to what they really want. And sometimes they want more than they should have—think of this:

A man wants to be your knight in shining armor. He doesn't want any other man to be your "best friend." He wants to be your only "man friend," even if he's lousy at it. He wants to be seen as your protector and your counselor. He wants to know that he is important enough in your life that you consider him in most all of your decisions. He wants to believe that he is the most atractive, most masculine man you have ever known. And—you're going to hate this—he wants you to belong to him.

You're biting your lip, aren't you?

That's a bad thing, the belonging part, isn't it? Sadly, it is the way it often happens. A guy takes "ownership" of a woman and smothers her and bosses her and swallows up her identity in his. But that's not how it should be. The proper way is she belongs to him, and likewise he belongs to her. The two individuals become one, loyal and true to each other (both protecting their union from outside forces), yet able to be distinct and separate people. They have personal interests, but they build a life where most of what they do, they do together.

If you think about it, even your husband, whom you describe as being inattentive and absent, was wanting to be the knight. That's why I prefaced this by saying that people sometimes act in direct opposition to what they really want. The main cause of divorce is selfishness. We're living in a world that's become increasingly focused on personal desires—selfishness. If you'd have enthusiastically participated in all of his activities and made yourself available to satisfy his every need—and done this submissively, without any sort of obligation from him to satisfy your needs—guess what would've happened? He would've been the knight. He would have assumed that because all seemed well in the kingdom, he'd earned his knighthood. All the "good" things he thought of himself would've been justified.

You can take a man with the most inflated ego in the world and reduce him to ashes, deserved or not, by taking away his knighthood. This can be done by doing nothing more than complaining to your mother about him or getting your advice from a best friend. Depending on the man, it could happen by simply commenting on the good looks of some guy on television. It'd definitely happen if a woman were to be unfaithful and commit adultery. This is why we're supposed to be so careful when we choose our companions. One emotionally healthy and mature person cannot make a marriage a success. It takes both people being unselfish and determined. The problem with many marriages is that neither person is prepared for what is required—that was my own experience.

You said that you rather resented the fact that Heavenly Father was requiring you to be escorted to the celestial kingdom by a MAN. That is a fairly poor way of looking at it. Personally, I see myself as a priesthood holder at half-mast. I can't do what is required without the right woman to sustain me. It's all in her court at this point. I have become all I'm going to be without her. Things will continue to happen in my life, and I'll continue to have new experiences, but it will only begin to go forward again when "she" and I find each other. When that happens, I'll be progressing again (only not alone). I will not be allowed to enter that highest kingdom without *her*.

This is getting long. I'm sorry. I hope that I have expressed this in the way I intended. I do trust you with my thoughts. Besides, what can you do to me? You're, like, 3,000 miles away? I'm kidding—but really, what can you do to me?

Goodnight Moongoddess,

Papabear

♥

From: Selena

To: Duane

Subject: That is a lot to take in . . .

Date: Thursday, November 16, 2000, 10:09 a.m.

I appreciate your perspective on the whole fidelity thing. And, as much as a man wants to be the knight in shining armor, a woman wants to have that knight in shining armor. A woman wants to be protected, not smothered. Cherished, but not owned. Worshipped in a way that will make her want to drop to her knees to worship a man who can love her so much. A woman wants (oh, who am I trying to kid—I'm speaking mostly of myself and can only assume other women feel these things too) to move forward with talents and skills and be supported to this end by the man of her dreams.

I felt like a trophy wife. I was good to take to the company parties because I could hold my own, even when younger women entered the "competition." I'm just too old now to take that as love anymore and too wise, I think, to be content with being hand-fed like a bird in a gilded cage, never being able to magnify who I was meant to become in this mortal life. I also would rather spend the rest of my days, and even eternity, alone than to be with someone I don't feel safe with in every way. If I can't have the knight, I'm not settling for less, and if it means being alone, so be it. How's that for attitude?

I've come to believe that all people operate according to two basic needs. There are others, of course, but these are the ones that never change from person to person. We all want to be understood and we all want to avoid pain. We want others to see how incredible we sometimes believe ourselves to be and understand and not judge us when we fall short of the incredible mark. And we'll do almost anything to avoid being hurt. It wouldn't make sense to deliberately set ourselves up for hurt and anguish.

I made many terrible choices years ago. I have come to a time and place, though, where I can look back at the girl I was then and feel pity and sadness for her rather than judgment and contempt. I paid a high price for those choices in repentance and humility, and I knew when I went to the temple that the slate was clean. Of course, in this mortality, no slate is ever clean and there will always be people to remind you of past mistakes, sins, choices, errors, and so on. But that's not who I am, and I don't dwell on it.

Thanks for listening—oh, and any other words of wisdom you can think of, feel free to share. I'm glad you felt the Spirit. ☺

Selena

From: Duane
To: Selena
Subject: Not judging
Date: Thursday, November 16, 2000, 11:20 p.m.
Dear Selena,

I hope that you did not think that I was a "people" reminding you of past indiscretions. I was offering you a perspective on the human male animal (I'll bet you independent women types love that description). What I mostly want you to get is that your husband may very well be the biggest jerk in the world—but all those things I describe to you still apply. Let me tell you a little story and let's see if you get the analogy:

Several years ago, a pair of missionaries and I were eating at this restaurant near my house. This waiter came over and asked us about the Church. Long story short, he was an ordained minister and the

missionaries and I taught him the restored gospel. His church became
angry with him and stripped him of his ordination. He was baptized
(by me!) later on. I started getting to know him and we became friends.

Bill was a good guy—he had endured a pretty rough life. He was
always telling me about his grandmother who raised him, and how
she was never pleased with anything that he did. She was critical and
made him feel like a nuisance.

When Bill was only five months old, his mother left him and his
father, never to return. At the age of two, his father committed suicide,
and Bill was left to be raised by his grandparents. His grandmother
would tell him, for as long as he could remember, that no one loved
him or wanted him. That his mother left because of him and his dad
could not handle the pressure of raising him alone. Bill believed that
he really was the cause of these awful circumstances because of his
grandmother's words.

One day in Church, I was talking to a couple, who coincidentally
had a five-month-old baby (the same age Bill was when his mom left).
I made Bill hold the baby. Bill is a dear man, and you could see that he
really liked that baby. I asked Bill after a few moments, "What could
this baby do to make you hate him?" You could see the lights come on
right away—Bill's eyes welled up and I knew that he understood that
there was nothing that he could've done as a baby to cause the grief
that he had experienced. I think he gained a lot of ground that day and
began to see things a little bit differently.

One day, Bill invited me to go to the nursing home to meet his
grandmother—oh goody! When we went into her room, I was a little
surprised to see this little frail woman. After all that I'd heard about
her, I somehow expected a much bigger and stronger woman. She was
a pitiful sight—blind and bedridden, with her face all twisted with
pain. She was nice to me and told me how glad she was that "Billy"
had made some good friends. Before our visit was over, I was treated
to a little of Bill's world. She fussed at him for something that had
apparently happened ten years ago as if it were just last week. She
belittled him in front of me and a nurse. Bill looked like a little seven-
year-old boy standing before her—taking his scolding.

But then, as I observed this sad family dynamic unfold before me,
I became aware of something. When Bill was born into this world to

less-than-ideal parents and things began to go so bad, his grandmother was the only person able to take him and his dad in. So when his father died and his mother was nowhere to be found, there was this baby. His grandmother took the baby in and raised him, albeit reluctantly—and there was never anyone around to praise her for doing this (frankly) noble act.

She did abuse Bill. Not physically, but in a still cruel way. She was crying out where only he could hear, "I'm doing a wonderful thing! Look at this sacrifice I am making for this child! No one else would do this but me!" I'm sure that it was quite frustrating to her and her husband, and the little dysfunctional family grew from there.

Bill's grandmother was not acting on illegitimate feelings; no, the feelings she had were quite valid. She was justified to see herself as something of a martyr. Many people in her situation would likely feel as she felt. The big difference is how she responded to those feelings. She loved Bill and didn't intend to make him the insecure, emotionally immature mess that he became as an adult, but that was the end result of her actions.

Last night when I wrote that bit for you, I was hoping to show you a glimpse into your husband's world. I hope that you didn't take it as me standing in judgment of you, because I certainly don't mean to offend you. The story I just wrote is about a woman trapped in a situation who is starving for some kind of recognition—her feelings are completely understandable, but her actions are on the scale near where the "horrible" mark is located.

People sometimes have way better intentions than their behaviors would suggest. A man (not me, of course, but some man) can fail to show appreciation for his wife for a long time, but then one day he discovers she is unhappy and slipping away from him. His reaction is likely to be immediate and not well thought out. When that happens, all the personality flaws start coming out!

I want you to know that I'm not defending your husband, or even suggesting that you patch things up. I'm sure that your eighteen years of experience with the man are a better judge than me to determine the likelihood of that happening. You should just know that the world isn't against you. We are all jumping our own hurdles and suffering our own trials in life—even your husband, the big jerk.

I'll let you digest this. I feel like I need a big hug. Everybody's in bed except for me and my Old English sheepdog, Lizzie. She's a great little snuggler, but she doesn't have any thumbs (or at least that's what she tells me), and you may not know this, but thumbs are somehow essential in a properly executed hug. She can't pour a glass of milk either. You know . . . thumbs.

G'night,
Duane

♥

From: Selena
To: Duane
Subject: Aha!
Date: Friday, November 17, 2000, 1:34 p.m.

I think I'm beginning to see a little light here. Your stories were good and make sense. You're a pretty smart guy, did you know that? I think you're right. Steven desperately started trying, in his own way, to "fix" me and make our marriage what he thought it should have been. He didn't mean to hurt me in the process; he just didn't understand what I needed and couldn't understand what I tried to tell him I needed because it didn't make sense to him. Now he's consumed by anger, and I believe that is borne of the hurt and sense of loss he is feeling now. How am I doing? Am I going to get an A in this class? ☺

Do you mind if I ask you a question? It only occurred to me today that perhaps it is not wise or appropriate for me to be so forthright when asked about my marriage. I mean, we've only become acquainted recently, but I dumped pretty much the good, the bad, and the ugly right in your lap. Should the day ever come that I would give up my dream of becoming the wise old crone, living at the edge of a small village where everyone is a little afraid of her—but still go to her for advice and healing because she is, after all, the wise old crone—should that day ever come that I meet a man, when and how would it be "right" for me to divulge all those things that I've already told you about?

Now enough about me. Let's talk about you. Tell me about your current relationship with the mother of your children. Tell me which stage of the healing process you are at, where your history with her is concerned. Tell me how you feel about yourself. And last of all, tell me about the happiest day of your life.

Sorry you had to rely on a thumb-less pooch for emotional hugs last night, but your sacrifice is duly noted.

Selena

PS I'm really glad that you've become my friend. I think I'll become a better person for having known you (that is the sign of a really good friend). Have a marvelous day.

From: Duane
To: Selena
Subject: Your grade is . . .
Date: Friday, November 17, 2000, 10:56 p.m.

Wow, you nailed it! Your husband was desperate all right. He was also way behind in his attempt to "fix" things. This has a tendency to blow up in your face—you know, too little too late. People (and I'm thinking of a certain former spouse) are prone to believe that their behavioral changes are way more established than they really are. They spend six days acting in a near acceptable fashion and insist that it has been six months of good behavior! You do get an A.

As for your second question, I don't know. This is the exploration of baggage that I spoke of earlier, meaning that you would do that for me. Somehow, it didn't occur to me that you would have baggage—you just seemed so . . . together. ☺ I have not told anyone some of the things that I have told you. These are not things that I would want to keep from an eternal companion, but self-disclosure is a tricky thing. You give up too much at the wrong time and pretty soon the other person is looking at you like my dog looks at me when I'm standing around shirtless: head cocked sideways with puzzled eyes. Reading that over, that may be too much information.

The reason I've told you the things I have is because you are far, far away. You can like me, hate me, love me, feel indifferent toward me, be angry, whatever. At this point, I would really miss you if I didn't hear from you anymore, but a "broken heart" is way easier to mend from this distance. I'm going to have to think on these things.

Where am I with the mother of my children? It's very over. I feel bad for what she has to go through, but I'm glad that I'm no longer a part of it. I don't love her anymore. I think that's a shame, but I don't hate her. I feel lonely sometimes, but I don't miss her. It actually bothered me at first that an emotion could change so much in two years. I did sort of ask Heavenly Father to give me relief during the most intense times—I believe I got it, and then some. She doesn't look the same to me, and I don't feel the same. We see each other about once a month, if even that much, and I don't feel the need to call and chat.

As far as healing goes, I think that my period of mourning is over. I guess the natural expectation is that, considering my past, I would worry about my new companion being unfaithful (maybe some loyalty issues?), but I don't think that I think that way now. There are no perfect people. But if my sweetheart and I are sincere and determined to love one another and endure the hardships together, I believe we will be fine. Something else to consider, after the experiences that I have been through, my new wife will get a much better husband than the ex-wife got.

How do I feel about myself? I suppose my confidence level is little low. That's probably how I got so comfortable dating the woman who strokes my ego, but I think things are getting better with time. Once upon a time, I had lost everything because of my drug and alcohol use, but I've bounced back. I have a great job, great kids, and great friends. There is the depression factor. I have had bouts with depression ever since I was a little kid. I remember being upset by the thoughts that I would have and being so scared of . . . well, I don't know what. I'm sure that depression was a primary reason that my substance abuse problem escalated the way it did. I went many years after joining the Church without having even a mild episode of depression. I honestly thought that I was cured—like my conversion had cured me. But when all that stuff started happening with my wife, that was the catalyst for the mother of all depressions. I have been taking an antidepressant for the past two years, and I now see a time in the near future when I will be done with it. I'd have to say that, overall, I feel good.

I'm approaching forty years old, but I don't feel like it, or feel like I look like it. I love my children with all my heart and feel fortunate that I get to be their dad. I have great hope for what is coming in the future and look forward to being the grand patriarch of my family with a cherished wife by my side.

The happiest day of my life? I'm a pretty happy guy and I've had many happy days; it would really be hard to pick the best one. I believe that the happiest day hasn't happened yet. It'll be the day that I look into the eyes of my eternal companion across that altar in the temple and make those vows before the Lord. Am I starting to sound like a broken record?

Write me baaaaaaaaaack (that's how sheep say it).

Your friend,

Duane

From: Selena
To: Duane
Subject: Good morning
Date: Saturday, November 18, 2000, 9:56 a.m.

Hi Duane,

Are your free moments generally dictated by your children's activities and social lives, as are mine? I'm working this weekend and, in a way, work is my social life. Especially evenings and weekends. There's nobody in Administration but me, so I have the place to myself. I like to think I'm the queen of my little hospital castle, or maybe I'm just the hub of a wheel (queen sounds better).

Working in a hospital is interesting. I've had a lot of memorable experiences, some of them funny, some puzzling, and some deeply sad. I have the attention span of a gnat, so the ever-changing situations are perfect for me.

Have a great day!

Selena

From: Duane
To: Selena
Subject: I'm all alone . . .
Date: Saturday, November 18, 2000, 12:11 p.m.

The kids are off doing something today and I've got the whole (I almost wrote *hole*. And I don't know why I'm taking the time to tell you that) house to myself. I get weekends off when people aren't too thirsty. (Work for me is managing a satellite warehouse for the local Pepsi bottling plant.)

It's cool that you think of yourself as a queen. My kids call me the King of Christiansburg! I don't remember how it started, but it was funny when they were little. I would have adults ask my kidlets to tell them who the king of Christiansburg is and they would reply, "My daddy!"

Duane

♥

From: Selena
To: Duane
Subject: Hello from work
Date: Saturday, November 18, 2000, 3:34 p.m.

Hi Duane,

I got to thinking if it stayed quiet here, I might just be able to send you another email. All is still quiet. Lots of visitors, but no business for me. So I was rereading one of your last notes. One of the things you said caught my attention. Maybe you could elaborate? However, it sounds suspiciously like something I've had private anxiety about as well: loyalty issues.

In what context were you referring to these loyalty issues? Please explain. Then I'll tell you my thoughts about the matter.

Also, you mentioned jail—mind me asking about that? Don't worry, I'm not all freaked out. I'm just interested.

What do your kids think about you contemplating finding a new wife? How long have you been separated? How many more questions do you think I could possibly ask in one letter?

I'll send this now and see if you get it and will be quick to reply if you have occasion to write. Deal?

Selena

♥

From: Duane
To: Selena
Subject: Re: Hello from work
Date: Saturday, November 18, 2000, 4:48 p.m.

Whoa, slow down there, little lady. The "lil ol'" questions of you'rn are comin' faster than a cowpoke to a dinner bell. You probably can't tell, but that was the best Texas accent you've ever heard. It seems that I keep putting my soul on display and you manage to stay in the driver's seat with rapid-fire questions—doesn't it seem that way to you? Can you hear me? Okay, I'll play, but I better be getting a nice soul-baring response on this. You got it, sister?

My issue with loyalty isn't a worry over an inability for me to be loyal. I think, in that way, I've grown up. I believe that I am capable now of fully devoting myself to one woman forever. Though my marriage was a bit of train wreck during its final seven years, I still focused on being a good husband. It wasn't under the easiest of circumstances, but I managed to learn through good examples and the teachings of the Church what it means to be a good husband.

For my wife, I want to be the constant she can depend on. I want her to feel safe and complete with me. I don't ever want to give her a reason to regret her decision to be with me. I want to support her and help her become all that she can be, and then watch her in her glory on earth and in heaven. I want her to see her accomplishments and abilities as her own so that she knows she is fully capable and that she's with me, not out of necessity but because she chooses to be.

But I do have a little part of me that is concerned. My new life and relationship I'm seeking is still an abstract. I don't know for sure what it will be like when I'm living it. My hope is that being with a woman who is clean and sober will make things much easier. Even girlfriends that I had in the past, before there was a wife, were prone to substance abuse problems. Maybe because I'm ready, my perfect match is too?

And this relationship that I envision is possible—I mean, I know it's possible. I've seen it done. I guess the worry that my heart has is if she will desire that devotion that I'm offering her. Am I coming across as some hopeless dreamer? Does this make sense? Do I sound like a puffball? Are you making fun of me right this minute as you share this message with some big guy named Biff, who is inclined to believe that I need to be smacked? Oh, what was it I was saying about too much self-disclosure?

Stop laughing and write me back,
Duane

♥

From: Selena
To: Duane
Subject: Re: Loyalty
Date: Saturday, November 18, 2000, 10:01 p.m.

I am smiling, but not at what you said; just at how you have this way of framing something really serious and substantial in a light way. Keeps it less threatening somehow. Now you want a nice, soul-baring in response? Yikes! I'll have to be more careful about what I ask you in the future (reminder to self).

My loyalty issue isn't that I'm worried about my ability to be loyal either. I've learned a lot over the years, and maybe that's why I'm so leery of just jumping back into the relationship fray. If there's going to be a next time for me (wonder if there's openings at the convent for slightly used, older nuns?), I will be mature about it. I'll have spent the time necessary to develop a true and honest friendship with someone to the point where I won't be able to imagine living without him. I will be able to project us into the future and envision a life even when we're old. There's more to love, I think, than just youthful, heated romance. I want the kind that will carry me out of this world—literally. And I know that, even with the inevitable flaws, I will feel a loyalty that is unshakeable because the relationship won't be based on looks, money, or circumstances. The relationship will have as firm a foundation as any relationship can. Okay, so it's time for you to stop laughing at *my* little fantasy world.

What about the loyalty issue, you ask? Shoot, I was hoping with all my endless babble that you'd have forgotten that. Let's see, how do I put this delicately? . . . It has to do with intimacy. While I can't imagine being with my former husband again, it's almost inconceivable for me to imagine trusting somebody new with, well, me.

Holy cow. Talking about this is harder than I thought. Good thing this isn't paper or it might need some drying off. That was my particular loyalty issue, and I wondered what yours was.

Didn't I ask you a zillion other questions? Isn't it your turn to be in the hot seat again? It must be your turn . . .

Selena

From: Duane
To: Selena
Subject: Loyalty
Date: Saturday, November 19, 2000, 1:14 a.m.
Dearest Selena,

I'm really proud of you. You have shared your life with me, up to now, in sort of a "neck up" way. I mean, you have been forthright, but mostly what I have from you is the kind of thing that you could share without giving anything away. I really get the sense that you gave a little something away with that "loyalty" message. That makes me feel good. Thank you.

I get the idea that you feel that you could—or might—rather go through the rest of your life without a man. I sort of admire that. I am not insecure, but I do seem to be keenly disposed to the directive that a man should "leave his parents and cleave unto his wife." I have a need to cleave. But seriously, I have hopes and goals that cannot be attained without that special someone, and even if there were another way, I know me. I'd take the babe option.

I don't believe that you will continue to feel that way, but not being obsessed with the idea of finding the next mate will definitely be a plus for your healing process. I wonder, though, if you set your requirements unattainably high, you might possibly sabotage any chance of romance in the future.

Remember that you're not the young woman that you were when you married the first time. You are wiser. You are savvy in ways that the young Selena didn't even know to look for. You know, if you ever meditate, I have a fun activity I do that you might be able to benefit from. Ever heard of "the inner child"? It was a method of therapy that was real popular about ten years ago. Visualize yourself in the role of comforter and counselor to Selena eighteen years ago (or any time). Tell her about the wonderful things that are to come in her life. Warn her of the hard times to come and give her some pointers on how she should respond to those things. Give her encouragement to develop her talents and recognize her blessings. Be the adult voice that you needed way back then. It will reveal your wisdom to you and place in context all that you have endured.

When I read your last paragraph, I was touched. No, that doesn't express it quite right. I mean that I was stirred—no, that's not right either—I was deeply moved. . . . This is getting worse. Seriously, and I mean this in the most sincere way, I wish that I could hug you or hold your hand or something.

I don't mean to be trying to solve all of your problems. I guess I just feel a little elated to have been treated to such a soft side of you.

Thank you,

Duane

♥

From: Selena

To: Duane

Subject: You make me blush

Date: Sunday, November 19, 2000, 12:51 p.m.

I don't often blush either, but you've been really kind. And you'll have to take some responsibility for my softening, because you've made me feel like it's okay to go there. And if you weren't so darn far away, that hug sounded pretty good.

So it's funny that you bring up the idea of the older, wiser Selena talking to the young, inexperienced Selena. I have actually been doing that a lot over the past months because I've come to see my younger self as someone separate from who I am today. I have sadness for her and the bad choices that caused her (and the people around her) pain, but I don't judge her anymore for that. She was never bad, just foolish sometimes. So, because you said it's okay, I guess I'll continue talking to myself, even if that makes me look like Sybil.

Duane, do you ever get the feeling sometimes that the men in the Church rely on the women to carry the spiritual ball, even in their families? I carried that ball alone for so long, and I really don't want to end up with someone who's going to make me be the strong one all by myself again. I know I have to be careful about not setting unrealistic expectations, but I've already admitted I'd be willing to love someone fat, bald, and broke if he was my true friend and had an inner peace and strength I could count on. Doesn't that count as not having expectations set too high? Of course, it would be more fun to love somebody with those qualities who looked yummy to me and wasn't having to collect pop bottles to buy milk.

It never occurred to me that people might start trying to set me up with their brothers, fathers, friends, coworkers, and so on until you mentioned the woman at Church and her sister. Isn't that just a little frightening, the idea that soon it will be open hunting season and guess what? You're Bambi! That really scares me, actually. I have to admit to being "socially stunted," in that I have little experience with the flirting and dating game and can't even force myself to assume the role of the bubbly, effervescent ditz. I was never meant to be soda pop—I've always been more like a V-8 (do you have that in the United States?). You do realize that there are a lot of men who only want their women to be rather submissive and only smart enough to make cutesy crafts to decorate their homes but not to express themselves as individuals in their own right? That also scares me, because I won't be able to play that game. I won't be a hen pecking contentedly in the chicken yard, knowing I have wings.

Geez, I'm all over the place with my babbling today, aren't I? But you're a smart guy. Maybe you can sort through all this stuff and make some sense of it.

Don't you think it's time you told me another secret?

Selena

♥

From: Duane
To: Selena
Subject: Okay, Bambi, how about this?
Date: Sunday, November 19, 2000, 1:27 p.m.

You have raised the bar. As I said earlier, I have already compared one woman to you. I'm now including traits in my search that I hadn't thought of before because of your input. You say that if you thought you would be happy, you'd be willing to love someone who is fat, bald, and broke. What if you thought the perfect mate was 2,279 miles away? Would that be worth pursuing if you thought he was, as you say, "yummy"?

I'll never be bald. I make enough money to be comfortable. I refuse to be fat. And I know where there's a cow that no one's paying attention to in the event of a milk shortage. I am available to hold hands or massage feet; and talk about inner peace and strength—I'm oozing with it!

You talk of carrying the spiritual ball in the family—baby, you're preaching to the choir. I have been doing it all alone for most of the eight years I've been in the Church. I have a vision of giving one of my children a blessing, and as I am pronouncing the blessing, my wife has her hand on my shoulder. In my mind, it's symbolic to me of her sustaining my priesthood and supporting the desire of the bless-ing. I'm not perfect by any stretch, but you would not attend Church alone and you would never get grief for attending to Church business or events and leaving me with the household responsibilities. I would love to be "stuck" at the house with the children in order for my wife to go to a Relief Society meeting or some other kingdom-building activity.

A hen pecking contentedly in the chicken yard? Oh, you rural folk and your homespun analogies! I believe it would be a sin to suppress your thoughts. I love an intelligent woman. My ex-wife is an intelligent woman, and I have often wondered where her mind would have taken her if she had not been an addict. I would not only be willing to "let you fly," but I would be content to be in your shadow now and again when the spotlight is on you. I'm not all all interested in a ditzy female. I appreciate a woman who is thoughtful, smart, and can express herself and her thoughts and opinions well.

I'm not proposing marriage; I just thought that I'd let you know what's going on in my head. I'd love to get to know you better. All these miles apart and I have to admit that I am a little "twitterpated." No matter what, this is a great experience for me. You care about real things. I find your sensitivities endearing. I believe you have a great future ahead of you and the man who gets to share that with you will be incredibly lucky.

My friend's sister is actually the third setup for me. The first two went okay, but one was too young and there were just no sparks with the other. If I remember correctly, Bambi and the hunters were all in the woods together, but he fared all right. It's just a matter of staying out of the line of fire. Maybe it would be in your best interest to just say no to any suggestions of a setup—oh, sorry, I was looking out for *my* best interest.

You shouldn't worry too much about your social skills. People are people, and if you try to put others at ease, you'll invariably do the same for yourself. Whenever someone wants to introduce me to a single friend or relative, I try to get some information about that person and if anything strikes me as a red flag, I just say, "You know, normally I would be game, but I'm sort of interested in someone at the moment. But thanks for keeping me in mind though." If you think that going out with someone would be good company, I would recommend it. Human contact is good for your mental health; being with just kids all the time doesn't always do the trick. I do okay, but after a while I need to talk to another adult.

I hope that I haven't frightened you off with my boldness. I just felt like you didn't have enough to worry about in your life—I mean think about it, I am just as harmless to you as you are to me, and I don't have enough time to devote to stalking someone, especially if it is a long commute (I have work in the morning). I'm happy with the status quo and I could go on like this indefinitely with you. Which reminds me, I haven't told you about my exploits in jail (then he laughed like a madman).

Your friend of royalty and an unlimited soft drink supply,
Duane

From: Duane
To: Selena
Subject: Uh oh, did I scare you off?
Date: Sunday, November 19, 2000, 3:17 p.m.
Dear Selena,

Hey, it's me! Do you know that I have been writing to you a lot? You ask a lot of questions, do you know that? How can you ask so many questions? Are you naturally curious or what? What's up with that? Have you noticed that I'm not nearly as creative at this as you are?

What do my kids think of my searching for a new wife? They have been supportive. My girls have expressed an opinion that I should only be dating LDS women (if I'm going to be a good example). The kids have only known about one woman that I dated (because she had a daughter who went to their school) and they didn't seem to care much for her.

My wife and I have been "legally" separated for just over a year. I started the process over two years ago, but we tried to work things out after she made an effort to get help with her addictions. It didn't take.

Another secret? This isn't really a secret—to the people around me, it's probably more like an annoyance. I do impressions. Like cartoon voices, accents, and dialects of fun and interesting people. My son seems to have been blessed (or cursed) with the same gift as well.

I'm quite sure that it's your turn.
Your friend, His Majesty, the King of Christiansburg,
Duane

From: Selena
To: Duane
Subject: More scattered thoughts . . .
Date: Sunday, November 19, 2000, 3:43 p.m.
. . . for you to sort out. Want to borrow my butterfly net?

Yes, I have noticed that you've been writing to me a lot, but the same could be said of me, so we must be even. I think you do well, talking without my input. And I'd way rather hear what you have to say. But I suppose that defeats the entire purpose of corresponding, so here it goes.

Regarding separation. I guess it's fair to say that with few exceptions, our separation within the house began in January of 1999, so almost two years. I moved into my own place February 23 of this year, so that makes a physical separation of nine months. I didn't realize it until later, but that was twenty years to the day I actually met Steven. Strange, huh? A lot can happen in twenty years.

Yes, I ask a lot of questions and if it drives you bonkers, you'll just have to stifle it, answer my questions, and keep me happy. ☺ Does that sound ominous or what?

Do you think that there's a twelve-step program for people who get hooked on email? I mean, if you were to stop writing now, I might start having withdrawal symptoms. For the sake of my health, you won't do that without fair warning, will you?

Okay, that's all for now. I've got a patient going AWOL.

Later,

Selena

From: Duane
To: Selena
Subject: I believe I asked you a direct question
Date: Sunday, November 19, 2000, 4:37 p.m.

You may have missed it as it was cleverly hidden in the very first paragraph of the very first email that I sent to you today. It said, "What if you thought the perfect mate was 2,279 miles away? Would that be worth pursuing if you thought he was, as you say, 'yummy'?"

It may well have been the most important thing in the whole email, even if you count the foot massage and the offer to go out and abduct a cow.

Let's get it out there. I'm more than just a test subject, right?

Duane

From: Selena
To: Duane
Subject: Wow
Date: Sunday, November 19, 2000, 5:58 p.m.

You don't beat around the bush, do you? I have to say that I have been a little blown away by how quickly I've felt comfortable with you and by the level of "friendship" we've already managed to achieve. I was of the opinion that next time around, I'd have to know somebody for a couple of years at least as a friend, and only after I'd had a suitable healing period (probably years) after the breakup of my first marriage. You're sort of messing with that, you know.

Okay, I like you and you like me . . . so far. I suppose that's always subject to change, but for the moment I'm having a wonderful time because it's honest and real. I'd like to suggest we take the opportunity we have (because distance offers no option) to continue talking. I'm not perfect, and whoever gets saddled with me will have to know all the icky parts up front because I, for one, don't want to spring any nasty surprises after the fact. Here are some of my idiosyncrasies—file under the "strange but true" section.

If you spit on the sidewalk, I would probably cancel you for that silly reason. (I figure if I can swallow my spit, everybody else can too.)

Smell is big. Bad smells drive me up the wall and away. Bad breath, body odor, whatever. Cleanliness is pleasing. (If my breath is vile, I want to know, and I also want to be able to reciprocate.)

My dad never belched or farted in front of us, and maybe that's why I hope for that in my future.

In general, I don't cancel people because of their actions (with the exception of spitting—don't worry, writing it down makes me see how ludicrous my inconsistencies are).

I used to be part of the judgmental Church crowd. "Ooh, so-and-so is drinking a soda with caffeine" or shopping on Sunday or whatever. These days, I think everyone's better off if I leave my judgment hat in the closet and spend a little more time looking at my own self in the mirror.

I actually had already made up my mind that I'd never submit to another "judging of worthiness" by a mere mortal man in the form of a bishop again. You're forcing me to rethink my position on the issue.

You've also made me think of my temple clothes. I'd put them way at the back of my mind. Will you help me out with some of my more Church-related issues?

Looks like we have lots to talk about. Let's keep talking.

Selena

From: Duane
To: Selena
Subject: Re: Wow
Date: Sunday, November 19, 2000, 6:56 p.m.

Dear Selena,

I'm sorry, but my extensive prison record is going to have to go to the back burner one more time. It's a shame; you'd be shocked.

Article I. My son, the athlete, thinks that I'm a big sissy because I fuss at him for spitting. I occasionally spit—but you'll never be able to prove it because nobody ever sees me do it. Even when brushing my teeth; when I rinse, I just sort of let the water run out quietly into the sink, and I have taught my children to not make that "spitting effort" when rinsing.

Article II. My fondness for kissing is the main reason that I keep my mouth clean. Nothing like engaging in a nice romantic kiss with fresh breath. I'm also confident in my bodily freshness, or I don't leave the house. I don't even have smelly feet, and that's quite an accomplishment for a man whose feet are covered in socks for fourteen to sixteen hours a day. I have been using the same cologne (moderately) for several years, and even my kids' friends want to know what it is.

Article III. So I too am offended by the deliberate escape of the lower gases. My ex-wife once asked me if there was something wrong with me because I didn't "express myself" in front of her or the kids. I tend to be somewhat private with respect to those things. We are all entitled to a little privacy, and this is the gift we can all give each other, I say. As for belching—I have for amusement sake let out a complimentary burp. I am in no way attached to this as a habit, and I believe it would only be an improvement in my near flawless profile to give it up. ☺

Article IV. Judgmental? Please, you see where I've been. Everybody is at a different level of progression and no one is immune from sin. I think sometimes we believe that our sins are more acceptable than other people's sins.

Article V. Now this is important stuff, so pay attention. ☺ I was a rebel all of my life. I did things my way and I didn't want to answer to anyone. Oddly, my parents were "cool parents," but even they didn't understand where my rebellion came from. And when alcohol, drugs, sex, and rock and roll (well, not rock and roll) brought me to my knees, I determined that I would never feel like that again, and I didn't want anyone I love to ever feel like that if I could help it. The best way I could come up with was to become a little more conforming.

I didn't have an avenue for that right away, but when I discovered the Church and was given a bishop to look to, I decided that I would offer to the Lord a special covenant. I decided that if the bishop were to give me a directive, I would follow it, that I would receive counsel from my bishop as the most direct way of getting a message from my Heavenly Father. I believe that the Lord selected him as my leader in our ward, and if I did believe in His Church, I should believe that my bishop is the best mortal help that I'm going to get.

I thought this had blown up in my face when my bishop counseled me to consider taking my wife back when she was coming out of rehab a couple of years ago. I had already filed for divorce, and his suggestion hit me like a ton of bricks. I was upset with my bishop for even suggesting such a thing and seemed to make the painful experience just that much worse. I reluctantly did it and it hurt just like I thought it would. I was sorely humbled by the experience. I forgave her and struggled through the experience as generously as I could. Now two years later, you might say that was bad counsel because she relapsed and it all ended in divorce anyway—but my bishop wasn't wrong. It took from her any reason to blame the Church for our breakup. There are other things too, but mainly he was correct in his counsel, and I'll not be forgetting that.

Bonus Article. Here's a mini secret: I wear my garment tops only. I don't want anybody asking me any questions about it, so I wear the tops for show. I'm nearly ready to go and talk to the bishop about getting where I need to be to attend the temple again. I just want to make sure that I'm really ready to make the commitment. I don't want to go at this halfheartedly.

You are precious and this is fun,

Duane

From: Selena

To: Duane

Subject: Finally home from work

Date: Sunday, November 19, 2000, 10:19 p.m.

Hi Duane,

You probably won't believe this, but I could hardly get through my shift at work in anticipation of coming home to another email. I'm not sure what exactly has come over me, but it feels a bit euphoric.

Now, I'm going to be dead serious, so stick with me. It's almost like having hope again for the first time in these past years that turned my world upside down. I honestly believed that while I was capable of being a good friend to men and women alike, I was too broken to ever really be cared for just for who I am. I figured I would be able to give wise counsel to others and watch them live happily ever after, but that privilege would not be mine to even contemplate. And now, even though it's too soon to tell, even though I haven't felt the Spirit, I feel hope that maybe all is not lost. Maybe I'm not lost. Having hope is a gift I never thought I'd have again.

Now, I want you to know something about me—I want to do things for the right reasons. It was really important to me that when I left Steven, I did it for me and for reprieve for the children, not for someone else or for any other reason. I want to come to the Church because it's *my* deepest desire to humble myself (I think that I'm not all that humble right now) and partake of the blessings it offers, not because I've fallen for somebody for whom the Church is important. I don't want to be the type of person to do the church thing only for another person. And I don't want to commit to someone just because it's not easy being alone, or because I've gotten lost in the euphoria that accompanies a new love. I want to do all these things for the right reasons. Does this make sense to you or am I going to have to start speaking English here? I feel like I'm babbling in tongues for some reason.

Okay, you've passed the spit test (and that was a big one), but you can't be perfect. When you get angry, do you punch holes in walls? Do you lean toward the silent treatment? Is keeping a balanced cheque book beyond your control? Are you a Democrat or a Republican? You still have much to tell me about yourself, and I'll be content to listen.

So far, one of the first letters you wrote to me made me laugh and then the sincerity made me almost cry. You've touched me on some of my deepest emotional levels, and when I was writing to you about the loyalty thing, I was literally weeping great drops of tears (I didn't know I had that much water in me). Even if we were to meet and you found that the hump on my back or the third eye weren't acceptable, I want you to know that you have, in such a short time, become a dear friend who has given me so much.

I also want you to know I never expected this to happen. I was merely engaging in an unofficial anthropological study of the LDS male, with zero thought of potential attachment. How did you ever manage to penetrate the walls I so carefully built?

These and other questions of universal import will no doubt, in time, be answered. For now, they shall remain a mystery. And so I wish you good night. ☺

Selena

♥

From: Duane
To: Selena
Subject: Do you like me? Check yes or no
Date: Monday, November 20, 2000, 1:11 a.m.
Dearest Selena,

I've stayed up even though I'll be rising in three hours for my day's work, all in hope of receiving one more message from you. I don't know what the delay was. It looks like you sent this off a few hours ago. I am in the greatest mood—it's like being twelve years old and finding out that the prettiest girl in school is asking about you.

I'm almost afraid to tell you anything more about myself for fear that I'd reveal that one thing that'd totally disgust you. I mean, that whole spitting thing was entirely coincidental, not to mention that deal with the, um, expulsion of—you know—gas. So I have never been one to leave well enough alone and I must add at least a couple of responses now:

First of all, I *am* in search of a bride, only that isn't the reason that I wrote to you. I was drawn to you because of your profile. I just had to say something to that faraway woman who could make me laugh. I'd been writing exclusively to women within a couple hundred miles radius because I felt like it was the most expeditious way to reach my goal.

So what has happened? I have all but quit answering the random inquiries (though I do feel guilty if I don't at least acknowledge having received a message). I was talking to you for fun and suddenly I have found someone who is actually interesting to me. You engage me in intriguing, thoughtful discussions that lead me to think about what I want and what I believe. I want you to know that I appreciate you letting me into your inner sanctum. You can be confident that I do care for you and about you, about who you are. I have little more to go on than those words that I enjoy reading so much. I have that profile picture (I can make out a woman in overalls, sitting on a rock) and the pictures you sent me from ten years ago (which I look at occasionally after you send me a message—I don't know why), but the pictures are not enough to sway my opinion. I'll admit, looks are important to me, but I'm not consumed with them. As long as your hump is healthy, I think that I'm good.

Hope. That's the salvation of people who go through what we have been enduring. I got my boost the other day when I felt the comfort of the Holy Spirit. You know, I hear tell that there are only a few things that can't be overcome by the Atonement of Jesus Christ and prevent someone from being fully redeemed and making their way to the celestial kingdom. When you consider all of God's children and all the sins that are committed as they progress through their individual lives—and just how many stories of redemption there are—you and I are not so far from reaching that ultimate goal. We know what needs to be done. There are lots of reasons to have hope, for both of us.

I have a couple of rules of my own, concerning the desire to do what is "right." I will not try to convert a woman to the Church for the purpose of matrimony—neither she nor I would know if it is genuine. I also don't believe in taking a "test drive." I think people are just conning themselves with the game that they're "checking for sexual compatibility."

One more thing before I call it a night. Maybe you could modify your vision of becoming the wise old woman of the village. I believe that I've told you about the car that I passed a while back, where I witnessed an older couple holding hands. So what if you were part of a wise old team? What if you discovered true happiness and determined all the factors that go into making a happy marriage, and then you went forth with your companion and shared this wisdom to an admiring youth? Would that work, or is it entirely necessary to be a little more intimidating and mysterious? I think you can still be that way if your mate is willing to go along with it.

Good night. Thanks for a lovely day,

Duane

From: Selena
To: Duane
Subject: Just a quick note . . .
Date: Monday, November 20, 2000, 5:21 p.m.
Hi Duane,

Yesterday was certainly a day I hadn't anticipated. No matter what, though, we're grown-ups, so let's try to sleep at night, okay? (I know, I haven't been sleeping too much myself.)

I'll write copious amounts later, but this will have to do for now, at least.

Selena

Duane's Journal
November 20, 2000

There is a line that divides nurture and codependency. A healthy caring for someone and the mental illness of obsessively trying to fix people. My life has not been a history of healthy relationships. It's been mostly the opposite.

I've done well these past eight years, considering my marriage to Marie and the insanity that occurred during it, to learn how to be a more responsible husband, son, father, friend, employee, and so on. My strongest desire at the moment is to find the emotionally stable woman of my dreams and then get married, but today I find myself questioning whether I have made any progress at all.

A few months ago, I was just sure that I had come so far and was able to go and pursue this "ideal" relationship and start a new life. I just *knew* that I was healed and ready to go, but now I'm not so sure of myself.

My "Internet girlfriend" has shared her history, her fears, and her personal torments with me, and there is a feeling inside of me that I must don a cape and fly to a faraway land and save her. Not just save her, but *prove* to her that all men are not pigs and that fairy tales can come true. That's a red flag.

BUT . . . what if? What if two people were meant to be together for eternity but had to live their earthly lives separate for many years to learn valuable lessons that they would not have learned otherwise? And what if when they did finally meet, they were a little broken and the miles apart helped them to ease into their destiny together? What if a little desire to "rescue" is a normal response when people have discovered that their eternal companion has been enduring ongoing peril? Would it look any different than what I'm experiencing now? Or am I just trying to explain away puppy love?

It could be that I am behaving in a codependent manner, but if I am, why didn't this happen before now? How can I know? My heart is saying "love" and my mind is saying, "It's not possible." I feel like poking a fork in both of them.

From: Duane
To: Selena
Subject: In the light of a new day
Date: Monday, November 20, 2000, 7:45 p.m.

Okay. I got my head on a little straighter today. I had a discussion with a guy from work (all the people I work with are geniuses), and he gave me food for thought.

His car broke down and I gave him a ride home. He started telling me about his "Internet love affair" (his words, not mine). He said, "So we're, like, sayin' we love each other and all that."

And then I thought, *What a dreamer (and by dreamer, I mean loser) this bozo is.* But then I got to thinking, *You know, if I had a New York accent and garlic breath, put on about twenty-six pounds and lost some hair, and my car was broken down—why, I'd be him sitting here talking to me.*

"You gotta watch out for that stuff," I said condescendingly.

"Don't worry about me," he said stupidly.

I'm not worried about him. I'm worried about me.

You don't suppose a person could be so hopeful and desirous to be "in love" that he would allow himself to get carried away? I mean, not an intelligent guy with brains of steel like me . . . hah! Brains of steel—what does that even mean?

I've long admitted to myself that I want to be in love. I'm a romantic. I see myself and the girl of my dreams dancing to soft music in a dimly lit kitchen after washing dishes together. I see her and me holding hands on some of my favorite beaches, with the tide carrying away all of our stuff as we stare into each other's eyes. I see her and me drinking sparkling white grape juice in a hot tub with candles all around, and my dog lapping up a drink from the foot end of the tub.

Do I want these things so bad that I would just "make" myself feel like I've been feeling about you? If that's true, why did I not feel like this six months ago? How'd I talk to twelve dozen (that's gross—get it? Gross? You see, 144 is a gross. It's a play on words *and* numbers) other women without feeling like this? I'm going to let it ride. I don't know why I would want to question good feelings anyway; it's not like I've been blessed to walk around feeling like this all the time. I'm going to take your advice and get some sleep tonight. I'm enjoying that I have something to look forward to that doesn't involve my children. I think I must neglect myself in that respect. Maybe that's part of the elation. I've connected with someone with whom I can make a real friendship, and it's wholesome and safe—I am not used to having anything like that.

Please write to me. Tell me what you've been thinking today. I'll admit that I've been thinking about you mostly and going over all of our correspondence—you know, checking to see how I got where I am. I know that I haven't just put a Bambi in my sights and zeroed in. There's much more to this than that; there's a spiritual connection with you and me and that can't be faked.

Duane

♥

From: Selena
To: Duane
Subject: Everything is clearer . . .
Date: Monday, November 20, 2000, 11:15 p.m.

. . . with the light of day, even if partly sleep deprived. I was thinking to myself today how it doesn't make sense that I feel like a schoolgirl with butterflies in my stomach (if you're done with that butterfly net, could I have it back, please?). It goes against all common sense that two people could connect so quickly. That just doesn't happen in real life, you know. It also doesn't happen in Internet life either. I've talked to people for almost three years now and become friends with some men and some women, but this is somehow different. Please don't take that to mean that I know something you don't or that "it's meant to be" or anything else. Maybe you're right—maybe there is a spiritual connection of some sort that just can't be faked. And can that ever be a wrong thing? I mean, even if I end up giving you advice on which of six women to choose from while I pursue my lifelong old crone dream, how wonderful to have such a friendship.

So I remain content to learn from you and about you. And you're faced with the challenge of some of my doubts (Church related) and idiosyncrasies. And I look forward to every last bit.

I've been feeling wonderful at a time when things could all seem bleak and yucky. I hope you have a good sleep. Did I ever tell you that I'm really glad you wrote me?

Good night (or morning, whenever you get this) to you,
Selena

From: Duane
To: Selena
Subject: I took a walk around the world to ease my troubled mind
Date: Tuesday, November 21, 2000, 4:22 a.m.
Dearest Selena,

I'm wide awake and still high from your last letter. I have a busy day ahead, but when I get a chance, I'll catch up on some of the stuff you've asked about—it will be waiting for you this evening when you come home.

So I don't punch holes in walls. I grew out of that when I gave up alcohol and drugs. I have an even temperament. I don't like conflict; I know that it happens, but I'm usually quick to compromise. I don't like the silent treatment either. I experienced that as a kid, and it hurts (and deliberately hurting the people that you're supposed to love is mean). I do believe in taking a timeout to get your bearings before the conflict resolution begins, but not the silent treatment.

I would love to be in a relationship that would resolve never to go to bed angry—even if there is no resolution. Is that possible? Life is too short to be angry all the time, and *my way* isn't as important to me as *my people*.

Democrat or Republican? Well, look at the time! I have got to get to work. Big day ahead of me and all. I've got a great deal of thinking to do today; you've given me a lot to digest. Be careful in your travels today. How about if we both die without a mate, we look into the possibility of pairing up on the other side? Deal?

Your friend and anthropological test subject—LDS classification,
Duane

From: Selena
To: Duane
Subject: Kryptonite
Date: Tuesday, November 21, 2000, 7:21 a.m.
Dear Duane,

I too was treated to an early morning letter, and what a nice way to wake up! Everyone else is still sleeping, but it's only a matter of time.

Now, I'm going to throw you my first Church-related curveball. Did I mention how angry I was after my miscarriage? Well, Heavenly *Father* is male and also was on the receiving end of that anger. This has to do with prayer. I concluded that prayer was not only a waste of effort, but it might even be preferable not to pray. Here's why:

- We are supposed to pray that His will be done.
- We are supposed to trust that His will is always best for us.
- When we pray, He's going to do whatever He wants anyway, so what's the point?

If by some chance we could sway Him over to our way of thinking, then we might be making a huge mistake, not knowing what is best for us because we don't have that "all-seeing eye," so not asking for things is better than asking unwisely. Sometimes I will lift my thoughts above, but I will only thank Him for something. I don't ask for anything anymore. What do you make of all this? Please let me know, because while not my most humble self these days, I am teachable.

For now, I'm off to reality and work and whatever the day brings. I'd rather be sleeping! I hope your day is marvelous.

More later,
Selena

From: Duane
To: Selena
Subject: I'm so sorry
Date: Tuesday, November 21, 2000, 5:27 p.m.
Dearest Selena,

I'm afraid you have me where you want me. I have no answer. I've been thinking those exact same thoughts for two years. In some ways,

I'm more critical than you. As you read the following, be aware that this is off the cuff with no rehearsal:

I don't believe in predestination. I believe that our agency cancels that concept. So I don't believe that there are absolutes put upon all of our actions or circumstances. For instance, I believe that even Jesus Christ was not without choice when He atoned for our sins, and that is the reason that it was the most magnificent event in all of human history.

I do believe that, given a set of circumstances, our Heavenly Father can predict with great accuracy what choice we will make because He knows us. And somehow, the choices are all ours. I don't believe that our Heavenly Father is a micromanager, yet I see evidence all around that He intervenes in the lives of His children.

If we were always blessed when we were obedient and were always cursed when we disobeyed, human beings would cease to act according to their agency and only act to get the blessings. Likewise, we simply can't have everything we pray for. Therefore, the most important thing that we could pray for is a knowledge of His will for us. It is written that we should ask for what we want—and in this, I join you in your confusion.

I hope you don't mind if I were to comment on your miscarriage. I certainly do not want to make you sad, so let me know, okay?

I think that your miscarriage was an appointment. Heavenly Father selected you to be a mother for a special spirit who only needed the opportunity to have a body for a brief moment. I believe that there are lots of these spirit children, and Heavenly Father has to have mothers for them. One day, I believe, there will be a reunion for you and all these special moms, and this purpose will be revealed. One day, you will not only know the special nature of these children, but also the royal stature of their mothers.

I'm sorry that I don't have good answers to this question. I can say that I know our Heavenly Father loves us very much, and the purpose of that experience wasn't meant to be punishment. I can't imagine what that must've been like for you, but ever since you shared that story with me, I have been drawn to you—it's as if I have the answer inside of me, but I can't find it. I'm sorry that you had to endure that suffering alone.

Dang it, now I've made myself cry. Good thing this isn't paper. I wish that I could hug you and make everything all right, but I can't. I'll work on this, I promise.

So I have got to go run to the grocery store. I'll write more when I come back. One other thing though, I love babies! I know that our Heavenly Father is way better at the love thing than I am, so I'm not pulling this out of the sky to make you feel better. His selection of moms for these little ones is an indication of what special women they are, that you are. I mean, I already know that you are special, and I'm sorry again—

I'm babbling. I don't know whether to send this now or not. Heads! You should be about done reading this.

Duane

♥

From: Selena
To: Duane
Subject: It's okay
Date: Tuesday, November 21, 2000, 9:18 p.m.
Dear Duane,

I'm okay now with what happened. Maybe not that it did happen, and maybe not the way it happened, but I'm doing okay now so I don't want you to be bothered by it. I appreciated your thoughts and hope that my doubts in no way ever taint that sincere faith and humility you have. See, wouldn't it just be the crummiest thing for me to be Satan's tool to wreck your life?

I think it's time for a subject change. When the heck are you going to tell me about jail? You tell me about jail and I'll tell you about the time I got heck from a doctor . . . lol (the joke is they're always crusty and giving us trouble).

Selena

♥

From: Duane
To: Selena
Subject: Okay, I'm all better now
Date: Tuesday, November 21, 2000, 10:19 p.m.

Wow, you got a play-by-play on that last note. I really got flustered. That was me in real life—no edits.

I'm not going to even pretend that I have any kind of answer for this one. Everything that you said about prayer, I have thought about myself these past few years. I'm not bitter now; in fact, I'm a little ashamed of myself for my lack of faith. It was different for me than it was for you. The anguish that I suffered was a direct result of my disobedience and defiance years earlier. It all had to be rectified. I have no doubt that when I repented and made my baptismal covenants that I was wholly forgiven. I'm sure of it. However, the Lord promises that those things will be blotted out, but I don't believe that means it's taken from my memory or that the consequences of my poor judgment are going to be completely removed—if it were, what would I have learned?

Can you stand another story? "He didn't even wait for an answer. He just started yakking away," she said with a sigh.

After my wife went to rehab, I decided to forgive her and give her an honest and fair chance at a fresh start. It was a miserable feeling, coping with all that had happened while at the same time trying to make things as amicable for her as possible. I was determined to make a clean slate and put forth my best effort, and I mostly did that, but I slipped into a depression. Out of fear of causing my wife to relapse, and out of desperation to feel some measure of relief, I went to go talk to a counselor.

The therapist that I went to is a doctor of psychology and a member of the Church. We discussed what it meant to forgive, as I was promising to forgive. When he was thoroughly satisfied that I understood the commitment I was making—he told me, "One day you will be exalted and you will wear a crown," which was cool because my fondest hope at the time was to "not die" of the seemingly perpetual anguish I'd been subjected to daily. But Dr. Dennison presented another promise. He said that I would find reward in the healing of my marriage and find new love and appreciation in my wife—but that this was contingent upon her ability to adequately repent and forsake her sins. He told me if, for whatever reason, this did not work out and she was unable to be my wife, then I would eventually find happiness with a woman who would agree to be my eternal companion.

Based on these circumstances, I could pray myself blue and it would not make a difference. My ex-wife had her agency and she held all the cards in what would determine our future, if we would be together or not. The Lord made me a promise (I sincerely believe that Dr. Dennison was speaking like a prophet that day) that if I sincerely forgave her and did what was right, I would either have a successful marriage with her or a successful marriage with someone else. Probably rather than pray that God make her do the right thing, I should have prayed that she would become strong in her desire to get well, regardless of the benefit to me.

I think that sometimes we pray for what we want exactly and don't leave any room for alternate blessings. Granted, I was given the two possible scenarios, and most times people don't even get that. What I learned about this is to not focus on the exact thing that I want, but rather what is best according to the will of God (there's that pesky *will* again).

How's that? You can at least give me a couple of bonus points for penmanship.

Write me back,

Duane

From: Selena
To: Duane
Subject: Re: Okay, I'm all better now
Date: Tuesday, November 21, 2000, 10:41 p.m.

I had a thought. Maybe I'm just afraid that He won't answer my prayers. That, for whatever reason, they will go out somewhere in the universe and never come back to show me they were worth the air they were sent upon.

A friend of our family and former home teacher was a hardworking, humble, faithful farmer. He got a brain tumor. He was only in his early forties and hung on for a couple of years and probably thousands of prayers and blessings. He died anyway. He was such a good man. "Thy will be done."

So what should a prayer for him say? That he'll be spared the effects? The blindness, the inability to walk, the incontinence? A brain tumor is a physical thing. Nope, he won't be spared the effects. Okay, that he'll have peace? The sheer frustration of watching Church and community come together to build a metal shed for his farm machinery brought him to tears. They were tears of gratitude, but it was also hard for somebody who'd been so strong and healthy reduced to sitting in a wheelchair, watching on the sidelines. I don't think he had much peace.

I suppose if I were to say one good thing about Keith and the brain tumor, it'd be that he lasted two years when it should have been months. The month before he died, we spent New Year's Eve with him and his wife and some other couples. Even though he was resting on a hospital bed in the living room while we played games, blind and weakened, he would still pipe up occasionally and tell a joke. I really miss him.

What should we have prayed for? Were any of our prayers answered? Clearly it was Keith's time to go, but what about all the prayers of faith offered up that he be healed? Did they do anything to sway Heavenly Father to letting him live longer? Did they make any difference in his quality of life? Okay, I'm going to stop beating that drum. Heavenly Father may be trying to tell me something here, and maybe I should listen.

I'll write more soon.

Selena

♥

From: Duane
To: Selena
Subject: Here's one that I owe you . . .
Date: Wednesday, November 22, 2000, 1:23 a.m.

My prison record. Well, not prison so much. It was usually a drunk tank for a few hours and then home to the little woman. I really hate this part of my past, but I'll just run it by you as part of the "baggage exploring" process.

I can be the nicest guy you ever met that wasn't trying to sell you something (or am I?), but something would happen to me when I was drinking—especially when I was in an episode of depression. I was just an arrogant and mean little cuss with a nasty mouth and a superiority complex. At 5'6", I just don't inspire fear in most men. If only they would've run away! I'm a little like the Incredible Hulk. I got in fights with people who sort of deserved it and the audience would cheer, but I would still be in trouble.

One night just before Christmas in 1985, my wife and I went to pick up her child support from her ex-husband. She was concerned about the way he sounded on the phone, so I went with her. My being there agitated him. He's a nice-looking man, a little taller than me and about eight years older—he had been aching for a fight for a long time, and I guess he'd decided that this would be the night. An argument began between us and he pushed my wife. She was about five months pregnant with our daughter. I hit him a couple of times, took him to the ground, and held him in a choke hold. He begged me to let him up and after a while I did.

Just a few minutes later, he started taunting me for letting him up (that's just poor form). As I was opening the car door for my wife, he sucker-punched me just over my left temple. Oh, that was it! I lost my mind. I finally stopped punching him when he stopped moving. There was blood everywhere. When I stood up, I heard sirens, so we got in the car and went home. I was arrested the next day with a felony assault. Her ex-husband and his mother reported that I had beaten him with a weapon. It wasn't true—my hand was shredded from the fight. The case went to trial and fortunately my attorney was able to get all charges dismissed.

You know, I used to be pleased with myself for what happened that night, but when I joined the Church, that all changed. I realized that I'd literally tried to kill that man. I've only ever told this to one other person before (as part of the repentance process), but I didn't just beat him because he pushed my wife—I did it because he had previously been with my wife, because he had a daughter with my wife, because he had eight years of marriage to my wife, and because the woman that

I loved and married used to love him. It was about seven years later when I came to understand what I had done, and I felt horrible about it. There was nothing wrong with that man that wasn't also wrong with me. I have experienced godly sorrow over that event and it has changed me.

On another occasion, I was on the riverfront in Savannah, Georgia, bar-hopping. Some friends were driving by and they stopped to talk to me. A police officer asked me to stop blocking traffic. I ignored him at first and when he walked over to me and put his hand on my shoulder, I turned and punched him in the nose. I hit him a second time in the forehead and it felt like I had broken my hand. All of a sudden, I felt the pain in the back of my head—another policeman had run up behind me and hit me with his baton. After a good thrashing, they arrested me for assaulting a police officer. I went to court, the arresting officers didn't show up, and my attorney got me off with a warning and time served. I believe that was 1983.

There were some other times, but those were the two biggies. All of my experiences with jail happened as a result of being intoxicated. The last time I had a visit to the slammer was in 1991. Police found me sleeping in my car and decided to bring me indoors. Oddly, when I stopped using drugs and alcohol, those kinds of problems came to an abrupt halt. Weird.

I hope this doesn't change your opinion of me. After all, I've paid my debt to society.

Your eternal friend,
Duane

♥

From: Selena
To: Duane
Subject: What a day!
Date: Wednesday, November 22, 2000, 3:42 p.m.
Dear Duane,

I got the little chicks off to school and got ready for the day. It's Auriana's birthday. She's eight today, so I went out and bought her a present (a kit to make different kinds of jewelry—she's always saying,

"Mom, can I do a craft?"). Then I picked her up at school and took her to lunch.

She told me other mothers bring cake or muffins to the classroom when their kids have birthdays, but she knew I wouldn't (I'd already made arrangements with her teacher to bring something) because I was not "that kind of mother." She then said that those ice cream cone things I brought to her class last year were the best.

So anyway, she was thrilled with her gift, and when I showed up at her classroom a couple hours later with (you guessed it) the ice cream cone things, she got this great kind of shy but really happy look on her face.

Here's something that I recently learned in a mandatory parenting class that I think is a great idea: Help children buy or make gifts for their dad's birthday or Christmas or whatever. It makes perfect sense, but I never even thought of that. I'm determined to be a good former spouse. At the very least, I want to make things as easy on the kids as possible.

Gotta run!
Selena

♥

From: Duane
To: Selena
Subject: Miss me?
Date: Saturday, November 25, 2000, 7:14 a.m.

I've been laying low for the last couple of days. Been doing some soul-searching, trying to get things back down to earth—apparently I let things spin out of control. If I were twelve years old, my daddy would probably be asking me, "What the !@#$%^&*! happened to your grades?!"

I've read back over all of our correspondence from the beginning and I still feel the same way. I check my mail over and over again and I'm disappointed when there is nothing from you. So, even though I've made it a point not to write so much and think about you all day, I'm doing it on some level anyway. This week, I have been spending some time getting to know (through email) a woman I'm supposed to meet next month. It sounds promising: she's a doctor and she's rich—I can be a kept man! She's not really like that though. She seems really nice. I guess I'm not happy unless I can express a huge amount of sarcasm when I feel like this.

In an effort to stay at a non-emotional level today, I'm going to tell you a little about my experience Monday night. I finally broke things off with my friend—the one who whispers the sweet nothings about my wonderfulness. What an awkward event that was. Do you ever watch the TV show *Seinfeld*? There was this episode where George tries to break up with this one girl and she doesn't accept his resignation from the relationship. She keeps saying that it's okay and that she will help him work through every objection that he presents, that *they* are worth it. He continually tries to break it off with her and she meets his every challenge until he ends up coming up with some pretty zany plans hahahahahahaha . . . aahhhhh.

Well, that's all funny right up until it happened to me in real life. I told her how pretty I think she is, how sweet she has been to me, how I really appreciated her thoughtfulness (she's constantly sending me cards and little gifts), and how much I've enjoyed going out with her. Then I told her that there are just no sparks, that my intention is to find someone to marry and it would just be wrong of me to continue this. It was deceptive to both of us. I told her that any guy would be lucky to get someone like her, she could be with any guy she wanted, yada, yada, yada.

Well, she answered with, "That's okay." She then said that she could change my mind if I'd let her, that we hadn't explored the relationship fully. Well, that's really all I need to complicate my life. I left with the intention of never going back over there. She has called me a couple of times, and so has her daughter. She's playing it off like I never said anything at all and now has gotten more aggressive. You know what this all comes down to: I never told her about my beliefs in marriage and the Church. She knows I'm a member, but she doesn't have any idea what that means to me, and I don't think she wants to know.

I took her to see her mother a while back and ended up teaching her uncle (the sheriff in that county), a really smart guy who asked a lot of good questions. She sat there and listened for a while, but she got up and walked out of the room a couple of times. She didn't say a word about the discussion during the five-hour ride home. I think she's trying to convert *me*!

Well, crud. Now I don't have anyone to go to movies or dinner with. Now what? See how boring my life is when I'm busy not being in love with you?

That brings up something else: Could I be so eager to be in love that I've created it with you? And if so, why you? I know that this way is safe and you can take all the liberties you want with reality, but why would I wait until now to do this? I thought I was perfectly content with the direction my life was taking. I could have fallen into this psychosis with any female on this website, but I chose you! Did I perpetrate this hoax on both of us because I needed at least two thousand miles between me and my virtual girlfriend?

Whoops! I said that I was going to stay on a non-emotional level. Is there something wrong with me? Tell me what you make of all this. Perhaps I'm the one who should become a nun . . . er, I mean, monk. Are there many Mormon monks? Maybe I could start my own order: "The Honorable Order of the Monks Who Are Somewhat Neurotic and yet Are Intent on Spreading That Neurosis Around to the Female Population." There we go: HOotMWASNayAIoSTNAttFP. Clearly this needs work.

Don't leave me hangin', babe,
Your friend,
Duane

♥

From: Selena
To: Duane
Subject: Layin' low, huh?
Date: Saturday, November 25, 2000, 4:29 p.m.
Dear Duane,

It seems like our minds have been in the same place—the twilight zone. ☺

Yesterday was a tough day for me, and I found myself all teary and lonely when I came home to an empty house last night. (I realized this a.m. I'd forgotten my "crazy pill." I wonder if that's why?)

I dreamed strange dreams all night and was connecting with some man I'd just met. I was surprised at how easy it was to sit close to him. When he asked me to dance, I let those warm feelings of the closeness of someone's arms wash over me. This morning, as I thought about those strange dreams, I wondered if I would be so lonely, so needing to be loved and held, that I would forget my sensibilities and simply latch onto the first man who might show signs of being able to love me?

So far, none of this helps you with your problem, but I'm trying to figure out my motivation too. You've been speaking to my heart and saying all the right words. Not only that, you're so far away that it's easy to idealize you because, deep down, I'm sure that we would never be able to be together even if we were meant to be. (Seriously, have you considered the logistics? Former spouses with rights to see their children grow up, and how to make that happen over a distance of, you said, 2,279 miles?!) All logic aside though, my heart tends to be a little selfish and is more than willing to forget common sense and simply bask in the everyday (or every few days) exchanges that enlighten, lift, and cradle its battered little self.

Taking me out of the equation, how goes the wife-hunting war? So there's someone rich you're meeting next month? I've been told it's as easy to love a rich person as it is a poor one, so you may want to keep that in mind. Here's where I can come in as your online chick adviser. Though it sounds like my advice about your nonmember friend didn't turn out so great. Duane, it's a bad sign when your life takes on a *Seinfeld*-ish turn, but I can't tell you how bad it is to be living George's life! You did good, trying to be honest with her, but stopped just short of coming clean. It doesn't work when you leave the door open a little. Let me tell you why:

A guy came in the hospital and identified himself as my "neighbor." Much to my chagrin, he gave the right street address and turns out he lives two houses away. He's not remotely my type, being much older, not physically attractive to me, and not interesting to me. Just nothing there. But when he asked me out for "coffee," I thanked him and said, "Gosh, I don't think that would be wise, considering my current marital situation." Did I say, "Thank you, but no"? Did I say, "I'd rather join a convent?" Noooo, I left the door open by leaving the impression that if there weren't the divorce thing happening, I might just go. Ewwwww! So much for not wanting to hurt somebody's feelings.

The point is, in my case, this dude is watching me ("I see you came home for supper tonight") and I've since found out he has a penchant for wearing pantyhose, painting his fingernails and toenails, wearing bras, and has poster-size pornographic pictures in his house. Oh joy. It's really hard being just the right amount of nice but firm and decisive. Sounds like you're going to have to practice that a bit too. (Hey, if I have to learn to do it, you should as well).

I guess if I were to say anything of import to you, it might be to not let your desire to have a wife cloud your judgment and make you choose too hastily. I mean, you're determined to pick a "forever wife," and that's one heck of a long time if you discover she isn't someone you can spend that time with. You help me and I'll help you try not to let our desire to be loved take us in the wrong direction, okay? I won't hold out any expectations where you are concerned and I will try to maintain friend status so that I can help in your wife hunt if you need some input—from a distance. You've become a close friend more quickly than I imagined possible, and I will be content with that.

I like you because you're somebody my heart and soul can relate to, and that's not an everyday occurrence. I like the way that you talk and think, and wish for you to have the best wife in the world. Don't be a stranger. I like hearing from you as much as you say you like hearing from me.

Selena

PS I'm sorry you don't have anyone to go to dinner or the movies with anymore . . .

From: Duane
To: Selena
Subject: Did you miss my earlier question?
Date: Saturday, November 25, 2000, 5:38 p.m.
Okay, Baby Doll,

You know, you say all the right things too! I'm back to feeling good. If I had one wish right now, it'd be to hug you until . . . well, you know that feeling that you have inside the temple? That safe, secure, warm feeling? Don't you believe we both deserve such a hug? Think about that for a minute.

That brings me to a question that I asked you several messages ago (now, you wouldn't dodge a sincere inquiry, would you?). If something happens to us before we find eternal mates and we find ourselves on the other side, you think maybe we could hang out and see if it works for us? Don't leave me hangin'; give me something to hold on to.

All right, I've got plenty more to say, but I have to go to the grocery store and make dinner for tomorrow. I'm having the sister missionaries come over. You hold on and I promise good, deep stuff, guaranteed to draw you closer to your spiritual side.

Love,

Duane

PS My life has been more and more like television every year—I'm beginning to think that someone is following me with a clipboard or something. You're right, though; it's sad when I start running parallel with George Costanza.

PPS While I'm on the subject, you know that song "Maria Maria" on Santana's album *Supernatural*? I found myself singing that at work on Monday, only I was substituting Selena for Maria—and that was probably when I began to realize that I was obsessing. ☺

♥

From: Selena
To: Duane
Subject: I didn't think you were serious, but . . .
Date: Saturday, November 25, 2000, 6:12 p.m.
Yes.

♥

From: Duane
To: Selena
Subject: Woohoo! I got a commitment!
Date: Saturday, November 25, 2000, 7:18 p.m.
Dear Selena,

I've never been closer to stepping in front of a truck. You don't have to talk me down. I'm not going to do it. I'm sure that there are flaws in that plan that haven't yet occurred to me. I am happy though—thanks for your confidence.

I want to share something with you, but this will be the first time that it's ever ventured outside my brain, so bear with me, okay?

<OOOOOOOOOOOOOOO/XXX/IIIIIIIIIIIIIIIIIIIIIIIIIIIIIIII>

I hope that I can explain this with the kind of clarity that it came to my mind yesterday.

The angle brackets (< and >) represent the eternities. Os represent premortal existence. Xs represent this life. The slashes represent birth and death. And Is represent our post-mortal existence.

I was thinking about what you said about your friend who'd died because of brain cancer. Of all the things you have told me that show your hurt, that seemed to shake your faith the most. I believe it's all tied together though. Your other hurts are part of the same problem—mostly that you're not sure if you have control over your own destiny, if our Heavenly Father's intentions are only fair to Him, and if your pursuit of happiness is in vain (and I'll go out on a limb), meaning you feel that you are being dealt with harshly and are therefore doomed for the duration.

Okay, now for the diagram above. We're going through a level of progression. The tangible body that we have in this life, the Xs, is an intense part of our progression. A huge amount of growth and learning happens on this level. We are placed in an environment that is conducive to this mortal experience that we need to have and, compared to heaven, is pretty harsh. It is a completely safe (relative to our spiritual bodies) environment that is monitored by our Creator. It is governed by laws that are designed to execute the necessary requirements for us to move to the next level of our existence. Our perspective is limited to what we know of this life and is reflected in our fears—like the fear of loss and the fear of death. It is a relatively minute part of our existence, and yet it's all that we know.

Have you ever listened to one of your older children talk about an event in his or her life as a great and remarkable thing and you think, *Gee, that was such a small and insignificant occurrence, I'm surprised that they remember it that way.* That's heaven's way of looking at some of our experiences. Not that they're not important—just like you wouldn't discount something that is important to one of your kids—it's simply that, in the grand scheme of things, it doesn't shake all of existence.

The important thing is to remember that our Xs are so small compared to our Os and Is. As you look at your child's experience in context and evaluate it accordingly; so too does heaven look at our earthly experience and see the bigger picture—the benefit of the design. Think of the child who struggles and struggles and then finally, after a lot of hard work, catches the prize. That's us! Our Heavenly Father does not find pleasure in our suffering, but He does celebrate with us when we gain the convictions of truth that we were sent here to gain. It's about our progress.

I know a man who is agnostic. He's a good man. He takes care of his family as a good husband and father. He takes all his responsibilities to other people seriously as a good citizen and neighbor. He's also really charitable. While he doesn't have much in the way of formal education, he's done rather well, career-wise. He's traveled the world and has many, many friends and the respect of a number of important people. I think that the main reason that he has antipathy toward God is the examples that he's had in his life. He has seen hypocrisy and bad behavior by people who profess to be Christians and has no desire to be subject to the rules of "self-righteous" individuals who apparently don't follow the tenets of their own professed beliefs.

This belief, or rather lack of belief, in God creates a perspective that reinforces and perpetuates every time someone whom he loves dies. He looks at all the good Christians he knows who have suffered and died and can say, "What good did their god do them?" Now, to you and me, he seems to be angry with a god that he doesn't believe in, but to someone who has no belief in any god, the concept of life after death doesn't even exist. Just think what that one belief does for your own perspective and ability to cope. The more you develop that belief (build your faith), the better able you are to endure the trials of this life.

The fact is we all die. When we learn all that we are supposed to, when we touch the lives of those who need us, and when all of our influence has expired, so will our temporary bodies. We all have to do it in some manner or another and, to our Heavenly Father, the separation of our spirit from our mortal body is just a process.

I'll bet that on the other side of the veil we don't even think much about our death (except as some dinner party trivia: "Hey, guess how I died? Nope, got sucked into a high performance automatic milking machine"). Heavenly Father probably grants us extra time here and there when we ask for it, probably teaching some individuals about faith and trust that way. But not everyone gets an answer in the affirmative. Imagine if we were always punished for bad behavior and always rewarded for good behavior—it would be like taking down the veil. The Lord is wise and knows how to respond to us to best direct our experiences in this life.

I hope that I have explained this as well as I understand it in my head. Ask me questions if you think of any. I feel a strong need to comfort you, like an assignment. I don't want to fail.

Write me back,

Duane

From: Selena
To: Duane
Subject: Glimpses
Date: Sunday, November 26, 2000, 11:16 a.m.
Dear Duane,

Every now and again, I get glimpses of what I used to know and believe when you say something, and I think that's what was happening as I was reading your last email. Who knows? Maybe someday I'll reunite with the "old Selena" and stop having to squint to see her in the distance, standing on the other side of the Grand Canyon. Keep talking because it might just do the trick.

I was reading over some of the letters you first wrote to me and found myself smiling again. It's good to be able to smile, and you do make me smile. (Let's see how many times I can use the word *smile* in one sentence, eh?) I figured I'd give you some more weird things about me. Are you ready?

Every once in a while, I'll write something in my sleep, usually poetry. It's actually only happened since this whole life-changing event of mine began about three years ago, and I'm always surprised. This morning, I woke up with a nonsense kind of verse. Usually it's something serious or, at the very least, shrink fodder (more on that later). So it starts with the children's verse about Jack, and then "dreaming me" adds a verse:

Jack be nimble, Jack be quick,

Jack jump over the candlestick.

(Now here's where I come in, and apparently borrowed from "Jack and Jill.")

Up Jack got, on fire he'd caught,

So he stopped, dropped and rolled,

And put himself out. (Sounds like someone in self-preservation mode.)

Okay, here's my shrink fodder one:

Here

In this Soul

Is Heart

Where

In this Heart

Lies Love

Divided

Honestly, I dreamed this one. I wonder what a psychiatrist would have to say about that? Actually, I'm not sure I want to know. What do you think?

Did I ever tell you how much I love animals? I used to want to be a veterinarian, and growing up on the farm gave me lots of opportunities to practice a little unofficial medicine. I remember mothering nine orphan bunnies and using a doll bottle to feed them milk because they were so little. I had to perform an amputation on a barn swallow to save its life. I cried for three days a few years ago when I had to kill a weasel. I used to climb trees to check out the eggs that birds had laid and remember sticking my hand in one nest to feel, instead of the eggs I was expecting, the hot, mushy bodies of baby birds (I may have screamed). I had a pet rooster who actually protected me once from another rooster (because he loved me, no doubt). I still have the horse that I grew up with, Baby Doll, who turned thirty in July. And I've got this great three-year-old gelding that I saw being born and bonded with ever since. This year, I started working with him and he's such a sweetheart. I'm glad I've got him because when Baby Doll dies, the grief will be lessened because I have him.

Okay, back to serious stuff. You know I stopped wearing my temple garments many months ago. Since then, I have bought items that are sleeveless and some shorter than would cover them. I'm no Amazon warrior, and I've discovered that the shorter length is the most flattering on me. So there's this vain part of me that questions what makes a woman's shoulders too sultry to go sleeveless and doesn't really want to go back to looking granola in clothes made for women who are 5'8" or 5'10". I feel rebellious without meaning to. I'm not looking tart-ish by any means, but my new look isn't always accommodating of the temple garments. What do you think?

Well, I know I've tossed you a mixed bag for Sunday, but I think you can handle it. I hope you have a wonderful day and I'm envious of those sister missionaries for being able to eat a meal you've prepared. Did I ever tell you I'm awful at cooking meat? But great at making breakfast. Here's to breakfast,

Selena

From: Duane
To: Selena
Subject: Re: Glimpses
Date: Sunday, November 26, 2000 1:36 p.m.
Dear Selena,
I wanted to write you a quick note—I have got company coming over soon.

Do you know that the finest vet school in the country is six miles from my house? In fact, my friend from Alberta is a professor there. So is our stake patriarch. I would be a great place for an intelligent young woman to make a fresh start on life, if she were willing to take such a leap. . . . Do you know anyone like that?

I called you "Baby Doll" earlier. I'm not stalking you—I had no idea that's your horse's name. If I were stalking you, I would've already presented myself for one of those aforementioned hugs!

You're welcome to come to dinner anytime. Standing invitation.

Also, have you recently looked at my LDSSO profile? Would you check out my greeting and tell me what you think? I redid some of it.

I'm going to respond to your nocturnal creativity later this evening. I participated in a study a few years ago in this area. I think I may have something to contribute to your experience.

Write me s'more, okay? I'm still way up there, flying high from last night. You are so special.

After I feed all these people, I'll sit and write when I can think at the same time.

Hugs and stuff,
Duane

♥

From: Selena
To: Duane
Subject: Glimpses . . . with a twist ☺
Date: Sunday, November 2000, 5:41 p.m.
Can you spot the Freudian slip in your letter?

♥

From: Duane
To: Selena
Subject: What Freudian slip?
Date: Sunday, November 26, 2000, 6:11 p.m.
I read my email several times and I don't see anything. What have you conjured up? I'm sure that it's all in your head, whatever it is.

I'm doing some cleaning up—what a mess. Good thing I've got built-in maid service, eh?

I'll write more later. What "slip"?

One of my guests was a girl from my ward, the president of the Young Women. She is pretty and nice, but alas she is only twenty-three years old. Is that too young for me?

What "slip"? I didn't see a slip—there's no slip, is there? Show me the slip. I dare you. . . . I double-dog dare you! I'll be "write" back after I finish my chores.

Sessik dna sguh,

Duane

♥

From: Selena

To: Duane

Subject: Re: What Freudian slip?

Date: Sunday, November 26, 2000, 9:31 p.m.

"I would be a great place for an intelligent young woman to make a fresh start on life." Note, *I* instead of *It*. Looks Freudian to me. ☺

♥

From: Duane

To: Selena

Subject: Re: What Freudian slip?

Date: Sunday, November 26, 2000, 9:45 p.m.

Selena,

What did you do with my "t"? I'm quite certain that I would never be so careless as to overlook something so obvious.

. . . But you know, *I* am a darn good place for a young intelligent woman to make a fresh start, now that *you* mention it.

One of the sister missionaries commented that I might make some woman a "wonderful wife" someday (because of my cooking, and not because of my looks or my mind).

Duane

♥

From: Selena
To: Duane
Subject: Well, was it Freudian or not?
Date: Sunday, November 26, 2000, 10:05 p.m.

Dear Duane,

Twenty-three is not too young for you, and I think it could work if she was always free to feel womanly, intelligent, and beautiful and not become a lost soul amid the babies, laundry, and Relief Society casseroles. A good man can help a woman feel that way and if anybody can do it, I think you would be the person. And, hey, maybe you could teach classes and be praised by women far and wide for "enlightening" the menfolk. ☺

But that's enough about you, let's talk about me! Sorry, it's just that tonight has been pretty emotional for me, with my daughter's sixteenth birthday around the corner and trying to figure out how I can be part of it, or if that's an unrealistic option these days. I gave away a shift (which is a sacrifice because I only have about ten a month) to make sure I had the day free for her birthday. Even thinking about trying to celebrate as a family seems crazy and awkward to say the least. I knew I had to talk to Steven and was somewhat reluctant (in case you didn't know, recent communications have not been entirely positive) but I bit the bullet and made the call anyway.

Last night when I was dreaming (I tend to have a vivid dream life), I dreamed I was sleeping and woke to find Steven kissing me and calling me "Baby." I was inclined to respond, but I remembered that it would never work and that it would go back to being a negative experience. (I know, this was a minor detour, but you'll see why I included it soon enough.)

The call began in a frosty, terse way, and he still had to vent, so I allowed the call to continue, amid periodic interruptions of having to answer the switchboard, direct visitors, and help patients. He told me some of the reasons why he was so angry and then he wanted to know if he could ask me a question, which was something like, "Would you consider forgetting about the divorce?" I had a flashback to that dream and said, "You don't love me anymore. You don't even like me. Why would you even ask a question like that?" Anyway, he said something like, "I know," and so on, but it continued to be emotional from there. He said he wished we'd been able to talk like this earlier. It sounded like he may be understanding some of what I've been trying to say for so long. He started to cry a little and said he can't imagine not having me belong to him.

I told him I just wanted to be able to do what we did for my oldest son's eighteenth birthday. We all were there at a restaurant, but he was at one end of the table and I was at the other. We barely spoke, but the kids were all together and happy with their parents. He didn't want to, and then said he'd show me he could do what I didn't think he was capable of—and that it would be uncomfortable. I told him those were the wrong reasons to do it and if we were to do it, we should be doing it for the children, not to show we could do something the other didn't think we could.

I'm probably not making sense, but it was an emotional night and now I'm a bit numb from it all. It's so sad to have a marriage break up. And who knows? Maybe he and I could reconcile and I could continue the compromised life I led for so long, but it would be peaceable. Just how much happiness should a couple experience anyway? I sure as heck wouldn't know.

So I just read your new greeting on LDSSO. It's really good and should tug at the heartstrings of mushy Mormon women everywhere. I miss one part though, where you said you have three teenagers and that alone makes you quite the catch. This one is a bit more serious, but it's still good.

You're a good man, Duane Pannell, and I have no doubt you will draw the right woman to you with your irresistible magnetism.

Selena

From: Duane
To: Selena
Subject: Further analysis
Date: Sunday, November 26, 2000, 10:57 p.m.
Dearest Selena,

Freudian slip? Typo? Can't it be both?

I enjoyed your midnight prose and found them to be quite deep—mysterious in a way, yet not indecipherable. That is, for you, not me. As for my take, I have no idea what that stuff means!

I can give you some of my theory on it and other brain activities, a combination of the psychological and the spiritual. It's something to think about and may even work for you.

The way I see the human brain is it's like a computer, complete with a memory that records sight, smell, touch, sound, and taste. It's constantly collecting information to build cognitive responses to our environment—primitively for survival, but it serves most of us just for coping in modern society.

The cool thing about the brain (that we take for granted) is that it records *everything*, whether we are aware of it or not. As we go about our day, the brain is busy picking up every sight, sound, smell, facial expression, weather variance, physical discomfort, and so on.

I would suppose that information from our pre-earth life is locked in there somewhere too. I believe that when we pass from this life that this area of memory is restored. I have often heard of people having near-death experiences and describing how their minds are flooded with knowledge—I believe that what they experience is recall rather than a blitz of new information.

I also believe that all the information in our brains is accessible if the necessary conditions exist, even premortal memories. Hypnosis is the art of creating those conditions. There is hocus-pocus that is called hypnosis, but it is also used *legitimately* in science.

Now, with that basic information, let's look at a couple things:

Reincarnation. Have you ever heard stories about people who recall, with astounding detail, centuries-old events that they couldn't possibly be privileged to know? Suppose that, as inquisitive young premortal spirits, we were insatiably focused on the events unfolding on earth—becoming so involved with the characters that are experiencing tragic, heroic, or otherwise outstanding occurrences of life—that we personalize them and store them in our memory. Then, during the course of a dream or during hypnosis, we "see" vividly these pictures in our heads, complete with feelings and even smells. It would be hard not to believe that we were the key players, and it would be easier to understand as reincarnation.

Prophetic dreams and ESP. A simple example might be like this: You have an acquaintance whom you see on a regular basis in a work environment. Your relationship is casual, and when you come in contact with that person, you're generally unable to spend any time talking because you're working. One day, you sit down for lunch and all of a sudden you get this terrible sinking feeling that your friend has been in a terrible accident. It turns out to be true—which, in your mind and by anyone's measure, is a really remarkable revelation.

It's easy to believe you have experienced some sort of supernatural event or ESP. And what actually has occurred is something of a miracle. Your subconscious picked up many points that you were totally unaware of in all of your brief encounters previously. First, history. Your friend has been feeling stressed lately and had told you that he was taking valium. Next, while it didn't strike you at the time, there was a mild smell of alcohol on his breath. Then, he had mentioned that his car was in the shop and he's driving a rental with a manual shifter. He told you once in 1992 that he couldn't drive a stick shift without running up on the sidewalks. And the last bit of information that your brain processed came as you stepped outside to go to lunch and you had to get your big coat because a cold front was moving in and the rain was turning to ice. So you have all this information marinating in your head and while your subconscious is processing and coming to an educated conclusion, your conscious mind is deciding whether to get the special or a big salad.

Dreams are what got me interested in this sort of thing to begin with. Since I was young, I have had what are called "night terrors." They aren't really nightmares because you have no recollection of what it is that frightens you and they're so intense. Just think about what occurs when you go to sleep—it's like putting your brain on auto pilot. All that information that has been collected all day begins to be sorted and filed. It gets cross-referenced with related information and makes association with known, previously stored information. Then the whole thing gets defragmented. All that random stuff and all the new information gets played like a movie during your sleep—much of it making no sense whatsoever.

Last week, I had a dream that I know you inspired. So I dreamed that I was going to the airport to meet someone special—I felt like I dreamed that dream the whole night. I went to the wrong airport, my car broke down, she was on the wrong flight, she called and said she was coming in on a different plane, and on and on. I couldn't find her. I couldn't touch her. I was longing for her, but there was a roadblock at every turn. The deck was stacked against me, and I was terribly frustrated. Not too hard to figure that one, eh?

Many dreams are more complicated than that and require lots more analysis. One point that you can use as a guideline is Freud said that we dream what we have experienced. We don't, for instance, come up with original characters in our dreams. So even a person who represents an unknown or a stranger to us is someone whom we have seen or come in contact with.

To sum up, the mysteries lie within us. We are the authors of these seemingly mystical events and, theoretically, we have the ability to figure them out. While a dream may not be a trusted way to predict the future, it is a good guide to what your mind is saying about the information it has been collecting. Those writings of yours have a definite meaning to you, but it's quite possible that only you could ever interpret them.

Well, that ought to be enough to chew on for one night. I hope that you'll write me back soon. Sleep well and if you must think, think of me.

Drbears

♥

From: Selena
To: Duane
Subject: I'm being silly
Date: Sunday, November 26, 2000, 11:36 p.m.

Sitting here, waiting for another email. I got the last one as I was finishing one to you, so I know you're out there somewhere at the same time as me, and I feel like I could sit here all night (which wouldn't be prudent, because a girl needs her beauty sleep—my motto, "live like a bat, look like a bat").

Thinking of you,
Selena

From: Selena
To: Duane
Subject: One good thing . . .
Date: Monday, November 27, 2000, 8:54 a.m.

Even when there's no new message waiting, I find there's a certain satisfaction in going over previous letters, savoring them again. Makes them sound like a coffee commercial, huh?

Selena the Queen-ahh ☺

From: Duane
To: Selena
Subject: Re: One good thing . . .
Date: Monday, November 27, 2000, 10:48 a.m.

My dearest Selena,

It's the word *savoring*. Otherwise you have no coffee commercial.

What do you see when you look over our old letters? Do we appear desperate? I don't feel desperate; I feel hopeful. Is it possible that you are the only woman in this hemisphere who understands and appreciates my words and stories? I've talked to a lot of women in the months past, and none of my online "relationships" even come close to this. I have this fantasy where you finally come clean and confess that you are actually a neighbor from down the street. But that is not going to happen . . . is it?

So I got mail last night from a funny chick—RLBLANCHARD on LDSSO. Maybe you could check out her profile and tell me what you think of it and her?

Or maybe you could just come clean and tell me where you really are? Sorry, it's lunchtime, and I think that my blood sugar may be low. Write me.

Knight in Shining Armor
White Stallion Avenue
Christiansburg, Virginia
"Rescuing damsels in distress since 1972"

From: Selena
To: Duane
Subject: Re: One good thing . . .
Date: Monday, November 27, 2000, 12:58 p.m.
Dear Duane,

I didn't dare hope for an email during the day, but here it is—ahhh! Who needs Juan Valdez and his old mountain coffee when you've got Duane, King of Christiansburg?

When I look at our old letters, I don't see desperate. In fact, I don't believe either of us are the "desperate" type. I think we both maybe believe in fairy tales and both love the idea of being in love, but as far as I know, that's not an indictable offense, at least not in Canada. And I have to agree on the hope factor. There's something about having a special friend (albeit far away) that makes one feel comfortable, and is at ease discussing important things and even silly things—that just can't help but give a person hope that maybe fairy tales do come true. I don't know how this will all end up, and I'm fully prepared to be your friend with estrogen, but I'll never be sorry that I got to know you and I consider my money for LDSSO well spent.

Now, RLBLANCHARD's profile. If I were a guy, she looks like a fun girl and someone worth getting to know. Her kids look like cuties too. She's got a testimony (that's a plus) and has some all-important domestic qualities—a good feature in any potential mate. Keep your options open; just because she's on the other side of the country doesn't mean she isn't "the one." And you do deserve "the one."

I hate to break it to you, but no, I don't live down the street. In fact, I live in the frozen north with sled dogs parked outside my igloo, waiting to be fueled up with whale blubber. It does seem kind of far away when I say it like that, doesn't it? Does anything ever come easy? (Actually, the answer is yes. I used to get pregnant really easy, hence the five children—but other than that, I don't think so).

I will write more later.

Selena

From: Duane
To: Selena
Subject: Fairy tales
Date: Monday, November 27, 2000, 6:22 p.m.
Dear Selena,

So you believe in fairy tales and you think I do too. Okay, I confess. *You* believe in fairy tales.

All right, all right, I do believe in something, possibly fairy tales. I don't know. What about . . . once upon a time there was this lonely old king and he met this hip chick from the Great White North, and together they figured out a way to make all their dreams come true. C'mon, help me out here.

I'll write more in a little while, I've got a crisis with my youngest to solve. A knight in shining armor's work is never done.

Duane Robert—as in *Robert* E. Lee—Pannell (an old family custom that I hope doesn't offend)

From: Selena
To: Duane
Subject: Re: Fairy tales
Date: Monday, November 27, 2000 9:37 p.m.

Okay, maybe the fairy tales are a girl thing. But there's something about a kind king living in a far land that makes a woman think twice about her decision to mentor a village in need of wisdom. So did you get your crisis solved? Want to tell me about it?

I just got back from having a birthday supper with the family. It was so great to see the kids all goofing around. The boys don't spend much time with me these days, and I miss their boyish ways. Still not sure how Steven was surviving, but he seemed cordial enough and looked relatively at ease. See, part of my problem is I don't see anything strange about us being together for important occasions. It all stems from my childhood.

Many years ago, I was born to Joe and Margaret. Joe was twenty-six years older than Margaret and, in fact, had a daughter older than Margaret by a few months. (If you need to make a chart, now would be a good time to get paper. I don't really have a family tree. It's more like an orchard, mostly comprised of nuts.) Dad's marriage prior to the one with Mom bore him four children: two sons and two daughters. As previously mentioned, the one daughter was older than my mom, and so the other siblings were all much older than me too.

My mom's a remarkable woman with a heart the size of Texas, and I believe she is to blame for my perception of what is normal. You see, I grew up with the belief that it was normal for the ex-wife and current wife to cook Thanksgiving, Christmas, and Easter dinners side by side while family milled around, playing *Yahtzee* or singing "You Are My Sunshine."

Only when I grew up and began having children of my own did it dawn on me that perhaps my adoration of these older siblings was not necessarily reciprocated. As a child, I'd assumed my place in their hearts. Of course, now a woman, I could now see how difficult—to say the least—it must have been for these sisters and brothers to have their father take up with a woman *younger* than the oldest daughter. How they must have resented the new children he fathered, who got to grow up with *their* dad. It boggles the mind a bit to imagine.

Okay, I've fed you a small amount of family information because that is likely all you can take in at once. Previous marriage with four siblings, all much older. Keep that in mind for the next installment.

Duane, I want to be your friend and to be able to give you good advice regarding those lovely women with whom you have begun corresponding. I also want to hop on the next plane, fly to meet you and your wonderful children, and see for myself if it feels the same in real life. So, you'll have to bear with me. Both inclinations are genuine and sincere, but certainly at opposite ends of the spectrum. And therein lies the dilemma.

Write when you can,
Selena

♥

From: Duane
To: Selena
Subject: So . . . you're saying there's a chance . . .
Date: Monday, November 27, 2000, 11:31 p.m.

Maybe it's one in a million, but nonetheless a chance that I'll one day stare into your green eyes across an altar in the temple of the Lord? Don't answer . . . just let that linger in the air for a minute.

Crisis was averted. My baby girl lost her ID card for the rec center. They're real strict and won't let people in without their ID and they only issue them twice a month. She was about in tears. I have a tough time with the maternal comforting portion of the job. ("I told you not to climb that tree—whoa, what do you need a hug for? Ah, now look, you got blood on my pants. Well, stop crying and tell me what to do.") I have to remind myself not to fuss at them when they cry about stuff that they do to themselves. I'm a fairly good dad; I'm not the best at being a mom.

You must be in a pretty good mood. I really enjoyed that portion of biography you shared. It never occurred to me that you might be from a family of "nuts." Now that's the kind of self-disclosure I can identify with!

I'm going to call it a night. If I'm going to continue to wear you down, I really must get some quality sleep.

That's not right, is it? I should be content just to know that you feel this way about me. Perhaps there's something I can do to make up for this "dilemma" that I have put us in.

When we talked about prayer, there was one thing I failed to say. You know Jesus Christ wasn't baptized because of any sins that He committed, but rather to "fulfill all righteousness." Suppose our prayers are like that. We feel impressed to do it and we have agency, but many times we exercise our agency to ignore the urge to pray. It could be that prayer is all-important in putting our blessings in motion. Maybe we delay our blessings by delaying our prayers.

Here's what I will do tonight before I lay down to sleep: I will put aside for now the fact that I have a crush on you (it's just puppy love really), the inclination that I have to send you a plane ticket, and all other desires that benefit me (which are usually at the top of my list of priorities). I'm going to say the most sincere prayer for you that I can. I will pray that you get relief from the stresses that you are going through, that you will also get relief from the things that are causing you sorrow, and that you will get all the good things that the Lord has in store for you.

You're a precious daughter of our Heavenly Father. He will know what to do.

See how I get late at night? I better go now before I start making kissing noises and scare the dog.

Good night, Queen Selena. Dream sweet things, and if some guy is going to smother you with kisses in your dream and call you "Baby," let it be me.

Duane (Action figure comes complete with everything you see here. Hovercraft and eye patch sold separately. Batteries not included.)

From: Selena
To: Duane
Subject: You make me smile
Date: Tuesday, November 28, 2000, 2:22 a.m.
Dear Duane,

Getting up in the middle of the night is always worth it when I find another letter. And I thank you for your thoughts on prayer. I'm going to do something I haven't done in months, which is dust off the old scriptures and take a peek and see if Heavenly Father has any wisdom pertinent to me at this moment in my small amount of Xs (a direct reference to your object lesson). I'll let you know if anything astounding happens, but it may take a while. I'm a particularly hard case. His Spirit may need the Jaws of Life® to get me out of the enclosed space I've backed myself into. I hear that patience is a virtue. I don't suppose you have any on hand?

Whew. I'm relieved my first installment of the family bio went well. "And so, fools rush in where angels fear to tread," she said as she thought, *Quick, send another before he has time to recover from the last bit.* Are you sure you don't want to start a chart? It may come in handy as this progresses.

Quick recap though. Previous marriage with four older children. It was marriage number two for Dad. We will leave it at that for the moment. It gets better.

Okay, so I'm a little kid who grew up knowing four older siblings because of family events and holidays, not because we ever really lived together. Age differences were too great. Remember, Dad is twenty-six years older than Mom. This becomes important.

Fast forward to high school.

My little sister and I were sat down for a talk. Our mom told us that we had two sisters.

"Yes, we know we have two sisters: Angel and Elizabeth."

"No, no," she said, "you have two more sisters."

Beg your pardon?! So, apparently, Dad was a busy man and had a weakness for beautiful women—and in this case, born in 1943 (my mom, my sister Angel, and now Florence). It seems Dad spent some meaningful time with Florence, a Cree woman, and went forth and multiplied upon the earth (or at least in northern Alberta). She was blessed with two dark-haired baby girls with hazel-green eyes named Shannon and Charlene. Keeping this in order for you would have me born first, a little blondie with green eyes, followed by Shannon about fourteen months later. Arlene seven months after that (my little sister, who's also fair with eyes the color of the sea) and finally Charlene about eight months later. The implications of this meant little to Arlene and me at the time.

All we knew as fifteen- or sixteen-year-old high school girls was we had two sisters the same age as us! Woohoo! We couldn't wait to meet them. We just hoped that they were pretty and fun. And of course, they were both those things and so much more.

Again, as self-absorbed teenage girls we never thought of the complicated dynamics involved with the arrival of these sisters in our lives who lived only about six hours north of us. We never thought of the two young women (both twenty-six years younger than Dad) who had been bearing him little girls at the same time. We never considered what it meant in their lives to have this charming yet obviously flawed man wandering back and forth, never really being able to support any of these children as well as he should because, let's see, he had four from his marriage to Lillian, two from his union with Mom, and two with Florence.

Nope, what we had was more shock value for the "normal" kids in school and church. We always had the oldest dad and the youngest mom, not to mention the mileage we got out of telling people that our oldest sister was older than our mother. This was sweet, being able to show up at high school with two pretty half-Cree girls our own age and saying they were our sisters! It didn't get any better than that. I wonder what teachers were saying in the staff room, now that I think about it.

Anyway, that's all for now. It's going to take some time for you to organize that chart. It's 2:16 in the morning now, and I am going to get my scriptures and see what there is to see. Heavenly Father is sure to bless you for making me feel like giving the scriptures another shot. Thank you for your prayers. And your friendship. And your enthusiasm. And your time.

Have a wonderful day,
Selena

From: Duane
To: Selena
Subject: How do you keep it all straight?
Date: Tuesday, November 28, 2000, 4:45 a.m.
Dear Selena,

I have never heard a story before where I had to draw little stick people *and* label them *and* color code them *and* draw a timeline. I think you're making a strong case against men—I'm not sure I even trust myself. For the past few years, I've been telling my girls that all men are scum. ("I know, I used to be one!") The only cure for this kind of history is to make your world bigger, and I think that I'm just the man who can do that.

You have a fascinating story. Have you ever considered writing some of this down? That's it! Forego your dream of administering village therapy and just publish your thoughts and anecdotes. Then with the money, you can establish two residences—one in Canadia-land and one here in Virginia. I just happen to know of a sweet little mountain home on seventy acres, not far from here . . .

Have a beautiful day.

Your heart-to-heart connection in the southland,

Duane

From: Selena
To: Duane
Subject: Re: How do you keep it all straight?
Date: Tuesday, November 28, 2000, 7:26 a.m.
Dear Duane,

You're such a good sport! And you're more than wonderful in your "human-ness." What comes to mind is another fellow who corresponds occasionally from LDSSO. Here is one man who stubbornly refuses to admit that he's human. I'm supposed to be dazzled by the trips and the fabulous dinners that he makes (flaming, no less) and impressed by his unpretentiousness (self-professed) and wisdom. The fact that any new wife he finds will be number four is no reflection on his own character. To him, it's only a sad reminder that the first three were crazy. Because, you see, there's nothing wrong with him.

Good grief! Have I told you how awesome your honesty is and how your sincere humility shines through like a beacon, even though you've never once thought to point it out? (Uh oh, that would be me doing a bit of comparing. I didn't expect that).

I'm highly amused at the thought of you surrounded in paper and covered with little stick people in different colors that are meticulously labeled. (I know you were joking, but it's not too late to start. "You know, there is more," she says in an ominous voice.)

Mwahahaha!

Selena

From: Selena
To: Duane
Subject: Change of pace
Date: Tuesday, November 28, 2000, 12:44 p.m.

Dear Duane,

Since your mind is probably still reeling from all the players in my family theatrical production, I thought I'd go back to the beginning and remember some of my early spiritual experiences. I'm afraid my scripture attempt last night was a bust. I just opened up to where it was blasting Korihor for leading others astray. Perhaps I'm too much like Korihor, but at the moment, with my current depression-induced detachment, I simply am not bothered by the idea of being burned as stubble or any other threatening thought. But never fear, I'm not going to give up.

I think my earliest spiritual belief came about in our association with the neighbors who lived half a mile up the road. The Jacksons moved in—two brothers with big families—all faithful members of the Church. My mom was the one who started asking questions, and so our family was soon learning about the Church and corrupting the missionaries by taking them on horseback rides, which was against the mission rules. Eventually, my mom, my dad, my sister Arlene, and I were baptized on Dad's birthday in 1974. I was eleven years old.

I don't recall whether this incident occurred before we were baptized or after, but it made a big impression on me—and as a young girl, my faith in the priesthood never wavered (at least not until the recent past, of which you are already aware).

One day, we got word of a terrible accident when one of the boys rode his bicycle to our house. His dad (the man who baptized us) had backed their three-quarter ton truck diagonally across his two-year-old son from hip to collar bone, the tire only missing his head by inches. We were to call the missionaries and have them meet the family at the hospital in Stettler, eighteen miles away.

When they got there, the nurses didn't want to allow the elders into the room, but Jay moved them out of the way to make some room for the missionaries. Little Sam was administered to, anointed with consecrated oil, and given a priesthood blessing. The doctor said things didn't look good and the child might not make it through the night.

He was released from the hospital the next day, however—the thought being that if he was well enough to jump up and down and play in the crib . . .

I had the simple faith of a child and could see that something huge and inexplicable had happened, and so I had a testimony of the priesthood. I didn't get to grow up with the priesthood, mind you, because my dad only remained active long enough in the Church for our family to be sealed in the temple. He wasn't particularly strong in the spiritual department (you may have already picked up on that, what with the tidbits about the family orchard). So I don't really have a knowledge of what a faithful priesthood holder would be like. Perhaps someday though.

But gosh! Look at the time!

Selena

From: Selena
To: Duane
Subject: Ready with your charts and crayons?
Date: Tuesday, November 28, 2000, 8:20 p.m.
Dear Duane,

So far, we have wife number two, Lillian, and my mom, Margaret, wife number three. You'll remember that when Dad was with Mom, he was also seeing Florence on the side. Getting to know Shannon and Charlene was a cool experience as kids. And that was that.

Or so we thought.

I was a young married woman when Dad sat Arlene and me down for another talk. Seems during his marriage to Lillian, in between child two and three with her, he managed to find the time to venture outside the bonds of matrimony and fathered another daughter, Carol. This makes her the third oldest of Dad's children. Or does it?

Remember that he'd had a first wife. As far as I can tell, he wasn't convinced he played a starring role in the paternity of the son she bore during their brief marriage, which was brought about because of her expectant condition. After coming clean about Shannon, Charlene, and Carol, he finally was willing to acknowledge he had a son named Terry. This son was actually three years older than my mom.

I vaguely remember meeting him as a little child, or maybe I only imagined meeting him. I knew that he existed, but he was really only a name. Of course, another thing about me you've yet to discover is that family has always been the most important thing. Even as a girl, there was this force inside me that made me do everything I could to become closer to those who'd gone before me. I would use horse pedigree charts to make up a family tree (too young to realize that I'd need several). Just knowing the names gave me a degree of comfort, and finding out stories about my ancestors thrilled me immensely.

Even though I had a boatload of brothers and sisters, just knowing that Terry existed always remained in the back of my mind. It seemed to me that my family would never be complete if I knew someone existed and I did not "know" them. Maybe that's why it says in my patriarchal blessing to "accept the call of being a gatherer, first of all in your own family." Anyway, I didn't know anything about him or where he was, and it was a delicate subject I was loathe to bring up. So I didn't.

Then at a family reunion a couple years ago, I found out that someone thought he lived in the same town that I live in. Are you kidding me?! I quickly ran to the phone book and looked for Terry Williams. There wasn't one. No matter how many times I looked, he wasn't there. I concluded that he must have moved.

Now, about three months ago, I was at work at the hospital. I was doing my regular job, which is in Admitting and Reception. Part of my duties include processing the forms of patients who have visited the Emergency Department. I'd separated them, filed them numerically, taken out the doctors' copies, and was ready to put them in the folder for Medical Records when there was something inside my head, like a dimmer switch going brighter. I flipped through the stack of forms and pulled one out. I read the name and thought, *Yeah, this is probably my oldest brother.*

He'd been to the hospital only a couple of hours before I started my shift. The birth date made him about the right age. And what the heck? The person listed as his next of kin—the woman he lives with—works at the hospital!

Keep in mind, I didn't know this woman because, since I'd come back to work at the hospital, she'd been on short-term disability and had only recently come back to work herself. This was a lot to take in. I figured I'd sit on it awhile.

Awhile came sooner than I expected, because two days later, when I was working as a unit clerk on one of the wards, I looked up to see her standing at the desk in front of me. I wasn't entirely sure it was her, so I introduced myself. When she said her name was Debbie, confirming that she was who I thought she was, I said, "You're just the person I wanted to talk to."

She looked at me kind of strange because she knew we didn't know each other. So then I said, "But it's personal, so could we talk in the conference room?" I suppose she was wondering what was going on, and she followed me in and closed the door. I told her about this form I'd found and that I thought this man was my oldest brother.

She asked me who my mother was and I said, "Oh, we don't have the same mother."

She said, "Who's your father?" When I told her, she said, "Yes, he is your brother."

Okay, that's a long story, so I'll leave it right there. Besides, it must be your turn to write.

Selena

♥

From: Duane
To: Selena
Subject: If I had anything to say . . .
Date: Tuesday, November 28, 2000, 9:59 p.m.

. . . then maybe it'd be my turn to write. I could go a couple of ways with this. I narrowed it down to either disturbed or intrigued.

You know, I've known a few men who have lived their lives much the way your father has. I don't know how they do it. It keeps me busy enough just disappointing one woman at a time.

But you know, ALL I WANT IS ONE WOMAN TO SHOWER WITH ALL OF THE LOVE INSIDE ME! IS THAT REALLY TOO BLANKETY-BLANKIN' MUCH TO ASK?!

I'm sorry you had to read me act like that. It's just a bit frustrating to know that this is going on all around me, and yet I'm alone.

So tell me more. From some of our past notes, I sort of gather that you love your dad. Have you forgiven him? Did you feel the need to? Do you resent men because of your experiences with us? Do you believe that I'm genuine and truthful with you?

I think that you are sweet. You're a good girl.

Duane

PS In answer to a question posed long ago: No, I don't punch walls when I get angry. I don't really have a hot temper. One thing though, if I do get angry and argue, I have a tendency to get louder and louder. I'm easily brought back down to talking volume by being alerted to the fact that I'm getting loud. (But first I'll emphatically state, "I'M NOT TALKING LOUD!" that is followed immediately by a much quieter, "I'm not talking loud.")

From: Selena
To: Duane
Subject: Re: If I had anything to say . . .
Date: Wednesday, November 29, 2000, 1:58 a.m.

Yes, I do love my dad. I separate my relationship with him from his past, and maybe that is how our father-daughter relationship survives and even thrives.

I also believe that I was blessed to grow up with an unusual family. Each of my siblings is intelligent, witty, and unique, and I'm glad to know them. Yes, you could say I enjoy my family and the strangeness of them all.

Having said that, you're right. My dad is one of the reasons I can't imagine a man not defaulting to the tendencies of the natural man. So you could say that my ideas of men began to form from what I knew, which didn't exactly fit in with my perception of faithful men in the Church.

I know I need to develop a healthier paradigm of the man-woman relationship. But I'm not going to beat myself up over the fact that I didn't choose the right one first time around. I'm learning, and I've come to view myself as one of Heavenly Father's children who's young and just learning to walk—barely a baby, really. He wouldn't be harsh with me for my learning process anymore than I would slap a toddler just getting his land legs for falling down on his or her trial run. It's time to be gentle and patient, with myself and with those around me. We're all in this mortality thing together, after all.

Whoever ends up with you as her husband will be a blessed woman, and I can say that because I've known you for what, three weeks or so? But you do have a certain something and, in seriousness, much to offer someone because of your growth. Would you trade your experiences and what you've learned for a less troublesome past? I think of my history and my family and I believe many of my best qualities are because of the difficulties and challenges I've had presented to me. I'm grateful for them.

We all go through junk in life. I've had some, but I don't fret about any of it because, honestly, I'm okay. I recognize I have certain issues, but I can, for the most part, relate those to their origin and know that I have to work on them. But it's all part of the process, and I'm learning not to fight it, instead trying to learn, grow, and then move on. Kind of like my marriage. It wasn't what it should be. But it wasn't a mistake because it brought me here: being a mother of five great children (motherhood rocks!), older, wiser, and more in tune with what I believe a relationship can and should be. Life really is good and good stuff is well worth waiting for.

So there you have it, all my nocturnal ramblings in a nutshell.
Selena

From: Duane
To: Selena
Subject: You go, girl!
Date: Wednesday, November 29, 2000, 3:08 a.m.
Dearest Selena,
You know, I'm so impressed with the attitude displayed in that last letter that I'm going to take my little Moongoddess stick girl (who is quite fine, by the way) and put a little gold star on her little forehead? Now all I have to do is find that little bugger. . . . There's, like, a whole bunch of these things in here . . .

"No, I'm not playing with dolls! Go back to bed!"

Everybody is so nosy.

"It's a chart, for cryin' out loud—go to bed!"

Why is it that I can't have any privacy around here?

"Even if I *could* explain it, you wouldn't believe me. Now, go back to bed!"

Gee whiz, can't a guy dress up a couple dolls . . . um, I mean stick figures, without getting grilled by people? What is this, Nazi-occupied Christiansburg?

Your attitude sounds quite healthy to me. I have said the exact same thing about my marriage—how could it have been wrong when I got these beautiful, wonderful children out of the deal? I will be with them forever, and they wouldn't be with me any other way, right? I didn't start off right with their mom, but eventually I turned things around. I believe that she will also make things right in her life and there we will be: two repentant people, better off for the experience.

Considering what you've experienced in your past, all your feelings and fears are not unreasonable or unusual. Do you realize that you are better equipped now to be happy then you have ever been? I hope that you can see that.

I think that I could talk to you forever, but it'd get mighty hungry around here if I don't stop and get ready for work.

Have a great day, okay?

Your friend who plays with [action figures],

Duane

From: Selena
To: Duane
Subject: One more thing
Date: Wednesday, November 29, 2000, 11:55 a.m.

Yes, I believe you're both truthful and genuine (which may explain my respect for and feeling at ease with you). Are you sure we really live this far apart? I mean, if we were to wrinkle up a map, wouldn't that make us live closer? Just wondering.

Selena

♥

From: Duane
To: Selena
Subject: Wrinkle a map?
Date: Wednesday, November 29, 2000, 2:03 p.m.
Dear Selena,

That's one of the things I like about you—always thinking. Me? I am thinking how I can get somebody else to pay my airfare. It occurs to me that maybe for health reasons, one of us needs to be in the other's location. If you could get your doctor to prescribe a visit to Virginia, insurance would probably cover the costs. I don't know what your ailment could be. Personally, I'm allergic to the cold (feel free to use that one if you like). I could masquerade as your special LDS therapist. Of course, lying about being a special LDS *anything* sounds like it might be wrong, and I don't want to put a curse on the relationship. Maybe we could meet on neutral ground, like in Detroit or Chicago?

Have you *tried* wrinkling a map? I feel like I'm doing all the work here. I used to have a map of the United States and it was actual size. Down in the right-hand corner, it said, *one mile equals one mile.* I don't remember what I did with it, but it must be folded up in a drawer somewhere (probably with a Steven Wright CD).

I'm in a good silly mood, in case you can't tell. Why don't you be my princess in shining armor and take me away from this loony bin?

You know what I think it is? I'm actually excited about Christmas! I've never been more prepared for the holidays than I am this year. I have so many good friends. Have I ever told you about this wonderful, sweet ward I live in? These people are so awesome, and I know they love me—it seems like everyone is watching out for me. This is going to be a Christmas to remember. I think I'm going to buy a present for every little kid in the ward and go visit them all! Pepsi products all around, I say! Write me back, sweetheart, I'm going to finish up some paperwork and go home. Did I tell you what a great mood I'm in?

Desperately wrinkling some maps for you (hey, that sounds like a country song!),
Duane

♥

From: Selena
To: Duane
Subject: Postcards
Date: Wednesday, November 29, 2000, 4:39 p.m.
I wish you were here. I wish I were there. Have you ever heard of ICQ?
Selena

♥

From: Duane
To: Selena
Subject: Re: Postcards
Date: Wednesday, November 29, 2000, 6:35 p.m.
I'm home! I just got my teeth cleaned and you know what? That's right! I am very kissable right now—what a waste, all dressed up and no place to go. Minty freshness. Wasted.

What's ICQ? Is it something I can eat? 'Cause if it is, I want some.

I'm glad you think that motherhood rocks. As you know, that's a rather endearing quality to me. No matter what you do, I'm just going to grow fonder and fonder of you, and there ain't nothing you can do about it!

I think it's time for the purging of more secret files—what do you think?

Sincerely, your friend with the minty-fresh breath and the winning smile who's not going to be kissing anyone tonight because the only one who'd kiss him is a big, fuzzy Old English Sheepdog (who, by the way, has less than minty-fresh breath) that is a good friend but is not much of a conversationalist—but is still sympathetic to my lack of a sweetheart,

Duane, the monk in training (who may or may not be more bitter than he sounds)

♥

From: Selena
To: Duane
Subject: Re: Postcards
Date: Wednesday, November 29, 2000, 6:50 p.m.

ICQ is a play on words ("I seek you") and can be downloaded. If a certain someone has it, he or she can see if another certain someone is online. If that's the case, both certain some-people would be able to initiate a conversation then and there. I happen to know someone who has it and wouldn't mind engaging in conversation with someone who is a monk in training due to minty-fresh breath with no place to breathe it that'd be reciprocally enjoyable. What do you think?

Selena

From: Duane
To: Selena
Subject: Re: Postcards
Date: Wednesday, November 29, 2000, 9:27 p.m.

I think that's a capital idea. You kids and your technology. I don't know how it works, so you'll have to coach me. Will you coach me? I would love to talk to you live!

Duane, two hours later and still minty-fresh and kissable

From: Selena
To: Duane
Subject: Quarantined
Date: Thursday, November 30, 2000, 11:36 a.m.

Dear Duane,

It was really nice talking to you last night. I have Auriana home sick today. She's not too bad, but too sick to go on a ski trip with her class. Oh, and I loved your bit about the little stick figures. Thanks for making me laugh.

Selena

♥

From: Duane
To: Selena
Subject: Re: Quarantined
Date: Thursday, November 30, 2000, 4:54 p.m.
Dearest Selena,

I thought I'd take a moment to write to you before I leave work for the day. All my little brain candies have been buzzing today. It's lucky for me that you took the initiative this morning, or I would've stayed up talking to you right up until it was time to go get ready for work!

Don't worry about me showing up on your doorstep unannounced. While I am so taken with you—and therefore more than likely a little bit punch-drunk—I'm not losing my bearings. As our friendship is developing, I'm finding myself more focused on what I want in my life. It's funny, a few months ago I was so out of touch with my own life that I had to be shaken to the realization that I wasn't pursuing the relationship that I always said I wanted—but talking to you has not only reminded me of what my goal should be, but it has me thinking about reconciliation to my old spiritual self. Between the two of us, we know what's right, and if this grows into more than a soulful friend-ship, it will only be more special if we do things with some measure of restraint.

So I've been giving something a lot of thought. I believe it's nothing short of child abuse to be raising your kids in Canada. It's the blistering cold that plagues your little one. How can she enjoy skiing when her little nose is blue? I want to be as objective about this as possible, and it's only after careful analysis that I have come to this conclusion: I think the only real solution is migration to a warmer climate. Not too warm. Not too far south. I'm thinking America . . . mid-Atlantic region, like perhaps, I don't know, Christiansburg, Virginia, comes to mind.

It would be blatantly manipulative and selfish of me to suggest that you move into my town, and for that reason alone, you can rest assured that I'm only suggesting it as a genuine solution to your immediate need to properly care for your little girls. Just another pearl of wisdom. No charge for it.

Sincerely,

Duane, not just another pretty face

From: Selena

To: Duane

Subject: *Yawn*

Date: Thursday, November 30, 2000, 11:36 p.m.

Dear Duane,

I honestly can't believe that I, of all people, am so "smitten." It's not like me to throw all caution to the wind and let myself be carried away by the good feelings of the day, but here I am. I look forward to the day when we can talk and see how real life translates these wonderful feelings from paper to people. As you say, even a soulful friendship would be a blessing beyond measure, so the way I see it is, we simply can't lose.

Selena, sending warm fuzzies back to you!

From: Duane

To: Selena

Subject: A date?

Date: Friday, December 1, 2000, 6:54 a.m.

A new policy has to be enacted and adhered to, effective immediately: From this point forward, all emails from you to me should be written while you are sleepy. I read your note this morning and I'm feeling good. I brought my little Selena doll—I mean, action figure—to work with me. We are having lunch together. If all goes well, we'll be going to a movie later. I'm just kidding, of course! She really is more of a doll than an action figure.

I've been meaning to ask you if you have altered or modified your dreams of becoming the wise old lady of a village? I believe that the last time you mentioned it, you said that you were "rethinking the whole thing." Have I told you about the abundance of village idiots we have here? There is a huge demand for your brand of talent.

I read our chat last night, just once, of course! Okay, twice. But just to make sure that I was understanding all the dynamics of the interaction. We're pretty sweet together—how's that for syrupy? My head tells me there must be something wrong here, but my heart's quite sure that all is well with the universe. I tried to print our chat (you know, for posterity, or the FBI, or whatever) but I couldn't get it done. Is there a trick to that? Or is it impossible? Or am I a village idiot? A fool in love? Who said that? I hate when people read over my shoulder.

Well, I guess I should go do some work. They have been paying me like they said they would, so the least I can do is work like I said I would. I'm in a great mood. You are such a happy feeling in my life, and it's showing in everything I do.

Best of stuff,

Duane, friend of Moongoddess

From: Selena

To: Duane

Subject: Done . . . finally!

Date: Friday, December 1, 2000, 3:32 p.m.

Dear Duane,

It seems like I've been living at the hospital this last little while, but now I get the whole evening off. Are you sure it's 2,279 miles to your house? The idea of a quiet evening at home (yours or mine) sounds great, but 2,279 miles seem a bit prohibitive, huh? And I don't suppose there's any way you could just skip over here and come to my Christmas party tomorrow night? Ah well, I have already been set up . . . with my friend's sister (who is going through a divorce, so Val thought that we'd make a nice couple). But I will not change what I'm wearing to match her purple outfit!

You might have to stop writing to me because the idea of talking all night sounds so lovely. Steven is an only child and he never really talked with me. We would drive an hour to the city to go to a movie and back home without ever really saying anything. Isn't it a shame that two people who are basically decent and good can't connect in the way that will keep them together when things get really rough?

It makes me sad and makes me want to try again, but that wouldn't solve anything because the bottom line is we won't change the other person we're with. We have to be completely satisfied with our choice "as is" because the hope of change isn't likely to happen. I keep reminding myself of that.

And then there's you. You say all the right things. You make me feel like I am worthwhile and special. I've never had that before in my life. Did you know that I can look ordinary and, in fact, less than attractive (that's being kind) when my hair is all messy and I have no makeup, with sleep lines on my face? Honestly, nobody would give me a second glance. I have one of those faces. Can be nothing or can be something lovely.

Let me tell you a story. It's about my dad. Looks are everything to my dad. All his women, whether they're his wives or daughters or a waitress in a restaurant, should look good. He's always liked dressing us up and seeing us look our best. One time a few years back, he had to have an emergency surgery. When my sister and I found out, we went straight to the hospital an hour away. I didn't have any makeup on, but my clean hair was pulled back in a French braid. We walked into his hospital room and he looked really gray and ill. Then he saw us, and when he looked at me, he found the strength to pull himself up and say in dismay, "You look awful."

It was then that I knew that, even though he loves me, if he calls me and says he's having chest pain or whatever, I will always take the time to fix my hair and put makeup on first. That's more important to him than if I get there thirty minutes sooner.

So the looks thing is kind of a weirdness with me. I'm not certain of my worth as a woman if I'm not looking my best, and I'm not sure it all goes back to that one place. I am trying to get out of that and will occasionally go out without makeup and feel good about myself, but even feeling good about myself doesn't take away the feeling that others might not agree with how I am feeling. Did I mention I'm not altogether altogether? ICQ tonight?

Selena

♥

From: Duane
To: Selena
Subject: It's a date!
Date: Friday, December 1, 2000, 4:31 p.m.
Dear Selena,

I will be home at nine my time unless the house caves in on me or, well, nothing—the house caving in is the only thing that might actually happen.

So . . . all this stuff about looks. You know I'm becoming attached to you, and I don't need to see you to know that you are beautiful!

"'Duane' the tub! I'm dwowning!"

From: Duane
To: Selena
Subject: You wouldn't stand me up, would you?
Date: Friday, December 1, 2000, 9:39 p.m.
Dearest Selena,

Do you have any idea how hard it is to know that you're there and I can't reach you? It's so frustrating.

I should have known you would stand me up on my dinner and movie offer. *Forrest Gump*, what the heck was I thinking? I should've said *You've Got Mail* or something. I'm such a dolt! Reel in the pretty girl, Duane, maybe just ask her over for a double feature of Jim Carrey movies. That is the last time I take dating advice from a guy working at a 7-Eleven!

I can do better if you'll just give me a chance.

Duane

From: Duane
To: Selena
Subject: Would you teach me . . .
Date: Friday, December 1, 2000, 10:14 p.m.

. . . to ride a horse? Not right now, of course. Tomorrow would be just fine. I'm kidding . . . about tomorrow, not about learning to ride.

So when I was little, I loved horses. Everything that I had either had a picture of a horse on it or smelled like one. I'm a city boy. When I got to be ten or so years old, I became interested in motorcycles and never spent any more time with horses.

My kids like to ride, but I haven't been on rides with them. I have limited knowledge of horses. I can identify one in a line-up. I mean, if you put a fire hydrant, a cat, a shoe, and a horse together, within three minutes I can for sure tell you which one's the horse. I'm not stupid.

But even with my limited knowledge, I am motivated by the pure beauty of horses. I would love to own some. My dream home would be a log cabin built up in these beautiful mountains with lots of land and horses grazing in the front yard. So what do you say, will you teach me?

The elders came by this evening and we played a trick on the senior companion's new "greenie." We pretended that I was an investigator whom they had tracted into last week. I started asking the new guy all these tough questions and he was doing really well, but then Jr. and me started making it hard on him. We began "revealing" a little at a time that we had some Word of Wisdom and chastity problems. I offered them money to baptize me and made an appointment to get baptized next week. The elder that was in on the joke started taking down my information and clearing his calendar for my baptism—and the new guy was looking more and more nervous.

So I took it up a notch. When the elder got all my information, he was acting really excited about being able to baptize Jr. and me. And I turned and said to the new missionary, "So it helps you guys when you can dunk somebody?"

He stammered, "Well, umm, it's not about us," and he started to explain the purpose of baptism, but I interrupted him.

"Well, heck," I said. "My girlfriend, she ain't here right now. See, she lives here, but she's in jail right this minute . . . but she'll be out in time for the baptism. You can dunk her too! She does whatever I tell her to do!"

That poor kid looked a bit like he was going to throw up, so we let him off the hook. I'm sorry for having to do that, but that's what he gets for being the new guy.

I missed talking to you tonight. I hope we can get together soon. I'll send you a picture of me from last Thanksgiving because you don't have LDSSO anymore. It'll come in real handy when you arrive here. You'll know right away who I am.

Good night, sweet princess,

Duane, as seen on TV

♥

From: Selena

To: Duane

Subject: I didn't make it up!

Date: Saturday, December 2, 2000, 9:27 a.m.

Dear Duane,

I was wondering how long it would take you to ask. Of course I'll teach you to ride!

So I was doing some reading and found this by William Makepeace Thackeray: "Remember, it is as easy to marry a rich woman as a poor woman." (You may want to give that nice rich lady from before some extra thought.)

You may also be amused by something else he wrote, "And this I set down as a positive truth. A woman with fair opportunities and without an absolute hump may marry whom she likes." While not rich, my hump is not absolute, so there may be hope for me yet. I'll leave you with one last thought of his (and my own echoes it): "I think I could be a good woman if I had five thousand a year." ☺

Good morning, Sunshine! I don't remember a time when I didn't have one horse or more at my disposal. Mom and Dad raised horses and, because of their great difference in their ages, Dad was semi-retired the whole time I was growing up. Mom was a trainer, riding instructor, and saleswoman. She used to compete in gymkhanas and even won a barrel race when she was eight months pregnant with my sister Arlene. Dad was the judge of fine horseflesh and brains behind a selective breeding program. He worked hard and learned to do much of the veterinary work and farrier work.

Eventually, though, we got down to about 30 from 150 horses, and Mom continued to train and give riding instructions. Dad trapped to make extra money, and we did all right. Arlene and I kind of raised ourselves because they were so busy with the horses, but we had our own and spent all our time riding. We made up games on them and were never bored.

Okay, I am going to stop talking about horses now, but remember that you brought it up, and I would be thrilled to have someone to go riding with.

If you write to me at work, I'll write back,

Selena

From: Duane
To: Selena
Subject: I thought it was going to snow?
Date: Saturday, December 2, 2000, 11:16 a.m.
Dear Selena,

Just as I wrote the words, I saw one, two, four, eleven . . . 612 . . . 1,459 . . . 16,232 . . . um, wow! There's, like, a hundred snowflakes out there! It was supposed to do this last night. Does Santa come now?

So did your sister Arlene come out okay? What with all the barrel racing and jostling around, she doesn't, like, walk into walls or anything like that, does she?

I'm off to the mall for more goodies.

Write to me. I'm thinking about you all day,

Duane, the pause that refreshes

From: Selena
To: Duane
Subject: The mall?
Date: Saturday, December 2, 2000, 11:38 a.m.
Dear Duane,

If you're reading this, I will have to assume you have gotten home from the mall and with any luck haven't had to endure too many stores.

Do they fill up there as much as they do here, with only twenty-two shopping days left until Christmas?

Yes, my sister turned out fine, but like they say on television, "Don't try this at home, kids." It just happened that Mom was riding all through her pregnancy, so the exertion wasn't anything out of the ordinary for her. Heck, if things don't work out for you and me, there's always my sister. ☺

And since you get to go to the mall and I have to stay here and wait for blood and bruises, I have no other option but to fill spare moments with another note to you.

Let's play a game. Fill in the blank (c'mon, there is no need to be afraid; this could be fun). One thing I have got to stop doing is . . .

Okay, that's as good as it gets on short notice. Now, it's time for you to sit in the hot seat. When did you say you were coming for a visit? (Oh, don't mind me, I am getting imagination mixed up with reality again.) Besides, it's getting a wee bit chilly here. You'd never find me among the igloos. I'd probably be out harpooning a whale or stretching sealskins. Now where did those sled dogs go? (They thought they saw a ptarmigan. Silly creatures.)

But enough of my endless rambling. Answer my question, if you dare.

Selena

♥

From: Duane
To: Selena
Subject: If I dare?
Date: Saturday, December 2, 2000, 12:26 p.m.

That sounds like a challenge, lady! What, do you take me for, some sort of chicken? I'll have you know that I have nothing to hide! I have no secrets . . . that I wouldn't share with you, anyway. I'm quite confident that I'll once again dazzle you with my wit and charm and leave you begging from more—if I'm lucky. So don't you worry, I am up to the challenge.

One thing, are you leaving yourself an out? Passing your leftovers off on your sister? I am shocked that you would even consider such a thing. If I'm not good enough for you, certainly you wouldn't want to burden your sister with the likes of me, would you?

I'll be back soon!

Duane, Man of the People

From: Selena
To: Duane
Subject: Re: If I dare?
Date: Saturday, December 2, 2000, 12:56 p.m.
Dear Duane,

I'm still laughing that you think I have leftovers to give my sister. Trust me, not only am I not that benevolent, but I barely have enough to suffice as an appetizer, let alone have leftovers! Surely, you jest. (Okay, I'll stop calling you Shirley—the joke doesn't translate as well when it's typed, does it?) Sure you can't make it for my Christmas party? You've got what, five hours before it starts? That should be plenty of time for you to get here, don't you think?

Selena

From: Duane
To: Selena
Subject: . . . And don't call me Shirley
Date: Saturday, December 2, 2000, 10:45 p.m.
Dear Selena,

See how funny that can be in print, if you do it right? I suppose you're surrounded by friends and family; meanwhile, I'm surrounded by a sick daughter, a sheep dog, and whatever that is that she just now brought in from outside—some sort of carcass. Her tummy hurts. The daughter, not the carcass.

Well, there's nowhere I'd rather be tonight than at your party. I look pretty darn pathetic right now, sitting here, wrinkling a map, pacing, wrinkling, whining, wrinkling some more. It's not an attractive sight.

What if I did show up at your party? If I took your hand and led you to the floor for a nice slow dance? And what if, in my slow southern drawl, I whispered in your ear, "You look beautiful tonight" and kissed you on the neck? What would you do then, huh? Oh, please, don't be a man!

Whoever marries me will have to like to laugh because, in my family, we can't help it! You may remember that the reason I first contacted you was because of your profile. It struck me as funny. It was as if you were playing a joke on a whole community of guys and you were content to be the only one in on the joke. I really didn't think you would give me beans for a response—I would never have thought that I would gain such an awesome friend.

Thinking and planning with you in mind. Just in case, you know? I don't know, you know?

Okay, I feel like I'm only learning more about me—that's enough about me, so what do *you* think about me? Just kidding. I would like to know what gets you angry and how do you handle it. You can tell me about a time when you were angry, if it'll help.

So I'm ready to buy one of us plane tickets. It's thirty-three degrees here—what do you got?

Duane, the wise old man of the mountain

From: Selena
To: Duane
Subject: Are you sitting down?
Date: Sunday, December 3, 2000, 3:11 p.m.
Dear Duane,

Your letters lately have given me butterflies in my stomach, but it's good butterflies. The strange thing is, the better you make me feel, the more my thoughts turn to Steven and I wish there were some way that we could make it work. I keep reminding myself though, that even if he did make important emotional changes, the Church isn't likely going to become a part of his life. Which brings me to the ever-constant little voice asking me, "What if the Church becomes important to you again, Selena?" This may not make sense now, but with any luck will become clearer as I try to explain myself. And if I botch it completely, let me have another go at it, okay?

I don't think that there's a way of doing this chronologically, so I'll just attack it from the angle that you asked me about: anger. On the bright side, I've never had any "incidents" involving an axe. You know, I'd always heard of people who were so angry at other people or even God, and I just didn't get it. It didn't make sense to me. For the most part, I'm relatively easy going. I am *not* a type A personality, and being adaptable is one of my strengths, so I always seemed to be able to adjust to the current climate of the situation, usually in the form of a peacemaker.

My thyroid went haywire (an expression of my dad's) after Cal was born and I went from being hyper to hypo, where it ended up staying. It ceased to function, and I spent years on and off the synthetic stuff. I didn't really understand what I was dealing with and would take myself off when it would start affecting my heart (my heart does weird things as well). The last time, I let it get so bad that my doctor said she didn't know how I functioned. The truth is, I wasn't functioning but had become accustomed to feeling so tired and "non-functional" that it'd become the norm for me.

At the point that my doctor wondered how I was functioning (it'll be three years in January), she also looked at me and said, "You don't know much about the thyroid, do you?" The truth was, I really didn't. As it happened, on that occasion, I'd taken Cal with me to see her about a sprain, so he was a witness to this conversation. She proceeded to explain how important the thyroid is and that it is responsible for controlling or running all the systems of the body. If left untreated, as I had been doing, it could eventually end up with these systems shutting down, one by one. This would be a bad thing. She added, "You could even get a goiter."

I said to her, "I couldn't get a goiter . . . could I?" She assured me I could, and I have not stopped taking my medication since. A goiter is not exactly something you can cover up with a string of pearls, you know?

This information was a lot to take in, and I was kind of glad that Cal was along (he'd been listening intently to our conversation) as sort of a support for me. I shouldn't have been so grateful. When we got home, he ran into the house ahead of me and apparently announced the news. Jasmine (thirteen at the time) met me at the door and said breathlessly, "Cal says you're going to grow *what* on your neck?" Thanks, Cal—that conjures up quite the vision, doesn't it?

I already told you about the miscarriage. How I went dead inside, except for this anger that I'd never felt before. *Now* I could understand what people had been talking about when they said they were angry at God or other people. I felt that anger inside and out and for many months. That was the emotion of the day because it was basically the only emotion I felt. It was just part of my persona; my countenance was rather dark for a long while.

(I'm making that nice rich lady look really good right about now, aren't I? I'll send my address so she can thank me later.)

In the months after my miscarriage, I didn't realize I was depressed and floundering my way through the whole aftermath. I did not want to succumb to the darkness and was doing what I could to make sense of it and make sense of me, who was now unrecognizable to my family and even myself . . .

Selena's Journal

December 3, 2000

Duane, the man from Virginia whom I met on LDSSO, has quickly become, almost too quickly, a very good friend and confidante. It's kind of scary to think how fast my defenses have come down and I have felt safe to tell him my "stuff." We have shared our lives quite honestly, and it's been cathartic in a lot of ways, but mostly fun. Up until now.

I think I may have guaranteed that he'll never write to me again.

He asked me, in passing really, about a time I've gotten angry. And did I dance around the question? Nope. Did I ignore the question, as I might easily have done? Oh gosh no. I just dumped it all out for him to inspect and dissect.

Hey Duane, you want to hear about how angry a woman can get when her thyroid stops functioning? Imagine some easily preventable if-you-take-the-medication-faithfully-but-I-didn't-because-I-didn't-know-any-better rages. Aren't I just adorable?

But did I stop at just one example?

"No, no, no. Tell me there isn't more!" he says, sitting among the shards of shattered illusions.

"Oh, but darling, it wouldn't be very fair to you if I didn't tell you everything," she replies softly (sharpening the axe—kidding, I don't own an axe).

Hey Duane, you want to hear about the time I ripped the shirt off my husband during an argument? Or the time I left scratches on him when I pushed him away from me? Never mind that I was quick to apply vitamin E as soon as I saw what I'd done. Really, I'm not out of control. It just looks that way.

What was I thinking, telling him those things?! I just feel sick to my stomach. And it's not even because I went and told someone else all those horrible, ugly things about myself.

It's really sad to me to think how two relatively decent people can bring out the worst in each other. I think that's what has happened to Steven and me over the years we were married. I'm ashamed to think of the bickering and even arguing we did in front of family and friends. Neither of us is our best self with the other, and that should be a giant neon sign that loudly proclaims:

THIS MARRIAGE IS NOT WORKING.

I suppose the reason I'm crying is because we've spent years robbing each other of emotional safety, of peace, of happiness . . . all the things that should exist in a healthy marriage.

I may never hear from Duane again, but this kamikaze exercise in brutally honest self-disclosure has taught me one thing, which is that regardless of the circumstances, if the person you're with brings to the surface all your character flaws and weaknesses, that's a huge indicator that you're bad for each other. I have to believe that a healthy relationship or marriage would enhance one's best qualities and attributes, and at the very least inspire a person to strive to be their best self instead of wallowing in the muck of mutual self-loathing.

I think I'm going to miss Duane. I've learned a lot, knowing him. Dang, I don't want to lose this guy. Guess you can't lose something you never had.

From: Selena
To: Duane
Subject: So . . .
Date: Sunday, December 3, 2000, 7:45 p.m.
Dear Duane,

. . . So I've given you the worst examples I can think of that show what I'm capable of. Rather disgraceful, when it's all written out in black and white. The reason why I am telling you these things is because, first of all, I feel safe enough with you to present the whole me to you (the good, the bad, and the ugly). And more important, if we really are to have a future together, I don't want to do a great false advertising campaign and dupe you into something more than you bargained for. That wouldn't be right.

Anger . . . yes, I know what it is now. I have felt it more than I ever care to again. I don't feel that anymore. I think, and hope, that it's a thing of the past. I feel sadness and sometimes frustration when I can't get through to Steven, but I don't feel the same lack of control that I've had in the past three years. I might raise my voice, but like you I am willing to tone it down if it's pointed out to me. I don't like condescension. I don't like being told how I feel or what I'm thinking. I think those are mostly the things that push my buttons.

In retrospect . . .
Selena

From: Duane
To: Selena
Subject: IN RETROSPECT!
Date: Sunday, December 3, 2000, 10:13 p.m.
My dear Selena,

That's not how we end a letter. "In retrospect [blank]"? That's just cruel.

Selena, I'm crazy about you. Stop sounding like you're spelling out doomsday. I love that you're being candid with me and I respect your honesty with such a sensitive topic; it makes me feel like you really trust me as a friend. As long as I'm a single man, we will be the best of friends. And if you and I are meant to be, then you have a best friend for eternity.

Please continue with confidence.

Love,

Duane

♥

From: Selena

To: Duane

Subject: In retrospect

Date: Sunday, December 3, 2000, 10:58 p.m.

Dear Duane,

In retrospect, I see things more clearly, as tends to be the case. At the time though, I was not seeing anything as a normal person would because, simply put, I wasn't normal. Sane decisions are not generally made by those who are feeling less than sane.

You have the right to know me with my imperfections and the right to decide if you can work with that—or if I'm too high maintenance. I respect you more than you know for your receptiveness that gives truth a place to go.

From now on, you may want to choose multiple choice questions for me. You'll be eighty-five years old before you wade through all my essay answers. ☺ Talk to me, okay, about anything that you feel you need to know?

Selena

From: Selena

To: Duane

Subject: Comic relief

Date: Sunday, December 3, 2000, 11:22 p.m.

Dear Duane,

I think comic relief's what we need after my last confession.

Anyway, I'm just thinking of you and didn't want to end the day on the "anger" note. I want for you to feel good and be happy. You've given me much to smile about, not to mention impatience beyond belief because I really, really don't want to have to wait to meet you.

It would be so much easier just talking, but then again, this keeps my typing skills up. So . . . anybody need a hug?

Selena

♥

From: Duane
To: Selena
Subject: A hug? I'll take it!
Date: Monday, December 4, 2000, 5:06 a.m.

Dearest Selena,

You've inspired a lot of emotion in me with the past few letters. I've felt similar anguish and frustration and I have no solutions, but I can empathize. I think a lot about what it might be like to be face-to-face with you and talk about all this stuff, but I have come to realize that we must be apart for a reason—and I suspect the reason is because I have prayed for the *right* relationship and our Heavenly Father is only accommodating that request.

When Marie and I got back together for our "last chance," we read a book together that Dr. Dennison had recommended. It's called *Men Are from Mars, Women Are from Venus*, by John Gray, PhD. I realized some things about myself, reading that book. Basically, I know that there is more to the differences in men and women than just physical attributes, and it's interesting to look at how men and women interact with each other and understand why we have conflicts because of our differences. What I discovered about me is that I am further away from the dark red, Neanderthal end of the spectrum and a little closer to the pastel magenta, Richard Simmons category (the fact that I know what pastel magenta even means is a good illustration of what I'm talking about).

I'm confident enough in my masculinity that I can admit to crying during a movie, but the caveat will be to quickly reveal that the movie was *The Wedding Singer* and not some soapy chick flick.

You've probably discovered by now that you're drawn to the "softer" kind of man—and that if you knew then what you know now, you would've picked differently. Deep down, you also know that though these things are true, they aren't your husband's fault. You and I do not have many similarities in our experience, but we have both come to the same fork in the road.

Marie and I simply can't be together. Knowing what I know about addiction, I am reasonably sure that if I'd forgiven her one more time (without consequences), it would have been a death sentence for her. I'm satisfied that divorcing was the right thing for both of us. Time will reveal your answer. I can't tell you if you and Steven should stay together (and considering how I feel about you, I'm probably not the best person to ask), but I do know this: The inclination to keep the family together is supremely natural and of God. So if there's a way to make that work, it should be done. But no one should have to stay in a toxic relationship, and you may be the only one able to make that determination.

One thing you are proving false: I've always been of the opinion that that the more you get to know of a person, the less lovable they become. I am getting closer to you with each passing day, and while you're sharing your "imperfection" with me, I'm becoming more comfortable with you. I'm glad that you're not as perfect as you might have been.

Duane—use only as directed

From: Selena
To: Duane
Subject: I have this problem . . .
Date: Monday, December 4, 2000, 10:34 a.m.
Dear Duane,

It used to be that my brain went mushy when I was sleep-deprived. Now I'm finding it's mushy all the time! What the heck have you done to me?! I was more than determined: "I wouldn't get married again for a million bucks! I'll never get married again. Why would I get married when I can be happier alone?"

Then a freak occurrence—ending up on LDSSO just to see Paige's sister and deciding to stay a bit to see if meeting some nice LDS men might teach me something and soften my opinions of men. I had no idea when you wrote to me and I told you that I wasn't interested in finding a mate that you would turn my world and heart upside down and shake both up a bit.

Duane, you're everything that I could dream of, from what I know of you so far. You speak, you're literate, you're smart and funny, and you listen to the ramblings of my heart. You're sensitive and charming and manly and desirable, and I'm not able to sleep anymore for thoughts of you. Do you realize I was trying to figure out how I could meet you this weekend? I usually work weekends, but I have this one off and I'm absolutely beside myself (did I mention my Siamese twin?). Just once in my life, just once, I want to know what it's like to sit in church beside a wonderful man, and because I'm so impatient I want it to be this Sunday! I'm that way too about getting my hair done. Pretty spur of the moment with some things. I really do have to work on being more patient, I think.

So I have this problem and I'm hoping you can talk me down from the ledge. One of us needs to be the voice of reason here, and I'm afraid I left mine back at the farm. Duane, I believed what you said about the more you get to know someone, the more reality sharpens the edges and reminds you of the glaring flaws. But the more I know about you, the safer I feel to be me and the more I want to know you. The true test of love is something I've often thought but never really verbalized until lately. I think a person should be able to picture themselves growing old with someone. Being able to picture yourself with someone after the youthful good looks have faded and the children have gone; being able to imagine still being interested in the other person and never running out of new adventures or discoveries about each other or love for each other surely must be the sign of true love. I know we've only met recently, but I'm beginning to . . . feel this picture of the two of us years from now.

That's one of the reasons I want to meet you sooner instead of later. If I'm losing my mind for what's destined to be nothing (if we are not meant to be), I need to get it back soon, because as long as I'm left with my imagination for a roommate, I'm afraid I'm going to be squeezed out of my place. The imagination's getting so big! More important, if we're destined to be an "us," please don't let me lose one more precious minute of time together.

Okay, so there you have it. My heart on a silver platter. I'm overwhelmed by the emotions you evoke in me, and yes, I think that I'm losing my mind. And it's all your fault!

Selena

From: Duane
To: Selena
Subject: Dear girl with problem . . .
Date: Monday, December 4, 2000, 11:07 a.m.
Dear Selena,

I'm at a loss for words, and if you knew me better, you'd surely be impressed at that accomplishment. You have just expressed some of the same things that I have been thinking and have been afraid to say. I have worried that you, being a little more grounded than me, would perceive me as lovesick and going off the deep end. Apparently, that was needless worry because little did I know we were swimming in the same end of the pool. I'm constantly testing my sanity, and I find that other aspects of my life are totally normal. I can only ascertain that there is something special and real here, and that it's okay to feel good about it.

I love what you said about growing old together. My children are so important to me, but I'm teaching them that a spouse is supposed to be number one in your life—it's scriptural. If they listen to my counsel, they will leave me one day, and I'll be alone unless I have that special someone in my life. Coincidentally, did I mention that I watched *The Wedding Singer* the other night? Growing old together is an underlying theme. I like to pattern my own life after what I learn in Adam Sandler movies. That won't be a problem for you, will it?

Seriously though, I really believe that our marriages are designed to be permanent. No matter what we believe or what our earthly experiences tell us, we're not designed for casual relationships that "resemble" marriage. That's why it hurts so much when they are severed. I believe that my divorce was not only necessary, but also the only option. That being said, it was a truly painful experience, and I didn't expect it to hurt so much.

Where do we go from here? I'd love to walk with you, talk with you, look at you, and hold hands with you from morning till, well, morning.

I have time off after the holidays. We should plan something. We really need to think this through and make it special and above board. If we're going to be together forever, then a few weeks to be thoughtful about this won't make a difference. Meanwhile, we should continue to write and talk and get to know each other.

I'm excited and finding it hard to contain my "twitterpations," so we'll have to keep each other in check and make smart choices, okay?

You're making all of my world look brighter. I feel . . . mushy.

Duane, the bewildered-looking chap with the intoxicating smile

From: Selena
To: Duane
Subject: Ah, the voice of reason speaks
Date: Monday, December 4, 2000, 12:35 p.m.
Dear Duane,

Thank you. I needed that. You're right. Waiting will make it "righter" and sweeter, and for you, I will do that. There's a part of me screaming that this is insane, to be contemplating something that just the thought of was abhorrent to me only weeks ago. So exercising a little wisdom, patience, and good judgment will surely only make me a better person.

Tell me more about you, okay? Don't ever stop talking. I hang on every word.

Selena

From: Duane
To: Selena
Subject: Re: Ah, the voice of reason speaks
Date: Monday, December 4, 2000, 4:33 p.m.
Dear Selena,

The "voice of reason" wants to issue a disclaimer: If you find your-self overwhelmed with desire to come see me, forget everything I said in the previous message.

Yesterday, when I hadn't heard from you for a while, my thoughts began to wander and I thought, *What if she's on the way here? That's dumb, why would she do that? But what if? Maybe I should go there. . . . No, no, not without talking to her. Besides what if we crossed paths? [Laugh, laugh, chuckle, chuckle.] No, that wouldn't happen. But I haven't heard from her for some time now. . . .* And my brain continued to ramble on in that general way until I finally got mail.

So as you can see, I want to be with you—and Mr. Spock had gone to the washroom, and I thought I would tell you about it before "logic came back."

"Don't ever stop talking?" Say, you are the girl of my dreams!

Well, I'm going to challenge your dreamy perception of me now, all right? I'm just going to release this first balloon and see where it goes: I don't know how much attention you paid to my LDSSO profile, but I'm only 5'6" tall, possibly 5'6.5" if I wear really thick socks. You say that Steven is 6'1"—do you prefer taller men or did it just happen that way? I can assure you that I'm really quite a bit taller in post-mortal life, about 6'1.5" or so.

I noticed that where women were listing preferences for body type that often they would say they preferred taller men. Some of them were like 4'11" tall and wanted to meet guys that were 8'9". Okay, so I exaggerated—but not by much.

There were lots of women who said that it didn't matter to them, but I know that it makes a bit of difference to me. I wouldn't feel all that comfortable waltzing down the street with a woman who's much taller than me; it just doesn't feel right, and I know. I have dated a few tall women. Me and Dudley Moore and Davy Jones used to do it all the time. It was hip.

So what do you think? Break it to me gently.
Sincerely,
Duane, Dudley, or Davy—you decide

From: Selena
To: Duane
Subject: Re: Ah, the voice of reason speaks
Date: Monday, December 4, 2000, 5:31 p.m.
Dear Duane,

I'm glad that you let Mr. Spock go to the bathroom. I liked what you wrote. And about the height thing, I'm a relatively clever girl and yes, that didn't escape my notice. Because I really haven't gone out with more than a handful of guys, I haven't really formed a hard-and-fast rule regarding something as serious as height.

Having said that, and this is important. . . . Hmm, how do I say this diplomatically? Most men of a shorter stature tend to show their insecurity about this by being braggarts and know-it-alls. Someone close to me married one, and he's his own worst enemy. If he'd just let the good-heartedness in him shine through instead of always reverting back to his glory days and being borderline obnoxious in a lewd and off-color way, we'd all appreciate him more.

Now, I haven't noticed any of these pesky quirks about you. You seem comfortable in your own skin, and, as I said, all the good stuff in you has made me lose all my sensibilities and throw caution to the wind. But you did worry about it enough to bring it up to me, so it's time to fess up and tell me how you handle being 5'6". All right, I'd say it's your turn to talk.

Selena

♥

From: Duane
To: Selena
Subject: Yeah, like I'll be able to sleep now!
Date: Tuesday, December 5, 2000, 5:43 a.m.
Dearest Selena,

I've thought of nothing but last night since we "hung up." I don't believe I really even slept. I have a lot to be grateful for in this life; many blessings, and I have to wonder if you're real—you're too good to be true, and I don't think you have any way of appreciating what I mean by that. You're so funny and sweet all at the same time. I didn't think that the Lord made women like that, or I would've asked for you many moons ago.

My kids think that I'm turning into an Internet junkie, but I really only talk to you anymore. I've got a few faithfuls that I email with, but for the most part, it's all you. I haven't checked my LDSSO for a while, except the other night because I got a message from a girl who served her mission in Roanoke about ten years ago, and she wanted to know if I knew any of her old friends here. Otherwise, I live for that unread message waiting for me from my Canadian girl.

So you told your mom and sister about me, eh? Well, well, well, I guess you are serious. Tell me this: I don't suppose you told your sister that you were planning to dump me on her as soon as you figured out what was wrong with me? I'll bet you kept that little nugget for yourself. Am I close? That's okay. At least I know that you're watching out for me, even if I turn out to be a real loser.

Write to me because I'm thinking of you a lot,
Duane of Sunny Brook Farms

From: Selena
To: Duane
Subject: I'm playing when I should be working . . .
Date: Tuesday, December 5, 2000, 11:34 p.m.
Dear Duane,
Something happened a couple days ago at work and it still haunts me. I turned it into a story. Tell me what you think.

Head down, she said, almost whispering, "I suppose I should be thankful he doesn't beat me."

Standing before me was a woman who has been married for forty years. As I opened her safekeeping envelope and counted out almost four hundred dollars, she confided that he was still mad that she'd been in the hospital.

She slipped all but thirty of it into a yellowing sock, made a knot, and tucked it inside one of the compartments in her black purse, saying she'd have to keep it hidden. "He won't let me have any money. I can't go to church and I can't have any friends. After forty years, I've learned to hide money from him." She said that last part almost defiantly and then added, sounding resigned to her lot, "But he is my husband."

She told me that the doctor had given her some medication to calm her nerves. She was clearly anxious about the prospect of going home with an angry husband. She left my desk and started back up the hall from where she'd come.

Not long after that, I saw a big man, eyes hidden by his dirty ball cap, coming down the hall toward the front doors, carrying a couple plastic grocery bags. She followed him, also carrying a plastic bag, likely holding a few of her personal belongings.

As they approached the automatic hospital doors, she turned to look at me, knowing now that she had a "sister" sympathetic to her plight. I saw her lip quiver. She left the hospital, following in the footsteps of a man she feared.

I've had people say to me, "Be thankful he doesn't beat you." Heck, I've even told that to myself.

I looked at that lumpy, frumpy, simple farm wife and wondered about the free spirit that had been consistently squashed and prevented from manifesting itself all those years. I admired the little piece of stubbornness that wouldn't give up entirely. I looked at her with a new respect for her womanhood and was angry that she hadn't been treated like a queen.

I don't want to be married if that's what it'll be like. I don't want to be with someone I fear, with someone who makes my stomach tie in knots. I don't want to be with someone I can't confide in.

It was just such a strange encounter. What do you think?
Selena

From: Duane
To: Selena
Subject: Re: I'm playing when I should be working . . .
Date: Monday, December 4, 2000, 3:39 p.m.
"The meek shall inherit the earth" (Psalm 37:11).
Sweetheart,

I know we are relatively new to one another, but I think I know why this touches you. I know you see your own worst-case scenario in this dear woman. You've never been where she has been, but you can empathize because you have been held captive on the inside.

I would not worry about her too much—she has learned to adapt, just like you are learning to adapt. One day, she will stand before the Lord and He will say, "Well done, my good and faithful servant." As for her husband, he has lorded over her in an unlawful dominion. He's treated her unfairly and cheated her out of joy, and he'll have to answer for his sins.

These people are everywhere, Selena. That's why it's important for you and me to regain our good graces with Heavenly Father. With a righteous will and the guidance of the Holy Spirit, we could possibly be privileged to help where the Lord needs His people. Have you ever thought of serving a couple mission in your later years? I have.

Duane

Caucasian [ ] African-American [ ] Hispanic [ ] Native American [ ]
East Indian [ ] Eskimo [ ] Pacific Islander [ ] Honky Cat [x]

Selena's Journal
December 5, 2000

Tonight I "ran" into Duane's youngest daughter, Emily, on ICQ. I didn't mean to, and I know he prefers to keep his kids at arm's-length until we figure out if we're just being foolish romantics or if we actually are meant to be an "us." But I was so excited to see him on ICQ that I quickly said hello, only to be greeted by Miss Emily.

I couldn't be rude, so I talked for a few minutes before making an excuse to get off the computer. Turns out, she likes horses! She asked me about mine and I told her if she ever comes to Alberta, I will take her riding. She thought that was a great idea. She seems so nice and funny, like her dad. I keep looking for red flags in this situation, but she definitely failed the selfish, hateful, and "jealous that you're taking my dad's time away from me" teenager test. All I know is I feel a sort of happy, peaceful contentment. Weird, considering a lot of my life at the moment.

From: Duane
To: Selena
Subject: Sweet dreams
Date: Wednesday, December 6, 2000, 3:14 a.m.
Dear Selena,

Voice of reason here. I think I'm weakening. Call me the voice of "almost rational." I cheated and read your message before I went to bed. I have no self-discipline.

So you've told me about your stand on self-adornment. (I have two friends who are jewelers—I feel kind of bad for them). What is it that the people who love you do or give to you that makes you happy and fulfilled?

I also want to meet and start an eternal bliss and not waste another precious moment, but you've saddled me with the charge of being the "voice of reason." Couldn't we just trade off? Like every other day being the voice of reason? I'm so good at being spontaneous and reckless if someone with a backbone is in charge.

Sincerely,

Duane, apologist for fools in love and keeper of rapidly depleting rational thought

From: Duane
To: Selena
Subject: Getting to know you
Date: Wednesday, December 6, 2000, 11:19 a.m.
Dear Selena,

I hope that you're having a good time with your mom. I have been thinking about our phone call last night and I'm feeling closer to you all the time. I trust you know that I was not trying to be hard to get along with—I could easily agree with everything you say, but because we're trying to be real here (we are still trying to be "real," right?), I want you to know what's really on my mind and not a bunch of fluff. "No stone unturned!" That's what I always say. I don't want to leave out any critical pieces of information. You should know what you're getting with Bachelor #1.

Back to my homework:

One thing I have got to stop doing is . . . stalking OJ. He'll never catch the real killer(s) if I keep distracting him.

Okay, seriously now, I need to stop skipping Sunday School and priesthood. I go to sacrament every Sunday, but I don't like going to the classes because it always bums me out. If you'll notice, almost all the topics are about families, specifically husband-wife type families. You know, the kind that I don't have. But it is wrong of me to avoid them. Those lessons are important, and if I had any kind of faith at all, I would go to the classes and prepare myself for the day when I will be in church with my eternal companion. I'm probably missing things that would make me a better father. It's just hard.

I've felt so isolated over the years, it's unnatural to be sitting there without the mom part of my family. The sweetheart part of my life. I know you know what I'm talking about. I was so happy when I first joined the Church. I was that way for a long time, but then I quit reading and searching and serving. I took on the attitude that this is just the way it's going to be, and I don't deserve any better. And so I lost it—the inspiration, I mean. I feel a little guilty because now things are looking promising and I want that feeling back.

Now that I've met you, I feel so much better about myself. Even if you are not the one, I can say with confidence that this experience with you has changed my outlook. I believe that I have plenty to offer the right LDS woman, and my goal to be married in the temple is so much more real. I will raise my family up to the Lord and seek His approval in the way that I should conduct my life.

Well, I answered the heck out of that one!

I heart you,

Duane, a riddle wrapped in a hard candy shell

From: Selena
To: Duane
Subject: You'll never guess . . .
Date: Wednesday, December 6, 2000, 1:36 p.m.
Dear Duane,

I did go riding with Mom today and it was wonderful. The wind came up and chilled things a bit, but we had a good time and a good talk—mostly about you. My mom thinks me going to meet you is a good idea. She's behind us all the way. She likes you already. So that should set your mind at ease somewhat. And all I have to do is figure out when. Something to ponder anyway.

I am wondering how you could possibly disagree with me on anything I say? I'm quite certain I'm right about most things. Very seldom wrong. Well, we'll just have to test each other big time when we meet. I mean, if we're going to be hitched *forever*, it would be best to find out any potential landmines ahead of time, don't you agree? (See, I knew you'd agree. What can I say? I'm almost always right.)

Now, what can people buy or do for me, you ask? Well, I'm a bit weird where "stuff" is concerned. It's a necessary evil, so I'm not against it. And, heck, I like nice stuff as much as the next person. I just don't require it to live.

When I was living here with no furniture, it made perfect sense to me to take a trip with my sister (who had to bow out at the last minute because of an ear infection) and spend the money I had saved on that rather than furniture. Chances to form memories come around only once; furniture can be acquired at any time.

I used to think I wanted flowers and little gifts. Now I just want the memories and the moments of time that never fade or go out of style. Travel is never a waste of money or time because it makes memories and is educational to boot. Again, I like nice things as much as the next person—honest I do—but if those are used to take the place of really meaningful time together or used to impress me (translation: attempt to distract me from glimpsing a piece of someone's soul), I could not care less.

Does that even come close to answering your question?

Selena (I'm not a material girl but am living in a material world)

From: Duane
To: Selena
Subject: I feel too good to sleep
Date: Wednesday, December 6, 2000, 3:12 p.m.

I am sitting here when I should be in bed. I feel like I owe you so much for making me feel so good. I've had a million friends in my life, give or take a few, but I have never felt like the world's treasures were all opening up to me. That's the way I feel now. Like some wonderful premortal promise is being fulfilled, and if it's just been this experience that I've had talking with you so far and feeling this way, then it would still make sense. I am so grateful for the trust and honesty we're sharing. This is hands down the best relationship I've ever had with a woman—and you may think that's sad, but to me, I say, IT'S ABOUT DARN TIME!

It's hard to believe that someone I did not even know existed until October 24 could be such a determining factor in the way I feel every day. I'm glad you have your mom's support in this. It's really nice to know that someone outside of the world that you and I have created for ourselves believes in us too.

I'm sure you could stay with friends who live just a couple of blocks from me. If you decide that you want to bolt in the middle of the night to get away, it'll be okay, no harm done (other than my crushed dreams). If we spend a little time together and we feel like the bond is just as good as it is now, *then* I will want you to meet my kids. I have promised myself not to go parading numerous women in front of them. I want them to be able to take my relationship with the right woman seriously and not think that I'm, uh, I don't know, a jerk? What do you think?

As for your answer, somehow I expected nothing less from you.

Duane, America's top romantic vacation destination

From: Selena
To: Duane
Subject: Re: I feel too good to sleep
Date: Wednesday, December 6, 2000, 6:32 p.m.
Dear Duane,

Your idea about the kids is wise, and I respect that. They don't need a parade of women muddying the waters (though I'm willing to throw myself on their mercy if there's going to be a tiebreaker round). What I really want to accomplish with our first visit is to just talk and get to know each other. We get along so great here and no matter how this all turns out, you have my respect and friendship forever, and I'm a better person for having gotten to know you.

I have to thank you for that. And for making me feel so darn alive these days!

Selena

From: Duane
To: Selena
Subject: My perfect Christmas
Date: Wednesday, December 6, 2000, 9:26 p.m.

Next year, maybe I will enjoy the perfect Christmas. With all of my family around me, everyone that I love. And especially my parents, to whom I hope to present a new wife or fiancée. And as I have taught my children, she will be someone that they can love, too.

Duane

From: Selena
To: Duane
Subject: Re: My perfect Christmas
Date: Wednesday, December 6, 2000, 11:57 p.m.

Dear Duane,

You know, you've experienced a lot of crummy stuff in your life, but for someone like you, who can go from caterpillar to butterfly in one beautiful transformation, I have no doubt that you're in line for the richest of blessings. I admire your strength to overcome huge obstacles in your life. Many others would just wave the white flag and give up on themselves, but you really turned things upside down in your favor. That's so awesome to me.

Family has always been important to me—and maintaining those ties—and it looks like that's another thing we share. I want to assure you that my heart has plenty of room to not only accept but embrace and love the children of the man I love. So I don't delude myself into thinking it'd be perfect, but I have given lots of thought to making the transition easier for everyone, especially so that the man in question would never be put in the middle, having to choose between his new wife and his old children.

Geez, I think I'm starting to sound like I'm at a job interview. Sorry about that.

Selena

From: Duane
To: Selena
Subject: Rich Blessings
Date: Thursday, December 7, 2000, 7:34 a.m.

Hello up there. I'M RIGHT HERE! That's it, go ahead and send 'em on down. I'mmmmmm right here. . . . There we go. Just keep the blessings comin'.

Dearest Selena,

I'm so . . . well . . . my cup runneth over. I am also quite capable of loving the children of the woman I choose to marry. You know that I love family, and I say the bigger the better. I want to have them all around me as I grow older. I plan to help raise some grandchildren and even great-grandchildren. I want to create a home that is as big and warm as an earthly home can be, with loving and learning and a spiritual influence that will draw them all to us—oops, I mean to me and my eternal companion.

Yes, I want to provide roots for the whole bunch to call their own, a place where everyone will know that they can come to feel safe and loved.

You say that I'm in line for some rich blessings. Well, I've thought the same of you many times over now. I would love to think that the kind of trials I have had to endure are ready to go to the next level, and that the long and cruel lesson of finding the right partner for eternity is about to finally be behind me. But as the team of Papabear and Moongoddess have often said, "It was all worth it, if only for the grand friendship."

I'm walking on a cloud, taking you to work with me in my heart, humming Christmas carols, and looking downright smug. They all wonder what I'm up to. No one can be that happy that many days in a row, they all think. If only everyone was blessed to have a wonderful friend like mine.

Hugs,
Duane

♥

From: Selena
To: Duane
Subject: Finally
Date: Thursday, December 7, 2000, 10:27 p.m.
Dear Duane,

I found out today that I weigh 123 pounds. I think I weighed that when I was in grade six. Definitely says something for the stress diet. I found out because the doctor made me get on the scale. Because it was my first visit to him. Because he's a shrink! Hey, maybe that's why I only weigh 123. He shrunk me!

Actually, my mom urged me to go see him because she believes that I need to talk and work through some of my junk. My history is such that I kept everything inside until one day, like Vesuvius, I just blew. As you can tell, I am getting much better at talking about the things inside me, but this is actually a new thing for me. Much healthier, I think. We'll see.

Thinking of you fondly,
Selena

♥

From: Duane
To: Selena
Subject: Now I'm concerned
Date: Friday, December 8, 2000, 2:44 a.m.
My dear delicate flower,
Hey, what's the matter up there, sweetheart?

You are not sharing. In this relationship (the one restricted to the printed word going out over the Internet), sharing is all we have. I'm not going to press you on this, only to say that I care sincerely about you and what goes on in your life. You're a little package of thoughts, dreams, experiences, humor, wishes, and love that I don't want to do without.

However, if somehow your recent expressions of emotions toward me and the "magical" connection that we have made has you upset, I want to know. I would do anything for you at this point, and that includes giving you some time off to get some space and breathe. I have my concerns as well, but I'm at a different place than you, and maybe I don't always appreciate that your needs may be a little different than my own. It would not hurt my feelings if you needed the space for your mental well-being. If I'm totally out in left field, you can let me know that all is well. Just don't hold it in. We are still 2,279 miles apart—a reasonably safe distance.

I hope that I'm wrong about this whole thing and that you're still excited about meeting me, but if there is any problem, *please* share it with me. I care deeply for you and I don't want to be in the dark. I'm not saying that I'd put my life on hold for you, but I would put it on *pause* if I thought that I was causing you problems that would be better handled without my interference.

I won't be able to take my daily naps at work till I hear back from you, so please write me.

I am sincerely yours,
Duane

From: Selena
To: Duane
Subject: Darn it . . .
Date: Friday, December 8, 2000, 4:05 a.m.
Dear Duane,

I guess I don't always express myself as well as I intend. And seeing this doctor is something that was in the works before I met you. What the future holds for me seems to be less uncertain now than it was even weeks ago, but regardless, it is my responsibility to recognize that my suppression of feelings and issues (I think that word *issues* is beginning to annoy me) was not healthy and led to an upheaval in my life that I don't wish to repeat. So there you have it. This better be considered sharing or I'm going to have to come down there, hold you down, and share until your eyes glaze over from the monotony of it all. I want to assure you that this is only part of the process as I try to continue my healing and progress.

For spiritual healing, I look to other sources. The truth is that when I first met you, you were a part of that program. If I could just have my faith restored that not all men were hopelessly lost to their testosterone and that they were able to master the nature of man with a deep and true belief in Heavenly Father, that would be a start. And, of course, you have proven that to me consistently. You may or may not have noticed a distinct softening in my persona since we first began to correspond. I've noticed it immensely and believe it brings me a step closer back to my Father in Heaven, perhaps even preparing myself to be receptive to the Spirit that has been absent from my life for too long. I have always been acutely aware of the facets of a person's soul and those would not be complete without the spiritual aspect.

You may wonder why I chose my unofficial anthropological study (another tongue-in-cheek moment) over other conventional methods (prayer, scripture study, Church attendance). The truth is, I believe if something isn't working, try another angle. Scriptures became words to me, prayer felt empty, and Church meetings were just a frustration. Why? Because I didn't feel the Spirit. It was easier to stay hardened in that state than to think maybe Heavenly Father wasn't interested in me or didn't find me "worthy" of that blessing. I had even come to a place where I felt a certain peace in spite of the absence of that spiritual aspect of my life and thought that maybe it had served a purpose but was not going to be a part of my life again.

But a thought kept coming to me recently (perhaps the persistent whisperings of the still small voice?): "What if the Church becomes important to you again?" I could not ignore that and so followed those feelings in a new direction (still toward Heavenly Father, though just a different, scenic route).

I was actually just musing today about that. When Paige wanted to see her sister's profile, I distinctly remember the spirit in which I did it. I just about gagged at the idea of all this "looking for love" stuff and the questions I had to answer to even get in the door. I was absolutely hardened to the process and found it ludicrous that people would fall for it. You have to understand that in recent months, I had replaced my love of fairy tales and their happy endings with reading autobiographical books about war. Anything with love was off my list completely. Romantic movies and stories were something I'd come to mock, and I think it was all part of my wall-building process. I just didn't want to be hurt in this field again, and that wouldn't happen if I didn't care, right?

Something inside me was reluctant to throw away all my years of unwavering faith and devotion, and so I allowed myself to be drawn into the LDS circle of singles for a brief time. There I met you. And then I began softening (I actually preferred hard at that time because there is a certain amount of power in not feeling). As much as I could not imagine at that time PD (pre-Duane) ever feeling open and soft again, I'm sitting here trying to imagine how I felt so hard, because now *that* seems foreign to me.

If nothing else comes of our friendship, I will always be grateful for your help in getting me from there to here, because while I give up the power of not feeling or being affected by my emotions, I gain (dare I say) a greater power that is more real and honest and certainly more beneficial to humankind—and especially to the people whom I call my family and friends. I'm actually anxious to visit Paige again to see what differences she notices in me. I think I've changed quite a lot since I was there in mid-October. Heck, you've probably noticed some changes yourself.

I don't want to hold anything back from you and if it ever appears that I do, tell me, like you apparently had no problem doing just now. It's human nature to want to present ourselves (more like *misrepresent* ourselves) in only a positive light. I'm uncomfortable with these mental health issues that I'm working with because even though I understand their physiological basis, I still feel like it makes me look weak and unable to fix myself.

Well, I'm not a weak person, nor do I wish to marinate in grief and turmoil, so I'm learning compassion and maybe even some humility along the way. Basically, I don't want you to think you're dealing with a crazy person who would be too high maintenance to take a chance on. You've been really good for me and have lightened and brightened my days—and hey, I would totally miss you if you were gone from my life. Having said that, though, it would be unfair to make you a crutch on which I leaned instead of exercising my own emotional limbs and making myself strong enough to run on my own.

Selena

From: Selena
To: Duane
Subject: Re: Now I'm concerned
Date: Friday, December 8, 2000, 10:07 a.m.

Dear Duane,

Now in the light of day, I see I may not have even answered your question. ("Now she tells me," he says, after taking the ice pack off his head because of the eye strain of reading endlessly.) In a nutshell, there is nothing about you that causes me anything other than anticipation, happiness, anticipation, respect, anticipation, good feelings, anticipation, and so on. Did I mention anticipation? Everything I know about you is everything I would put on a wish list if I were making one up of my "perfect match." Now did I answer your question?

Selena, sometimes a delicate flower

From: Duane
To: Selena
Subject: I'll call you again in six months
Date: Friday, December 8, 2000, 11:46 a.m.

Just kidding! That was mean, but I owed you something for hurting my feelings. I have noticed a trememdous difference in you since the beginning, and that is why it scared me. I thought that maybe you had some sort of anxiety concerning me, that maybe I was being too pushy.

I don't know, but it just seemed and felt like you were trying hard not to tell me something.

There's a lot that I want to tell you, but I'm running late. I just got back from the lawyer's office and it looks as though I'll be a free man in about two weeks. I had a long talk with my bishop (who knows, maybe he will be your bishop someday) and I really only told him that I had been talking to you and that we were hitting it off. I didn't say anything about you coming to see me, but he didn't seem concerned that I was spending time talking to you over the Net.

Selena, you're so special to me (and I hope that doesn't make you feel pinned in). I want the best for you (which is probably me). I would do anything for you, and that includes leaving you alone (though I'd rather be kicked in the stomach three times a day) and giving you some space. I don't want to complicate your life. I want to hold you, not smother you.

You're precious and I'm lucky,
Duane

From: Duane
To: Selena
Subject: Timing
Date: Friday, December 8, 2000, 10:48 p.m.
Dear Selena,

I think that you came to me at a perfect time in my life. I believe that the timing was remarkable on your end as well. I suppose that, at least as friends, talking over the Internet, we're a match made in heaven . . . with heaven's blessing. I can hardly contain (and I don't) the happiness that I feel after I talk with you. I pray that we are a real couple on the way to making both our dreams come true, but if it all doesn't come out as I want it to, I believe I'll always love and appreciate all that you have contributed to my feelings of joy during these days together. It has already been worth it.

You are so special to me,
Duane (what is that on your sleeve—your heart?) Pannell

From: Selena
To: Duane
Subject: Re: Timing
Date: Saturday, December 9, 2000, 7:55 a.m.
Dear Duane,

I decided that because I have to drive to Calgary on Monday, I may as well continue on another couple of hours and see my friend Paige. I'm convinced this is all her fault and phoned her today to tell her a bit of what's been happening. She's so happy and can't wait until I get there because we've got tons to talk about.

So Cardston is the town where the Alberta Temple was built and dedicated in 1923. It's the temple where I received my endowment on the same day as my sister Arlene. That was pretty special, being able to do those things together. We were treated so well by the temple matrons. We felt like queens. It was like stepping out of the world and experiencing a little bit of heaven.

Paige was so excited to hear about things going well because she remembers my crustiness when I was there in October. She told me she'd put my name on the temple prayer roll and thinks maybe I'm being blessed. I need to go and talk to her and have some serious chick time: giggling, taking care of the kiddies together, and so on. Maybe even go and sit in the temple foyer and do a bit of pondering. I'm really hoping Heavenly Father is willing to help me out right now with all the details of my life.

Selena

♥

From: Duane
To: Selena
Subject: I'm doing well
Date: Saturday, December 9, 2000, 9:35 p.m.
Dear Selena,

I've got to say, this could've been a bad day, but having spent some time with you chatting made all the difference in my attitude today. Even now, I am singing those Christmas carols and smiling like a big dumb chimp.

I was doing some shopping and noticed something a bit different in the way I was feeling. I have had this (I feel dumb for this) problem in recent years. Seeing all of these couples out in public—you know, the happy-in-love ones—and I would experience feelings of resentment and bitterness and that feeling has irritated me. Sort of like you were saying about all that goofy love stuff on LDSSO. It just felt wrong that other people are allowed to walk around all happy in their relationships while I was being screwed over. I have the capacity to be the best *in-love* person out there, and it made me mad to know that I was being deprived of the opportunity to participate.

Don't get me wrong, Marie and I had our moments. We'd call each other Schmoopy and say "I love you" every day (in fact, the more things would slip away, the more she would tell me), but underneath it all was impending doom, and it was a dark cloud over my heart.

Not today though. I am so full of hope. And it doesn't matter where you are, I can feel the hope radiating from you, and it is giving me a whole new perspective on life. I can't say enough that I've gotten more than I really believed I would get from this experience and I'm forever changed by it, no matter what happens from here forward.

I don't know if you caught on the other night because you didn't say anything, but I was talking about "leaning" on me. I understand that you have to be self-sustaining and a whole person—I believe that too. However, there is nothing wrong with supporting one another, and *leaning* is not a dirty word. I believe that to be what the scriptures mean when they say that the two become one (concerning marriage). There is a difference between a healthy merger and codependency. I would never allow you to abandon yourself and become dependent on me, even if you would do it (which I can't see that as ever being an option for you ayway).

So . . . don't be too rigid in that department. I understand it and want the best for you as well.

Thanks for being the star of my dreams, day and night.

Write me,

Duane, the dreamer

From: Duane
To: Selena
Subject: That was awesome
Date: Sunday, December 10, 2000, 9:54 a.m.
Dearest Selena,

Talking to you was like talking to someone I've known all my life—is that weird?

It occurs to me that it may be time to start thinking about giving up my photo collection. I've been thinking about buying a real good camera and taking pictures of more substantive subjects. You know, like my kids, you when you visit, my dog, you, some of the beautiful countryside here, you, close friends, you, and things that have meaning to me, like you. Oh, did I mention that I would like the chance to take your picture?

If you ever have need to call me (like from the airport in Roanoke, taking a plane to Christiansburg when you surprise me with a visit tonight), my number is 1-555-867-5309. I thought about it the other day. If I get knocked in the head and get amnesia or I get abducted by aliens, you might want to call here and find out whatever happened to me. Memorize this number, as it could become the most important number you have ever known.

Duane, putty in her hand

From: Duane
To: Selena
Subject: And then panic set in . . .
Date: Sunday, December 10, 2000, 6:43 p.m.
Dearest Selena,

It occurs to me that if you are with Paige for the next couple days, where will I be?

Lost, lonely, forlorn?
Duane

♥

From: Selena
To: Duane
Subject: Re: And then panic set in . . .
Date: Sunday, December 10, 2000, 11:37 p.m.
Dear Duane,

You're right, I'll be with Paige, but you forget that I'm in the same boat as you are. A few days without you is going to be strange. I've grown accustomed to your . . . font? I am trying to remember your voice and all I know is I sure liked listening to you. We might have to talk more often, maybe in person, just so that the memory lasts longer. What do you think?

I've been thinking of your famous photo collection at work. You know, it wouldn't bother me if you kept it, and I honestly mean that. There's just one catch though: I don't want my picture in there, okay? Otherwise, no problem, and you can continue to wow all the dudes who walk by.

Steven wants to take me out for supper on our "anniversary." That's a rather strange request, but it's certainly more preferable than the semi-threatening he's been doing up until the last couple of weeks. Divorce is strange. Winter is strange (it's so cold out that my coat was crackling). Technology is strange. People who'd otherwise go about living their lives nicely oblivious to the reality of another person now have the means to connect instantly. Amazing.

Keep replying to your LDS Singles emails (you are right that it'd be poor manners not to) and keep your mind open. There may yet be someone just like me who actually lives in the neighboring state. And at this point, I care enough about you to only want for you to be happy in life.

So think happy thoughts, and I will certainly be thinking of you.
Selena

From: Duane
To: Selena
Subject: Temporarily out of service
Date: Monday, December 11, 2000, 4:38 p.m.
My dearest Selena,

I'm taking myself out of the availability pool for a bit. I hope you don't mind. And even if you do, there's nothing you can do to change my mind, unless of course you want to come down here.

And while we're at it, I'm not concerned about any other woman in even a *neighboring town* who might be *something* like you. I'm so sure that we're going to be compatible when we meet that I'm not looking any further until I am proven wrong beyond a shadow of a doubt. If this isn't going to work, I'm confident that it'll be some other heart-wrenching reason that is completely out of both of our hands. The first of January is not too long to be out of the lineup. You have what is known, in legal contractual terms, as a first refusal option. I will be your reject for some poor chick who doesn't know she's getting seconds (with the possible exception of your sister).

Your picture would never go on my wall. I have a prominent place for your picture, where I will appreciate it and visitors wouldn't have a chance to drool on it. There is a belief I have gained from the Church that's part of the promise to cherish, so I wouldn't display you like that.

When are you and Steven celebrating your "anniversary"? Marie and I were married on January 3, and I don't believe we'll have dinner together this year. Last year, she mailed me a card. This year, I'm not really expecting anything.

Your biggest fan,
Duane

From: Duane
To: Selena
Subject: Thank you
Date: Tuesday, December 12, 2000, 2:22 a.m.
Dearest Selena,

You really put my heart and mind in a place that they haven't been since my teen years. And because I am experiencing this without the influence of drugs or alcohol, you're visiting uncharted territory. I'm so grateful to have met you. I want to be your friend forever. You have made such a difference in the way I feel about life.

You will be on my mind. As you go through your day, anytime you think of me, know that I'm already thinking of you and anticipating any little contact you might be able to sneak in (hint hint).

I may continue to write to deal with separation anxiety. So you'll have that to sort through. I can be annoying when I'm going through withdrawal. I hope you have a great time visiting with Paige. Please be careful driving and keep warm!

Your number one fan and not-so-secret admirer,
Duane

From: Duane
To: Selena
Subject: I miss you
Date: Wednesday, December 13, 2000, 7:45 a.m.
My Dearest Selena,

What a sad, pathetic man I've turned out to be. I'm ashamed. How did I get here? What have you done to me? Are you exposing my addictive tendencies on purpose? Quit being such a hottie. There, I've said my piece.

I'm going to share a little story with you, but I want to preface it by saying that it is not designed to extract sympathy from you. I have put this behind me years ago and learned an important lesson about gratitude from it. It is now even kind of amusing to me and helps me remember not to take myself too seriously.

When I went to the hospital in 1990, I was twenty-eight years old and feeling as though my life was coming to an end. I was horribly sick from the amount of drugs I was taking and the alcohol I was drinking. I weighed all of about 150 pounds, and my face was so sinister-looking, with my eyes sort of sunk in and dark. My marriage was about over and I wasn't even aware of it. Marie was infatuated with some guy at work and carrying on an affair. I was so absent (and psychotic) that she was able to keep her secret without all that much trouble. The main thing was I needed help, and if I didn't get it, I would die. I knew this. It's a long story, and I'll tell that some other time as to how I ended up in the hospital, not for one thirty-day treatment, but two. As I said, this is a story about gratitude, and it took place on the second day of my second visit to the hospital.

The drug treatment center at the hospital was on the sixth floor, and I was quite familiar with it. I'd checked out only two weeks before. I stood in the dayroom, smoking a cigarette and looking out of the window into the parking lot, wondering how I could possibly have ended up back in treatment. I was all alone and it was terribly quiet. I was so eaten up with self-hate that I didn't even want to be alone with myself or my thoughts.

I don't have anything, I thought. Everything that I had worked for over the years was gone. Lost possessions were one thing, but I had also lost relationships with people, some of whom were afraid of me and were better off without me. I had all but severed my relationships with my family, and the only thing that bothered me about all those burned up relationships was the fact that it didn't bother me. I knew that it should and that was my only concern. I wasn't *feeling* things the way that a person should.

I also had some cool jobs over the years that I had excelled at and I'd shown great promise in, but they were also gone by the wayside. There was no telling where I might have been if it hadn't been for my indulgences. Bosses didn't trust me any more than my family did, and it had become worse with each passing year.

As I stood there, looking out at all the people going about their day, I remembered how at seventeen I had gone to a clinic seeking help. I was already a full-fledged alcoholic and had been since I was a child. At the clinic, I talked to a counselor, and she gave me a drug that makes a person sick if they drink alcohol, but I just quit taking it. And then I read in one of the pamphlets that the first step was to admit that I was an alcoholic, so that's what I did. I admitted that I was an alcoholic and decided that I could live with it. There was so much that I didn't understand about its progressive nature, and I was now paying for it over twelve years later.

So there I was, looking out the window, all alone. I had nothing. I could see my car out in the parking lot. *What a hunk of junk that car is,* I thought. *Everything I own is in it. I must be the most cursed man in God's kingdom. He has taken everything from me. I have no home, no family; I'm a father, but I don't even know my kids. I'm homeless. I have nothing, just the clothes on my back and that stupid car. I HAVE NOTHING! I've lost everything a man can possibly lose and I might as well die. I have nothing.* I almost began crying.

Right around then, I saw a small truck pull up beside my car. It was my wife and her boyfriend. They both got out and were looking inside my car. I was perplexed and I put my tears on hold for a moment. They walked to the driver's side of my car and talked for a moment. Then he kissed her. Not one of those "thanks for the ride, stranger" kisses either. It was more of a "thanks for the ride and welcome to Slobbertown" sort of kiss. She then got into my car, he in his truck, and they both drove away out of sight.

I just stood there. I thought that something ought to happen next. "Roll the credits" or something. I remember thinking how I was power-less to do anything about what I had just witnessed, and how getting upset about it was useless. Just as I started to go back into my thoughts, I froze—would it be wise now to start whining about what I didn't have? I smiled and thought, *There is a God and He does have a sense of humor. A great sense of humor.*

I remember that episode every now and then when I feel sorry for myself for any reason. No matter how much I'd lost, there was still plenty more to lose. Today, I'm the richest man that I know and I also know that anything the Lord blesses me with is only mine as long as I am an honorable steward. And for that, I am grateful.

Your grateful friend,
Duane

♥

From: Selena
To: Duane
Subject: Hello hello
Date: Wednesday, December 13, 2000, 11:27 a.m.
Dear Duane,

I'm writing from Paige's computer because I really, really needed to talk to her about all the stuff happening in my life. She suggested

I send you an email (definitely don't want the withdrawals to be too painful for you).

Paige and I have done really nothing but talk about you, me, Steven, and my kids. She likes you already. I told her about something that happened recently that I haven't yet told you about. So I'm thinking if you're game, I'm ready.

After I saw the shrink and he talked to me about panic and anxiety, I thought about how my experience in the past had been with Steven's severe bout with it. Mine was definitely real, but relatively insignificant in comparison.

Then that night, at about three in the morning, I woke up and was startled by an epiphany. I've been hard on Steven for his absence in our marriage because I really needed a partner. I also know what it's like to be in a place where I am unreachable and unable to give even one more speck of myself to someone else.

This put me in the perfect position to remember him sitting on the edge of the bed, shaking, sweating, and trying to cry (he'd grown up not having permission to cry because he's a guy). How on earth could he possibly be a good husband to me when he was going through a hell of his own? I have often reminded him how I stood by him through his experience, but it became uncomfortably clear to me that while I was physically there for him—and he felt emotionally supported on some level—I had zero understanding and was certainly less supportive than he deserved.

What does this mean? I'm still trying to figure this out. You see, I'm not filled with the same anger I had in the past toward him. I now have an understanding of that period of our lives, so I apologized to him and absolved him of any responsibility for making me feel so lonely during that time.

I'm softer and more open now. There was a time (not so long ago, I might add) when it was inconceivable to think of him touching me or living with him again. Now, I might just be able to do it. No guarantees, mind you, because so much water has passed under the bridge. I also am a much different person now and am not willing to settle for half a life with someone.

Remember when the bishop counseled you to try again with Marie? How it seemed to make no sense, and there went another two years of your life? But at least now you know beyond any doubt that you did everything you possibly could to make that relationship work, right?

I'm not suggesting that I'm going to move back in with Steven. I'm sure not ready for that. But I think it's time I talked to him—really sat down and discussed with him his ideas of the perfect future for him and me and share my ideas of what I need and cannot (and will not) live without. I'm not sure how this will turn out. He's been good at saying all the right things but not following through because his heart wasn't in it. I want to be able to tell my children, when they ask, that I did everything I could to give our family a chance. I want to do this honestly and completely, not just halfway.

There is no doubt in my mind if I had no children involved, there would be no decision to make. As far as I can tell, from this distance, you are everything that touches me and makes my heart feel safe and happy. I think it's wise, though, for me to try taking my new, open, and approachable self to Steven and attempt to discuss the most important details of our life as it is and of our future, together or not. We will always be connected through our children, and they will be so much better off if their parents can communicate in positive and meaningful ways, keeping their best interests in mind.

I'm thinking of you and look forward to hearing what you think of all this.

Selena

♥

From: Duane
To: Selena
Subject: Hello back at you
Date: Wednesday, December 13, 2000, 3:31 p.m.
My dearest Selena,

I won't lie, nor will I hold back what I'm feeling (no need to duck, I haven't got it in me to be vicious). My heart sank when I read your message. I don't even know what I'm about to say as of yet; I'm just letting my fingers work it out.

You've become really precious to me. I've thought at least once a day how I've never had a woman respond to me the way you do when I share the things that I share with you. It has been such a lift in my life that I can't really explain. I suppose that I've put myself way out there as far as seeing a future for us. And as aware as I was that I was doing that, it felt way too good to pull back. I'm sure that there is a lesson in this, but being so determined to find true love and have someone to cherish is probably going to leave me doing the same thing, should I be given similar circumstances.

All that said, I can't argue with your decision. It's the best possible thing for everyone concerned to hold a marriage together if it can be made to work. I'm sure that Steven has way more to love about you than I do. He was your husband and deserves every possible chance to make things right. Certainly your children would benefit most from your reconciliation; all children want their mom and dad to love each other and be together.

As far as Marie and I go, it was an entirely different thing. The odds were against it working to begin with, and I knew it. I didn't do it for the kids. I knew the odds were such that they would be disappointed at the very least, and at the most they would likely be put back into an unhappy, volatile situation.

I did it because I didn't want there to be an asterisk in the divorce— a point that she could make that I left her for the Church. I loved Marie deeply, and it's only been about a year from the time that I could say I haven't loved her. Even though I loved her at the time that I gave her a second chance, I had to evaluate what I was likely to be sacrificing. I made a conscious decision to reconcile, knowing that I would give up going to the temple, at least in this life, to be sealed. I knew that I would have to continue to compromise my beliefs as far as illegal drugs were concerned (having them in my home). I knew she wouldn't go without marijuana for long and that I'd be back to that moral dilemma—she always pointed out that she was a smoker when I married her and that it would be hypocritical of me to expect her to change after what she had tolerated with me. I knew that I would still be sitting there in church every Sunday without a wife by my side and that I had to be prepared to continue keeping all my spiritual feelings and thoughts to myself (which included their slow but steady deterioration).

While some of that isn't much different than you and Steven, what does separates my problems with my wife and your problems with your husband has to do with the insanity of addiction. I had to give her that consideration because she was so reckless. I'm going to say something that I've never told another human being, not even my bishop. . . . This is so hard to say. I couldn't just cut her loose with the knowledge of her behavior that I had. She had told me things that led me to believe that she was a danger to herself, and even that aside, she was hanging out with dangerous people. I did not want to end up with her blood on my hands because of my stupid desires of a fairy-tale life.

I don't want you to think of me as some kind of jerk. I know that the story, as I tell it, is nobler than what I'm sharing with you now. I gave it another year and it didn't work. When I finally did cut her loose, it was as if I was saying I didn't care if she died.

You shouldn't think of your situation as one that's hard to overcome. It sounds to me like Steven is willing to try and work things out and all he needs is your cooperation. If you're willing to settle for a little less than the ideal and he gives a little, it could be that you'll be able to put it all back together again. You loved each other at one time. It can happen again, I'm sure.

That's all I really have. I don't know what else to say. Maybe if you have some time to sort through this, you'll have a better idea of what is important to you. I don't think that it's a good idea for you to be talking with me while you're in limbo because, I can tell you right now, I have put about all the "fair" in this that I can muster, and any other correspondence that I have with you will be a selfish design on my part to change your mind.

Selena, I want to do what is right. I've told you that over and over again. I cannot counsel you on this matter. I'm way too biased and I can feel myself right now wanting to delete this letter and start again to put my slant on it. I think that, as much as is possible under the circumstances, I love you. I want the best that the Lord has for you, and I could never be completely happy knowing that you had doubts all along. Please do these things prayerfully, and I'll do the same.

Love,

Duane

From: Selena
To: Duane
Subject: This is not a message
Date: Thursday, December 14, 2000, 7:30 a.m.

Dear Whoever Reads This: (It won't be Duane because he has more self-control than me),

I've been having a wonderful time with my friend Paige. Last night, we went to see the movie *Charlie's Angels*. They don't owe me money. I'll tell you why. First of all, we got in free because Paige's husband sometimes runs the projector.

It was really cold last night and when we got there at nine p.m., it turns out we were the first to show. The rule is there has to be at least seven people to show the movie. Two more showed up, so it was looking more promising. As Paige visited with the owner, he suggested if she'd turn off the projector at the end and lock up, he'd go home and we could see the movie. Now is that too good of an offer to pass up or what?!

Paige and I giggled and laughed throughout the whole thing. It was such a goofy, funny movie, and we decided that we could be Charlie's Angels too because they surely borrowed some of our sweet moves for the film.

When the movie was done, the couple left quickly, and there we were, all alone in this big theatre. Now, you have to understand the theatre in Cardston is big and even has a stage. Well, what were two girls all alone in a theatre to do as the closing credits ran and the music played? Get on the stage and dance, that's what! Not only that, but the shadows we made on the screen looked too awesome. We had such a great time, and I'm so grateful to have such a good friend. She is so spiritual and fun and has such a loving and generous heart. This visit will go down as one of the special snapshots of my life.

Now, onto more serious matters (where my flaws become apparent now as being selfishness and impatience). Your letter (I mean, Duane's letter, because he's not reading this) was exactly what I have come to expect from him. It was selfless and thoughtful and honest and good. It touched my heart and made me cry.

I don't know exactly what the next few days will bring. I expect I will be having a heart-to-heart with Steven. This while trying to leave the portion of my heart that feels like it's been given the unexpected gift of hope and connection out of the equation.

The prospect of losing the other half of my heart doesn't appeal to me and I am rather reluctant to let go of someone who has become so important to me, first of all as a friend. Do you know how darn hard it is to find good friends? I really don't want to let go that easily. Did I mention my tendency to be selfish? Please tell Duane if you see him that I don't want to hurt him and that I need my friend. Besides, we were going to help each other through this whole singles thing. Well, I'm totally going to hold him to it.

Selena

From: Duane
To: Selena
Subject: Re: This is not a message
Date: Thursday, December 14, 2000, 9:43 a.m.
My dearest Selena,

I do not have the self-control that I pretend to have. I've read your message and now I'm responding like the fool that I am. I'm glad that you are having a good time with Paige. Knowing that you went up on that stage and danced after that "wonderful movie" only solidifies the profile of you I have in my head. I really don't need to know that you are *more* like the girl of my dreams—if you guys rob a liquor store or something, tell me that instead.

I was up most of last night thinking and I'm of the conclusion that my first instincts on this are right. We cannot be talking to each other if there's even a miniscule portion of a fraction of a chance that you and your husband will reconcile. I don't trust me; how can you? I'm not going anywhere any time soon and will be here for you when you know for certain what it is that you want. Plus, this way I can use this time to think.

I started on LDSSO last night for about ten minutes and realized that my heart isn't in it and that maybe I should be concentrating my efforts somewhere else. I didn't think that I was susceptible to this sort of thing and was doing quite well keeping my wits about me before. I need to figure out how I let my heart get so far out there. Anyway, I'm here for you if you decide that you want to give it a go.

I'm going to offer you some free counsel that I'm sure won't be misconstrued as an attempt to sway you my way. Whenever you have made up your mind what it is that you want out of life, if it includes a man, particularly if it includes your husband, you need to give up close male friendships (even those on the Internet). Women and men are totally different creatures (which is usually a good thing). If you were to poll all the women and all the men in the world and ask them about platonic relationships, you would get polar results. Women would respond 95 percent that they are fun and healthy; men on the other hand would respond, again, 95 percent, "What's a platonic relationship?" We don't believe in them. Most men believe *platonic* is Greek for "woman you haven't been intimately involved with."

You'll just have to trust me on this one. As much as I know you might not like the way this sounds, I have to say it, your husband (as with most men) knows this. It's not as much a statement of the foolishness of women as it is the sleaziness of men. Some men are predators, in that they mask their intentions (even from themselves sometimes) and then declare their love at the most vulnerable of moments. It is the oldest ploy in the book for the passive in search of love—some women do it, but *all* men who masquerade as "friends" are to be considered highly suspicious. You should be willing to be wholly devoted to your husband—no matter who he might be—make him your friend and confidante, and never look outside of the marriage for what should be *in* the marriage.

I can't continue with you if you and Steven get back together—it wouldn't be fair to him, and you certainly wouldn't want to hear me constantly lament that you aren't mine (which I'll do, I promise). Enjoy your time with Paige and as you drive home, think about what you want out of life. If you are sincere about reconciliation with Steven, don't do it halfway. Give him everything that you have. Be his wife and don't expect him to be somebody that you already know he isn't. It would be a horrible waste of time to do it any other way.

And I will say it again, I have already received far more from this relationship than I ever could have hoped. I love you and I want the absolute best for you—keep your head level and do what your heart tells you to do.

Your friend forever,
Duane

♥

From: Selena
To: Duane
Subject: The plot thickens
Date: Thursday, December 14, 2000, 11:46 a.m.
Dear Duane,

I appreciated your response to my letter. As always, your reply was thoughtful and absolutely correct. Your counsel was wise and true.

The last years and months of my life have seen me go through many changes. I continue to evolve, but I believe I'm much closer now to becoming a beautiful butterfly (as opposed to a common caterpillar with fuzzy legs). I'd already concluded that true love would fill me and leave me complete without the benefit of any other male friends. This is quite something, because there was a point in time when I actually believed that no one person would ever be able to fulfill another, and therefore I would need a handyman, a mechanic, a poet, and so on.

But as I said before, your counsel to me confirms what I've actually been thinking in my private moments. All I really want is someONE to love and cherish and serve, and I think that my time with you has shown me just how important it is to have this spiritual element in my life.

You are right. If I contemplate a reconciliation, I must do it with my whole heart, never looking backward, forsaking all others (including you . . . ouch), and being prepared to accept him as he is—not looking to change or shape him into who I'd like.

He shouldn't have to change for me. And therein lies the moment of ultimate truth. Are we suited for each other enough to be content and happy "as is" for the rest of our days here on earth? Let me assure you, this conversation will be happening at the earliest possible moment because there is too much at stake.

I'd be untruthful if I said this moment in "our" time is not causing me a certain degree of anxiety. The more I know about you, the more I can't imagine my future without you.

At the very least, if you need a glowing letter of recommendation to the future Mrs. Pannell, I believe I'm in a position to write one in all sincerity and honesty.

Duane, I'm not going to say the words here, but I believe you are in tune enough with me to know how I feel about you through every molecule of my being. I am truly changed because of you. I am better because of you. I want to be even better than that—and all because of you.

Now just try concentrating at work. ☺ (Did I mention my mean streak?)

Selena

From: Selena
To: Duane
Subject: Just thinking . . .
Date: Thursday, December 14, 2000, 2:10 p.m.

I'm only thinking, so this can't count as being a message, letter, note, or any other thing closely related to correspondence.

Last night as I settled down to sleep on the living room couch, I heard Paige and Mike go into their room. I listened to their voices as they talked and went to sleep.

I envied that closeness. There's so much I've never experienced that I look forward to.

I realize that you will likely maintain some distance for now, and I understand that. But if you think I'm not thinking of you, you're sadly mistaken. Maybe that's why I send this "thought" out into space and hope it finds a comfortable place to settle.

Selena, queen of an empty theatre

From: Duane
To: Selena
Subject: Re: Just thinking . . .
Date: Thursday, December 14, 2000, 4:57 p.m.
Dearest Selena,

For someone I'm not speaking to, I sure am spending a lot of time writing. I'm happy for you. I think this visit was just what the doctor ordered. I've been (sort of) a jerk and I want to clarify something. As long as you're feeling good, like the way you sound right now, I'm not concerned, but (there's always a big, huge, giant one and sometimes it's me) I'm totally available to you if something happens and you need someone to talk to. At least now in the interim until you know what Steven has to say. I really care—I do. I probably always will, no matter what happens.

I am thinking of you. As much as it pains me, I know that you're doing the right thing. It's just hard to be here and not with you—which is probably the right thing too. When you said you listened to Paige and Mike talking last night, it reminded me of all the time I spend looking at the happy couples at church and the mall and EVERY STINKIN' WHERE I TURN—sorry, I got carried away. It is not beyond my reach, I'm sure of it, but I don't want your letter of reference until you are darn sure that you don't want me!

Be safe. Remember the things that we've talked about concerning life and love. I've given you some of my best stuff at the risk that it won't be used on me. So use it with me in mind.

Bear hug,
Duane—fresh, never frozen

From: Duane
To: Selena
Subject: Re: Just thinking . . .
Date: Thursday, December 14, 2000, 6:06 p.m.
Dear Mean Streak or Dancin' Queen of the Empty Theatre,

You have no mean streak. Not like yours truly. I've been giving it some thought and I have decided to take you up on an offer that you recently made—an unsolicited offer, I might add. I don't know what the future holds for me, but I do know that uppermost on my mind is securing matrimony before I'm too old to have the fun of growing old together. You know how important it is to me to find that one woman whom I'll cherish and hold dear for eternity; we've talked about it at least once or twice.

I like the way you write and I think that having a letter of reference from you would be an invaluable asset. It would help me to remember what it is that I can offer the girl of my dreams and highlight some of my finer qualities. Maybe writing down what you think might trick some chick into giving me a closer look and I could see my way clear to let you off the hook for ditchin' me. How's that sound? Though you weren't just sayin' that, were you? You really meant that you would help me, right?

Anxiously awaiting your reply with soft lips and minty fresh breath a wastin'—I am truly yours,

Duane, practically sells itself

♥

From: Selena
To: Duane
Subject: Just got your request
Date: Thursday, December 14, 2000, 9:01 p.m.
Dear Duane,

Wake up, Sleepyhead! Yes, writing a letter of reference will not only be easy to do, but it'll be enjoyable as well.

However, you will have to wait a bit for it because Paige is taking me downstairs so we can watch Shakespeare's *Much Ado About Nothing*. Apparently, it's a great spoof on marriage.

She's also praying for stormy weather so I will be stranded here and be able to continue the saga of "us." I do mean this in a good way. She has been fully apprised of our entire situation and has come to think of you as someone really good and worthwhile and is keenly interested in how "we" turn out.

In fact, the poor girl just told me to go and check "our" email. Can't tell she's a mother with small children, right? By her own admission, she doesn't get out much, and this whole thing here is a real "edge of the seat-er."

I will be thinking all night of what might be helpful to the potential Mrs. Pannell's and promise a reply tomorrow. If I'm forced to stay here (which would not be a sacrifice—I'm having a ball), I will write in the morning. Otherwise, you can look for something from me tomorrow afternoon. Sleep well, my friend . . .

Selena

PS My soft lips and minty fresh breath are also going to waste.

From: Duane
To: Selena
Subject: Re: Just got your request
Date: Friday, December 15, 2000, 7:48 a.m.

Selena, girl of my dreams (oops, let that one get away from me),

Just so you know, it doesn't take me all night to write a smart-aleck letter. I was reading our chat from Monday night and playing *The Way We Were* on CD. That was a great conversation. Those were the days—we were so sweet together back then.

I went in to wake up Emily a little bit ago and gave her some of my rapid-fire kisses. She was laughing and told me to stop (which is baby girl talk for "please don't ever stop"). I told her she'd better enjoy it while she could because my New Year's resolution was to get her a wicked step-mother. She said to me, "No, you're not. You're going to get me Selena! And she's nice."

"A lot you know," I said.

"Oh, I know," she said with a big, beautiful grin.

See what I'm dealing with here? (Speaking strictly as a single father with only his children's best interest in mind.)

I hope you can sleep at night.

Duane, the down-trodden

From: Selena
To: Duane
Subject: I've changed my mind
Date: Friday, December 15, 2000, 10:36 a.m.

I don't think I need a man after all. I just had a couple of Paige's ginger cookies—now I'm complete. Apparently, this makes me a simple woman with simple needs.

Signed,

My mean streak is bigger than your mean streak ☺

PS I'm composing your letter of recommendation as we speak (I'm stranded at Paige's and will be here for another night at least), so you can look forward to it (if you dare) a little later.

From: Duane
To: Selena
Subject: No, you have a cruel streak . . .
Date: Friday, December 15 2000, 12:11 p.m.

Dear Mean Streak,

I'm beginning to think that you're a bit competitive. Do you really think that I'm going to fall for the old "Paige's gingerbread cookies" trick? You're hardly a simple woman, and I plan to complicate your perception of needs to the best of my ability. My letter better net me a woman way better than me or I'll be sending it back for corrections. I can't seem to stop writing you and I'm not even going to pretend that I'm not talking to you, so keep 'em coming.

Signed,

Mine's *just* a mean streak

PS By the way, if you are sitting there with minty fresh breath and soft lips for no good reason, it's your own fault. By my calculation, you should've been here about six days ago.

From: Selena
To: Duane
Subject: **Formal Letter of Recommendation**
Date: Friday, December 15, 2000, 5:42 p.m.
Preface: If another uterus-toting, estrogen-loaded being is reading this, Duane R. Pannell is still free and single. What follows are a few impartial observations regarding his qualities, talents, and abilities, as noted by myself in our brief acquaintance.

It's important to note at the start of this that while most people tend to be somewhat out of balance in the four main areas that encompass personality, Duane seems to be the exception to this rule. These four areas are physical, mental, emotional, and spiritual, and when they are combined, they make up a complete and whole individual suitable for pairing with the right companion.

Physical: The subject in question is quite pleasing to the eye and is the perfect height for petite flowers (Amazons need not apply). Duane prefers to play sports rather than watch them on TV, which immediately sets him apart from the couch-potato variety of the male species. He enjoys dancing (this does leave some doubt as to whether or not he really is part of the He-Man Woman-Haters Club) and has expressed a great interest in learning ballroom and Latin dancing. Duane wants to learn to ride horses, which will be a blessing to his children and future wife, who will enjoy his company during one of their favorite activities. The jury is still out regarding his swimming prowess, though he mentioned something about "being in the deep end of the pool" once. He does not indulge in coarse male activities directly related to bodily functions and maintains a clean body and minty fresh breath. These are examples of a man who likes to move and to take care of his mortal temple, which makes him a good partner for numerous couple activities.

Mental: Duane is clearly open to learning new things and is interested in a wide range of topics. He's literate, articulate, knowledgeable, and interesting. He's also an incredibly good speller. He has the ability to think clearly under stressful, adverse, or tempting situations. He's an excellent listener and displays wisdom borne of experience, education, and common sense. He has used his abilities to work hard and provide a good and happy home for his children.

Emotional: Here's a gray area where Duane's level of testosterone comes into question. Duane is sensitive, thoughtful, and can be trusted with one's deepest thoughts, feelings, and fears. He takes seriously any question or topic and is honest and forthcoming with wise counsel regarding the same. He also has the gift of humor and uses it to add spice and life to deep and complex subjects. It's apparent he has a big and generous heart, as shown by his love of family and the children who bring such immense joy to his life. Because his capacity for love and joy is great, so also may be his hurt. It is a risk for him to trust someone with his heart, and if he gives it freely, it must be considered a great and precious gift to be treated with utmost care and kindness. Doing so will only enhance the relationship because his deepest desire is to cherish and honor the lady of his choice. From all indications, he is stable and steady and not at all prone to such negative emotions as jealousy and anger.

Spiritual: Duane is a walking example of how a man can change with the influence of the gospel in his life. His faith is beautiful and honest. He's humble and has righteous desires. He's can think beyond the moment and wants to be married in the temple to a sweet woman for time and eternity. He wants to provide a warm, loving, and spiritual home for children to return to with their families and is determined not to settle for anything less than that. His intentions are pure and honest. His weaknesses have become his strengths and he will be the kind of man a woman can count on as the righteous priesthood leader in the home.

Conclusion: Duane R. Pannell is a prince of a man (in fact, he is the King of Christiansburg) and may be considered the most excellent candidate for a potential husband.

Caution: These conclusions have been drawn through correspondence, two chats, and one telephone conversation (and this in less than a two-month period of time). The advertisements warn if it sounds too good to be true, it probably is. This may be the case "in real life," but it is highly unlikely a sociopathic jerk would be able to maintain such a steady, continuous flow of humor, gentility, and intelligence and seems to pose little risk for anything other than causing a woman to become irreversibly smitten with him. Love at your own risk.

The end (or the beginning?)

♥

From: Duane
To: Selena
Subject: I hope you're satisfied
Date: Saturday, December 16, 2000, 7:22 a.m.
Dear Selena,

I'm becoming so use to the great conversations that we have, and addicted to the feelings that are brought to the surface, that I'll have to be weaned off a little at a time, in the event it becomes necessary to abandon ship. I hope you're happy with yourself.

I couldn't just get up and go take a shower this morning without jotting you a couple lines. I had such a nice weekend with you—you're real special. Thank you for your sweet comments last night. It means more to me coming from you than anyone else. My letter of recommendation is filled with proof of your caring and detailed understanding of my heart and my motives. I grow closer to you with each passing day, and boy am I mushy this time of the morning!

I hope you have a wonderful day. Pray some, okay? Pray for what you want without thinking about "destiny" or complicating Heavenly Father's will. Pray for the tools to effectively do what you need to do, and don't forget to express gratitude for all that you have and all that you have accomplished. I'll pray for you this morning also. That'll get us both off to a great week.

Hugs and kisses,
Duane

From: Duane
To: Selena
Subject: What to do, what to do, what to do . . .
Date: Sunday, December 17, 2000, 6:01 a.m.
My dear Selena,

I hate to be such a disappointment to Paige. I had every intention of staying away but I simply couldn't do it. Last night's phone call was great, and I don't see me leaving you alone until you just come right out and ask me.

That's the only thing different about what I told you concerning you and Steven though. All the other stuff remains the same, and I'll abide by it and support you as you work through this. I just want to maintain the relationship with you until such a time that it becomes necessary for us to part or go forward, okay?

Note: I think you're covered for life on all your inner beauty. I'm thinking of you and I hope to cross Internet paths with you today.

Your friend and admirer who is not a secret by any stretch of the imagination,

Papabear, hipster doofus / romantic goof

From: Selena
To: Duane
Subject: Re: What to do, what to do, what to do . . .
Date: Sunday, December 17, 2000, 9:32 a.m.
Dear Duane,

I understand the dilemma. It's hard to give up what feels so good and right, and you certainly make me feel all those things. I'm anxious to tie up loose ends and begin with a clean slate. I'm currently in a bit of a conundrum where church is concerned. As I mentioned, it is a drive to a neighboring town to get there, and not only do I work just about every weekend, but the way my shift falls and church meeting times are making attendance difficult.

I hope you don't mind me thinking out loud. I guess I just want you to know that I'm thinking about church and trying to incorporate it back into my life. Don't want you to end up with a dud of a wife (umm, on the off-chance I may be in the running).

Have a wonderful Sunday. I'll look for you tonight. Sorry it makes you be up so late. By the time I get home from work and get the chicks to bed tonight, you're going to be rubbing your eyes and wondering if the sleep deprivation is worth it.

Selena

From: Duane
To: Selena
Subject: Re: What to do, what to do, what to do . . .
Date: Sunday, December 17, 2000, 1:49 p.m.
Selena,

Okay darling, what happened to you between the time I hang up with the best phone call of my life and mid-morning the next day? "On the off-chance I may be in the running"? *You* are the only one being considered and currently have only to say, "Let's go to the next level" and Duane is following you like a puppy—that portion is entirely up to you and your circumstances. Though it may appear on the surface that I have options, it isn't possible for me to do anything but let this play out as far as it will. I am soooooo enamored with you that I will not be able to pursue any options until I'm absolutely positive that this will not work.

Next is the Church thing: As far as I am concerned, I just want to know [as my potential wife], would you be an active member, seeking to be obedient and gain all that the Lord would bless us with, and sustain my priesthood and be an example to *all* of our children through the years? Would you stand with me in trying to be as conforming as two people like you and I can be, accept callings, and share your spiritual thoughts with me forever?

I know you know that these things are important to me. Do you have doubts about where your heart is? I don't think there's a problem here. While I know that you don't want to do these things motivated by me but under the strength of your own desire, you certainly can see how a marriage to me could take on celestial tones in this life, and sooner rather than later, right? We'll talk.

As far as talking to me goes: I'll try to curb any remarks that might suggest that I'm the only viable choice in your future, if you'll agree to talk to me every day until such time that our relationship must be severed because of your reconciliation with Steven. Deal?

Bear hugs,
Duane

PS I see that you had a little chat with my baby boy. He's funny. I see that the conversation was low key and non-threatening and friendly, so no big deal, right? You should have seen the big smile on his face when he told me that he talked to you. You would think that he'd just met the girl of *his* dreams. I think that it's sweet. He would never say it out loud, but he wants me to be happy and knows that you do that for me.

♥

From: Selena
To: Duane
Subject: Re: What to do, what to do, what to do . . .
Date: Sunday, December 17, 2000, 4:40 p.m.
Dear Duane,

What a great surprise to come and find an email here at work! As for the "off-chance" comment, I didn't want to appear presumptuous.

And as far as the Church goes, there was a time when I didn't feel much of anything about it and questioned certain things. Being able to work through these things with someone who has the patience and faith to help me would be a really cool experience, I think. I would never sell myself as an eternal companion and then say "just kidding" after making the commitments. The fact is, I've invested many, many years of faith and service, and that's why I was reluctant to just forget it, given my current situation.

I believe this will be the clincher in the discussion that Steven and I will have, regarding our ideas of the future for ourselves as individuals and as part of a couple. I just don't want to carry the spiritual ball alone—and when the children are gone, I want there to be something of substance that my mate and I have in common to hold us together. People can change, but I'm not sure that activity in the Church will ever be important to Steven.

I spoke to him today and told him that I want to talk. He's curious. Heck, I wouldn't mind even getting this over with tonight, but I really should pace myself and be prepared. I will let you know ASAP what happened when it all goes down. Talk to you soon,
Selena

From: Selena
To: Duane
Subject: Got a minute?
Date: Monday, December 18, 2000, 12:58 p.m.
Dear Duane,

Okay, I'll rally to the challenge. My tough question of the day: Why do men grow facial hair? I'll let you think on that for a while.

Today is a tough day for me (so much for the boost portion of the letter), and I'm trying to get in the Christmas spirit. Went over to the other house to go through some of the Christmas things and I couldn't find any of the stuff that I'd carefully wrapped each year. All the stuff in the Christmas boxes is just a bunch of junk. I was hoping to decorate the place so the little chicks could come home and ooh and ahh, but I think that's out. On the bright side, I did come across the Christmas music, so all is not lost.

I'm still going to have to pick up a few things for Christmas. How many days did you say were left before then?

You should tell me some of your favorite Christmas traditions. I'm thinking of you, as always these days.

Selena

From: Duane
To: Selena
Subject: Re: Got a minute?
Date: Monday, December 18, 2000, 2:23 p.m.
Hi Beautiful!

I hope that you're having a good day. I've been thinking of you and wondering what it might be like to be celebrating on your end.

Now, the tough question. Why do men grow facial hair? You came to the right place, dear lady, for you know that I won't tell you a lie, nor will I seek to sugarcoat my answer. The real reason men grow facial hair is because it gives us magic powers and is good luck during the hunting season. Also, Hollywood chicks dig it. Okay, that's not *exactly* true. I can only speak for myself.

The biggest reason I first grew a mustache is because I could. I was only about thirteen or so when I discovered it there. I shaved once or twice. Next thing I knew, I had a nice dark mustache. It separates the men from the boys (only psychologically, as I grew mine when I was thirteen). It's like belonging to an exclusive club. My father has a full beard and mustache, and I remember when he first grew it thirty years ago. He was so proud that he had my mom take pictures of him with it. He had been out of town and came home with his face all furry. Mom didn't like it at first, but she'd fight you for it today. I would suppose the old adage could be said of us Pannell boys: the more face you can cover with hair, the better off we are. The only thing I can add to this is if it was the only thing standing in the way of eternal happiness in marriage, it wouldn't stand in the way long. I'd shave my head for the right woman, if that's what you—I mean, *she* likes. I have stayed with the long hair and mustache because it seems to look normal on me. Though I do see men who look totally '70s with hair like mine, it doesn't really look like that on me. I hope this satisfies your wonderful curiosity.

Big bear hugs,

Duane

♥

From: Selena

To: Duane

Subject: Re: Got a minute?

Date: Monday, December 18, 2000, 3:39 p.m.

Dear Duane,

Thanks so much for the great messages today. It's been one of those days and you've made it brighter. You're awesome. As for the moustache, I've always preferred clean-shaven, but I'm willing to experience something new. Of course, if I decide it's just not for me, I may do what I did when Steven grew one. I told him I wouldn't be shaving my legs until the moustache was gone. (I do believe we had a mysterious moustache disappearance within the half hour.) How bad am I?! Are you sure you want to get mixed up with me?

Selena

♥

From: Duane
To: Selena
Subject: Ready for mushy?
Date: Monday, December 18, 2000, 7:40 p.m.

My dear Selena,

This morning I prayed so hard, with every ounce of my being, that you and I would be together. I want the greatest of the Lord's blessings to be poured out upon you, but I want for those blessings to include me. You might find a man on this planet that would offer you more than I as far as convenience, wealth, or power, but no man could ever exceed my appreciation of your wonderful personality, wit, beautiful humor, and sincere heart.

I truly want to be part of you, heal with you, love with you, learn with you, and take on the world with you. You fill me up and make me feel like I am serving a greater purpose; it's like I have so much more potential and I feel eager to explore things (especially spiritual things) that take on a much sweeter meaning with a companion, a companion who'd care as deeply as me. The way that you respond to me is addictive, and I could not script our conversations to be more perfect.

The most wonderful thing is it's not temporary. I believe we could talk to one another like this forever because it's real. Sometimes I think that I need to pinch myself, but I know it's real. Pray hard, Selena. Pray like it'll make all the difference. I'm making my appeal to Heavenly Father as we may be at a crossroads and our prayers may be the deciding factor. I don't worry that I might be praying for the "wrong" thing because if He helps us to be together, I believe the righteous desires of our hearts will ensure us His blessings for our lives together from that day forward. Will you join me?

Have a wonderful day. Know that I'm thinking of you every second with a big smile on my face.

Love,
Duane

PS It just started snowing. It's a Festivus Miracle! *Seinfeld* 1998.

From: Selena
To: Duane
Subject: Now I'm hooked . . .
Date: Monday, December 18, 2000, 10:42 p.m.
Dear Duane,

I'm so glad you found me and wrote to me and didn't think I was weird when I said I wasn't looking for a husband. You are everything I've ever wanted in a man and more. I hope and wish and pray you will be mine, with Heavenly Father's blessing.

Love,
Selena

♥

From: Duane
To: Selena
Subject: Are you avoiding me?
Date: Tuesday, December 19, 2000, 4:22 p.m.
Dear Selena,

You owe me. Big. I'll tell your mom stuff if you don't write me back. True stuff. I hope we have an understanding.

I forgot to tell you last night that Jr. insisted I show him the picture of your girls. He said that I had showed it to everyone but him and he wanted to see too. I think he was a little disappointed that Jasmine was not in the picture—though he said that your younger girls are pretty. "They'll be fine when they get older," I believe was the comment. He hinted around that he would be glad to look at any other pictures that I might have of your children, but I assured him that one was all I had. "Oh, I thought you might have some more pictures or something, heh." He's as transparent as I am.

Wanna go for a swim?
Your best bud,
Duane the pool guy

♥

From: Selena
To: Duane
Subject: Re: Are you avoiding me?
Date: Tuesday, December 19, 2000, 5:19 p.m.
Dear Duane,

Avoiding you? No, the truth is I've just had your letter on my screen most of the day and I do believe I was semi-hypnotized by it. Walking around all goofball, like nothing mattered in the outside world because Duane wants me. . . . He wants *me*! And no need to tell my mom stuff; you've already won me over.

Love,
Selena

From: Selena
To: Duane
Subject: Good morning to my most favorite Virginian in the whole wide world
Date: Tuesday, December 19, 2000, 11:19 p.m.
Dear Duane,

Even talking to you for such a short time buoys me up and leaves me feeling filled. You're a blessing in my life, and I'm so glad our stars collided. Coincidence? I think not!

Have a marvelous day!
Selena

From: Duane
To: Selena
Subject: Re: Good morning to my most favorite Virginian in the whole wide world
Date: Wednesday, December 20, 2000, 1:52 a.m.
My dearest Selena,

Your MOST favorite Virginian? C'mon, that is a lot to live up to. Are you positive I'm the *favorite*? You are right—we're no coincidence. In some ways, I can see where I've lived to share these moments with you. I feel my place in your heart and I'm staking a permanent claim there. It's so nice to have a "someone" to trust with my thoughts and feelings that I don't want to go back to the "other way"—you have set free an essence in me that most men have but never discover or admit that they have, and I just don't care to bottle mine back up.

I'm inspired to repent for this past year's behavior; not just because I was being a brat (child of God), but because I have been so obviously blessed by finding you that I know He was watching out for me all along. All the events that led me to you began to occur before I became a resentful little snot with a bad attitude. Does this make sense to you? I've been faithfully loved by Heavenly Father all along, regardless of my perception of the circumstances and at least the end result is the greatest friendship I've ever enjoyed—and the likelihood that it's the pinnacle event of my adult life may in fact be the case. I am humbled to believe this to be true. I have become so aware these past ten years that nothing happens that's convenient by my calendar; it happens too soon or it takes way too long. The good thing is good things do happen to me. I am sure if you examine it closely, you'll find the same holds true for you.

I wish you the best today. I am with you in spirit. Selena, you mean so much to me—this is the part where I *would* say "you'll never know," but actually, in time, you will know exactly how much you mean to me, I promise.

I am all yours. Love,
Duane

From: Selena
To: Duane
Subject: 'Tis the season
Date: Wednesday, December 20, 2000, 10:13 a.m.
Dear Duane,

I'm anxious and uncertain about how this conversation with Steven will go today. My friend told me about an interesting incident that came about last week. As you know, she has decided she doesn't like how her husband treats her when he has a girlfriend, so she's divorcing him. They continue to be amicable about the whole thing, and he will move out the first of January.

So last Friday, he had the day off and she asked him what he was going to do. He sounded all happy and said he was going to do some Christmas shopping. In a nutshell, after he came home that night, he seemed out of sorts. She asked him if he was okay, and he said, "I'm so stupid." It seems he'd taken his young thing shopping with him and they'd gone to a nice restaurant after for a cozy dinner. Except that day was the day members of our ward were in Edmonton at the temple. Guess what restaurant they went to afterward for dinner? Busted! The crummy thing is, I don't believe he'd have given it another thought or told her if he hadn't been caught. Granted, they are separated and only living under the same roof, but part of the ground rules were to behave until a physical separation was possible.

People have this incredible ability to hurt one another, don't they? Unbelievable power to hurt. That frightens me. I was telling her how, for the first time in my separation, I was at a peaceful and open enough place to even consider a reconciliation. Of course, I then added, I doubt that includes the physical closeness that'd be required. She told me then that I wasn't ready if that aspect wasn't going to be okay. She may be right. But I have to have the talk, don't I? I was thinking of running away to a tropical hideaway. Would that be so wrong? I mean, especially since it's so cold. I think I should be someplace warmer. Maybe even buy a swimsuit (surely NASA has come up with a fabric that will lift, enhance, hold, and flatter all at the same time).

Well, my darling Duane (see how brave I'm getting with the terms of endearment as we're getting closer to the dreaded hour of the final reckoning), I hope this makes your lunch hour entertaining at the very least. I am, of course, thinking of you, crossing fingers, toes, legs, arms, and eyes, hoping that Heavenly Father wants us to be an "us." If not, see you around, pal. ☺

Love,
Selena

From: Duane
To: Selena
Subject: The best promise you ever got
Date: Wednesday, December 20, 2000, 8:09 a.m.

My dear Selena,

I am amazed at the way people treat one another too. How people can swear their love to one another one day and forsake it the next is beyond me.

I can't tell you exactly how I felt the moment that I found out that Marie had a boyfriend, but some of the thoughts that crossed my mind were, *This isn't supposed to happen. People aren't disposable. Another person shouldn't be able to penetrate the bonds of a marriage. A family, a history. It's got to be more important than infatuation, right? If this can happen to the most important relationship that I have, are all of my relationships temporary? How much of what I believed to be the truth is actually the truth and how much is me being played for a fool?*

As for my promise to you, I won't commit to you unless I believe that I can fulfill. I want the bond of marriage to mean permanence, to be eternal and reliable for both of us—never a question of loyalty. I want it to mean that when really nothing else can be trusted, even our children, that we'd still have each other to turn to for comfort and guidance. I am afraid, as I have said before, of being abandoned again, but not so afraid that I'm willing to forgo an opportunity of eternal happiness. If you (let's say you) were to make me the same promise, of honesty and communication and loyalty, you need never fear losing my love.

And one more thing, I have noticed a recurring theme (not often, but often enough) over the course of our time together. The younger woman syndrome. As I've stated in the past, you're the younger woman. I'm eight years younger than Marie, but that doesn't even matter. I'm a different kind of man when it comes to this than any man you may have ever known.

I believe that the gospel is true, and therefore the doctrine taught by the Church is also true. These bodies are merely temporary—they are imperfect and they'll die. Not unlike losing weight or outgrowing acne, we are not what we appear to be right now, even at our best. We'll one day be restored to our "perfect frame" and there are many things more important than muscle tone, a flat tummy, and hair with all the same color strands.

There were times that Marie would draw so close to me that I could barely breathe, much of it was because she was afraid that she was losing everything, but it was also the comfort of being cherished. I knew in my heart many, many times that she was coming to me for security and that she was cheating on me. But I sometimes believed that I could love her to health (in spite of everything I know about addiction). I would put all of the problems of the world aside and just think of the fact that she was my wife and the mother of my children.

I was sincere and gentle. I would kiss her not-so-perfect tummy that had carried four children and kiss her face, which had many more wrinkles on it than it did twenty years ago, and enjoy and love the privilege of doing so. I had no desire to replace her, or any regret that she was not the same as she once was. I tried to be the kind of spouse that I wanted—you know, the golden rule.

I did this for a woman who cheated on me. A woman who didn't appreciate me or even like me sometimes. Do you think that I could be a good husband to a woman who was devoted to me, loyal, and loved me and showed it? Do you think that I've had more than enough practice with the highest degree of difficulty?

Don't fret. I think we'll be okay. I'm getting some good vibes and, with any luck, our problems will only be logistical and nothing serious. Keep praying. I'm thinking of you every minute of my day and will be anxiously waiting for the verdict from your talk with Steven.

I'm yours for the asking.

Love,

Duane

From: Duane
To: Selena
Subject: I may already be a loser
Date: Wednesday, December 20, 2000, 1:47 p.m.
Dear Selena,

I'm going to go ahead and write to you like I'm still in the running. I hope that's okay with you. I have to say, I'm feeling a little (and by a little, I mean *a lot*) anxious now, and it's only getting worse as the day goes forward.

I'm still on the edge of my seat. Don't leave me hangin'.

Love and kisses and hugs,

Duane

From: Duane
To: Selena
Subject: I hope today looks brighter
Date: Thursday, December 21, 2000, 7:19 a.m.
My darling Selena,

I hope you are feeling positive this morning and inspired. I really enjoyed our talk last night. I know having "the talk" with Steven was hard on you. I had a real strong feeling of the presence of the Holy Spirit during our conversation and one of the best experiences with prayer that I can remember having recently.

I can't seem to get it out of my mind that your oven isn't working, and that's just not right. During the night—I don't know—I must've been sleepwalking or something, or maybe it was gnomes; but my toolbox and a pizza coupon are sitting by the back door with my car keys. Be happy. It's Christmas!

Love and hugs and some other good stuff,

Duane

From: Selena
To: Duane
Subject: A little clearer in the light of day . . .
Date: Thursday, December 21, 2000, 10:05 a.m.
Dear Duane,

I have thought of nothing else since my conversation with Steven last night. I believed the pivotal moments would be based on things I said or questions I asked. In truth, Steven asked me the questions I felt deep down would decide the fate of our marriage, only I expected I would be the one to bring them up.

We were sitting in his truck, driving around when he asked me first how I was feeling about our attempt at reconciliation. I told him I should be feeling better than I do about "us" if it was the right thing to do. He then asked me if I believed in following my gut feelings. I told him I did and that I had done so when I moved out in the first place, and that it had been the right decision. He asked me what my gut feeling was about the reconciliation. I told him it felt bad. He then asked me if I had a spark of love for him and I had to shake my head in the negative. That's when he said, "Then I guess there's nothing more to say."

I believe Heavenly Father allowed the crucial points to come out and that there's no doubt now as to the status of our relationship. I'm deeply saddened by this, but I'm grateful for the knowledge. I'll move forward. I hope and pray Steven can do the same and live a good life. He deserves happiness.

As for you, mister, I guess I'm going to have to content myself with daily correspondence and the occasional sound of your voice. You have a soothing voice, did you know that? Meanwhile, I'll continue to strive to improve of myself and work on my relationship with my Father in Heaven. No matter what the future holds, I will still be stuck in this skin with this heart and mind, so I may as well make them as pleasant as possible (no point being trapped in a bitter body).

I just wanted to let you know that I am feeling a bit better about everything that's gone down. I'm still sad, but not devastated, if that makes any sense.

Love,
Selena

From: Duane
To: Selena
Subject: Re: A little clearer in the light of day . . .
Date: Thursday, December 21, 2000, 10:26 p.m.
Dear Selena,

I get a good feeling from that message. I've been concerned about you—not the events as you tell me that they took place, only how you

227

are reacting to them. I believe you're on the right track and you wouldn't be without having done the deed.

I can't really say that I know exactly how you're feeling right now, but I can empathize. When Marie and I finally separated, it was truly devastating to me. I wanted it done, and I knew that there would be no reconciliation, but it still hurt. I remember crying out to her, "How could you do this to us, to our family. To me?" It was a life-changing moment.

Then things seemed to make sense. I had been an eighteen-year-old boy rebelling against his parents. I got involved with a twenty-six-year-old woman who had a four-year-old child. We were both addicts. That it even lasted as long as it did is really quite amazing. I was facing the consequences of my choices, and I hated it.

I've reviewed my life with her for what was good, what was wrong, and what I have learned from it. I reflected fondly over what was good and I cried like a little girl over what hurt. I have learned a better way through the teachings of the Church, but that knowledge wasn't going to save me from the consequences of my poor choices. I have endured it, and I intend to make it all count for something in my life.

Now, when are you going to come and see me? Let's plan, okay? Tell me any and all of your roadblocks and I'll shoot 'em all down one at a time.

Love and sugar cookies,

Duane

♥

From: Selena
To: Duane
Subject: Still pondering
Date: Thursday, December 21, 2000, 10:47 a.m.
Dear Duane,

Hearing your voice was such a great comfort and talking of spiritual things was such an amazing blessing. All of this still hits me pretty hard because of everything at stake and the years already invested.

I didn't know how much I was hoping that I'd feel like something significant had changed with us till it was apparent that only the words were being spoken and that nothing had really changed. I even felt a bit like a fraud, knowing that I've got you. Granted, a zillion miles away, but still out there, writing to me, caring about me, and lifting me when I feel faint.

I imagine the next couple of days will be strange, simply because I know I hurt Steven with my honesty when answering his questions and I don't take any pleasure in knowing that I caused him this pain. Please bear with me in my out-of-sorts state, as I am sure to find my happy balance again. Thank you again for talking to me when I really needed someone. You're wonderful, you are.

Love,
Selena

From: Duane
To: Selena
Subject: re: Still pondering
Date: Thursday, December 21, 2000, 12:03 p.m.
Dear Selena,

I think that you're being way too hard on yourself. I know you've already had "the conversation," but maybe you should sit down and write out the pros and cons of reconciliation—this will help you to sort out what your motives are. You might also write down a list of what you could expect your life going forward to be like with Steven vs. not with Steven.

I'm *not* recommending that you use this to approach Steven again unless you discover that you didn't press him hard enough or that you were downright dishonest with him. The reason I suggest this is, like I said, to help you sort out your motives. It'll also help relieve some of your guilt (someone once told me guilt is an unproductive emotion).

You need to get that "time invested" phrase into perspective as well. I too have beat myself up over what seemed like wasted time, and it's really silly when you look at it in the grand scheme of things. Twenty years seems like forever to a thirty-nine-year-old; it's half my life. By the time I kick the bucket, it'll have diminished to a third, a quarter, and—if I'm to be a real burden to my family—only a fifth of my entire life on this earth. Then add the fact that Spirit Duane has been around at least as long as when the earth was created and will be around forever after that; well, it's an insignificant amount of time. Notice that I said *time* and not *an insignificant event*. You gained children that you love from your marriage, happy times with Steven, and most of all wisdom that will carry you through the eternities. Time invested is not wasted time and should not be construed as "loss."

I will provide whatever support you feel you need. If you don't feel like writing to me for a bit, or if you want to quiz me, or if you would like for me to phone you more or not phone you for a while, or if you would like me to write you more or status quo you (that sounded a little odd), or whatever you feel would lift you up, I'm here for you. Don't suffer alone, even if you're not talking to me. Call your mom or Paige or someone you can lean on. It's not good to get too far inside yourself; you'll develop tunnel vision and the distorted view from there will not produce desirable results.

Write to me and unburden your mind.

Yours truly (I've always wanted to write that and mean it!),

Duane

PS I know we talked about meeting after the divorce, but what if you happened to be in Virginia when I take my holiday in February? I am just throwing it out there. No pressure.

From: Selena
To: Duane
Subject: Supper break
Date: Thursday, December 21, 2000, 5:40 p.m.
Dear Duane,

I zipped home for my break so that I could read your message and send you another.

I've tried to figure out how I could meet you, but I can see no way that doesn't include deception, and that is something I don't want to have cast a shadow on what is beginning to be such a bright light in my life. I'd love to come for a visit, but not if it means having my kids find out their mom is dishonest.

Would you be willing to wait until the divorce is final? It sounds like things could be wrapped up as early as March. I'm not holding my breath, though, because I was originally told that the divorce could take anywhere from four to six months, but hey, you can always hope, right?

It's important to know how we proceed from here. We've got eight pairs of eyes watching to see how we make decisions. What do you think? Can you see another way? Believe me, all I want is to meet you NOW. Tell me your thoughts.

Love,
Selena

♥

From: Duane
To: Selena
Subject: Re: Supper break
Date: Friday, December 22, 2000, 4:00 a.m.
Hey Beautiful,

I've been thinking about this very thing all day today. You're right. I do not want to do it if it involves having to lie. My children don't know your circumstances and wouldn't ask, but your children would have to be told. Also, are you absolutely sure that it's going to take that long to finalize?

Anyway, let me know what you think. Of course, if there's any way to get together before then, I'd want to take advantage of it, but if not, I'd wait indefinitely for you. You *do* understand that, don't you? I'm quite sure of myself and my feelings for you.

And as for addressing you as "beautiful" at the start of this email, you're right. I don't really know what you look like. It was a reference to your inner beauty, the part of you that I'm the most familiar with at this point. Believe me, if you're as pretty on the outside as you are on the inside, you are *way* too good for me!

Can't wait to talk, but waiting is what this relationship does best.
Love,
Duane, not just another pretty face

♥

From: Selena
To: Duane
Subject: Four a.m.?
Date: Friday, December 22, 2000, 11:06 p.m.
Dear Duane,

Are you sure you're not a masochist? I mean, staying up so late to talk to me and getting up after only four hours of sleep?! I honestly don't know how you're surviving. But I'm glad I was able to talk to you tonight. I hope you feel better about "us." We've found each other; a few more days or even months is going to fly by and soon everything will fall into place.

Obviously Heavenly Father has His omnipotent hand in this, and if He's orchestrating it, who the heck are we to question how it's done? Just relax and enjoy the journey. I know I am.

Love,
Selena

♥

From: Duane
To: Selena
Subject: Re: Four a.m.?
Date: Friday, December 22, 2000, 11:43 p.m.
Dear Selena,

You're right. I needed to hear that. I know that I come off like a real know-it-all sometimes (I apparently have an opinion about everything), but I guess I'm no different than anyone else when it comes to needing a lift now and then.

I hope you didn't think that I was questioning our compatibility or our destiny; I just got down this afternoon, thinking about the circumstances. I guess I let the blessings get by me and forgot who is ultimately in charge of this merger of hearts. So have a great day, Moongoddess. We're one more day closer to being together!

I love you,
Duane

{ Part 3 }

♥

Selena's Journal
December 22, 2000

So much has happened in these past couple of months, my head is spinning. And now, as I ponder my future and the possibility that I won't be spending it alone as previously planned, I'm filled with more questions than answers. I'm so grateful to have the spiritual part of me awakening, but this only makes things more complicated because I'm not divorced. Plain and simple. And now there's a man in my life, one whom I did not go looking for, I might add. And in the Church, those two things do not go together.

I want to do what Heavenly Father wants. But this time, I want His input because clearly my own ideas are flawed, to say the least. As I've been reading the scriptures, I keep coming back to this,

> Wherefore, all things which are good cometh of God; and that which is evil cometh of the devil; for the devil is an enemy unto God, and fighteth against him continually, and inviteth and enticeth to sin, and to do that which is evil continually.
>
> But behold, that which is of God inviteth and enticeth to do good continually; wherefore, every thing which inviteth and enticeth to do good, and to love God, and to serve him, is inspired of God. (Moroni 7:12–13)

This particularly catches my attention: "*Every thing* which inviteth and enticeth to do good, to love God, and to serve him, is inspired of God." I don't understand how or why Father in Heaven would bring a man—of all things I'm pretty sure I didn't need—into my life *before* my divorce is final, but when I look at all the changes happening in my life and how they are all turning my heart to Him (not Duane him, Heavenly Father Him), I have to trust what He (Heavenly Father) says.

And finally: "For behold, the Spirit of Christ is given to every man, that he may know good from evil; wherefore, I show unto you the way to judge; for every thing which inviteth to do good, and to persuade to believe in Christ, is sent forth by the power and gift of Christ; wherefore ye may know with a perfect knowledge it is of God" (Moroni 7:16)

I know that this won't look good to other people and I get that. But I'm supposing that Nephi killing Laban wasn't man's solution to that problem either (not that I'm comparing myself to a prophet of God; far from it and more than aware of it). But I think if I cling to the word of God and keep my focus and my actions on my Savior and Heavenly Father's will, then I can't go wrong, no matter what the future holds in store for me and my family.

Duane's Journal
December 23, 2000

The first thought of the day? As my eyes opened, and even before my head raised off my pillow, my brain asked an important question: *You found the perfect girl. Now what are you going to do?*

A sense of panic has set in. As it stands now, I wouldn't have time to date a girl if she lived in our neighborhood. Selena is almost 3,000 miles away. We have kids and jobs and lives that are so far apart.

I don't understand my thinking sometimes. I recently challenged Selena to consider resurrecting the marriage that she put behind her two years ago; to go and talk to her soon-to-be ex-husband and see if there's any way to put it all back together again.

The apprehension that she'd reconcile with him was at least equal to the anxiety that I now feel. I've gone days hoping and praying that we are meant to be and that she would want to be with me. Now that she has determined that her decision to dissolve her old life was the correct choice and that exploring the possibility of a new life with me is truly what she wants, I'm discovering that I have cold feet.

I'm not going to give in to my fears. The next logical step is to meet in person, and I intend to make that happen. I don't know how these details will work, but I'm sure, if it is meant to be, that these worries will be overcome.

Will all of the many pieces fit together to make something whole? Are we more than just love notes in cyberspace? I have to go back to the night that I first became aware of Selena. It could have gone either way that night, but I made a decision to contact her. A little decision resulted in a wonderful friendship. If I let some anxiety about logistics dissuade me from the next step, it could mean forfeiting an even more wonderful experience. So do I ignore the temperature of my feet and push forward? I certainly will. My declaration today is that the remaining chapters of my life will be written with Selena as my companion, and together we will prepare for eternity.

Selena's Journal
December 27, 2000

Well, I have to give Duane credit for coming up with an ingenious solution. We talked about meeting but kept coming back to avoiding the appearance of evil. The fact that I am still not legally divorced is a huge deal, especially as we're both recommitting ourselves to our faith. Equally important to me is that I want to make sure my kids don't see hypocrisy in my actions.

And so with Steven saying our divorce should be final sometime in March, Duane and I have talked about the possibility of meeting when he can take a holiday in February. But we still couldn't figure out how to do this without it just looking bad.

Then Duane offered to buy another ticket for Mom to come with me to meet him in Virginia. He's even willing to pay for the days she would have to take off from driving the school bus. Hmmm, that's so crazy it just might work. I would have a chaperone, if you will, and an extra set of eyes to watch for red flags. This idea almost entirely takes the possibility of him being an axe murderer off the table. I mean, what axe murderer would want to deal with the mother as well? Especially if he knew mine.

This might really work. We might actually be able to meet in a few weeks, if Mom is up for the adventure. Wow. This is happening so fast! I wonder if real life could possibly live up to the wonderful images of him that I've conjured up in my mind?

Gotta run. I have to call Mom.

Duane's Journal
February 9, 2001

My phone rang a few minutes ago. Selena called. This is the gist of our conversation.

Me: "Hello!"

Selena: "We have a problem."

Me: "A problem? You're still going to be here, right?"

Selena: "I don't know. Ron's all in a flap about you being some guy on the Internet who may well be an axe murderer." (She also noted this seems to be a recurring theme.)

Me: "Who's Ron?"

Selena: "He's Mom's husband. I told you . . ."

Me: "Ah, yes! I believe I have a stick figure for him in the peripheral character pile."

Selena: "Peripheral or not, we need to figure this out. I can't come without Mom."

Me: (I thought I'd lighten the mood.) "Well, hon, it is the Internet. One of us is bound to be the axe murderer. I just always assumed it was you."

Selena: "Are you finished?" (She evidently did not appreciate my efforts to lighten the mood.)

Me: "Yes, Ma'am."

Selena: "Don't suppose you have any bright ideas handy?"

Me: "Well, I could give you some character references so you could call them to ask about me, but if they're friends with an axe murderer, I'm sure they wouldn't have any problem lying for me."

Selena: "You're not helping." (Again, showing no appreciation for my attempt at humor.)

{ Duane and Selena Pannell }

Me: "Okay, okay. . . . So how about this? We have a local Church website where Ron can contact anyone in our ward. I'm sure—well, pretty sure—they'd all be willing to vouch for me. [That should satisfy him.] Good-bye. Good-bye."

Our first in-person hello will be in three days!

Selena's Journal
February 10, 2001

Last minute crisis averted after an arduous phone call with Duane. I don't think he understood just how close our plans came to falling apart. Thank heaven Ron checked out the ward website (once again, Duane pulls a brilliant solution out of the hat . . . impressive) and he is satisfied that Duane is "probably on the up and up" without having to call anyone. I'm going to Virginia! Guess I'd better hurry up and start packing.

Selena's Journal
February 12, 2001

"Holy Attack of the Butterflies, Batman!" Only a few minutes until the plane lands and I meet the man I know so well who is, in essence, a complete stranger.

Mom is almost giddy because she is sure Duane is "the one," and that is not helping my anxiety level. She's supposed to be here for my support but he won her over with their first conversation, so I'm pretty much on my own. If he really is different, he'll appreciate my carefully chosen outfit. I suppose I have a twisted sense of humor, or maybe just an obvious mental block when it comes to being a man-pleaser. He's going to get the farm girl he signed up for. Ready or not, Duane, here I come.

Duane's Journal
February 12, 2001

I don't think I realized that I was pacing until Emily said, "What's the matter, Daddy?"

239

Now, in addition to pacing, I began talking fast. I said, "Nothing. Nothing's the matter. Why would something be the matter? She's just a girl. I'm just here to meet a girl. And her mother. I'm here to meet a girl and her mother. That's all. Maybe I'm a little nervous."

I forgot about my daughter for a moment and began to think, *I don't believe I've ever been nervous over a woman before in my whole life.*

"Aww, Daddy, it's gonna be okay," Emily said with all the wisdom of a thirteen-year-old girl.

I was only inches from her cute little face, and my eyes must've been quite wide when I said, "Emily, I really have no idea what this woman looks like. She could have a receding hairline, some missing teeth, a peg leg. . . . Oh crap, the hump! That thing could be the real deal!"

Emily never stopped smiling sweetly. "You have a couple pictures of her. Besides, she's beautiful. I can tell by her voice."

"Don't you know that some of the scariest looking folks in the world have the best telephone voices? Em, you have to promise me that no matter what, you won't laugh or make any embarrassing comments. No matter what she looks like—I'm in love with this woman and I'm going to marry her."

I looked back anxiously toward the runway as Emily said, "Daddy, she's beautiful. You'll see."

When the plane finally arrived and people began making their way toward us, I surveyed the crowd. I was looking, searching, scanning, trying to find . . . who . . . which one was she? I did make eye contact with a woman. She was a little older than I'd imagined and suddenly quite animated. A broad smile came across her face and she zeroed in and began running toward me. I think a little air escaped my lungs on impact, but my main concern was that my feet had left the ground. I was in an impressive bear hug, being swung back and forth as I heard her say, "I love this boy! This is my boy!"

So I met Margaret. As my little feet dangled and I gasped for air, I scanned again. I knew she had to be near. As her mother released her grip and I felt my feet return to earth, I saw Selena for the first time.

She peeked out from behind her mother, with a shy smile—the sweetest I'd ever seen. She was wearing overalls, just like in the picture where she was sitting on a rock in the middle of a stream. And she had her hair in pigtails.

I would've married Selena right there in Roanoke Regional Airport, but I was content to be near her as we made our way to the car to begin our ten-day adventure together.

Selena's Journal
February 13, 2001

So I don't know about Duane yet, but I could definitely get used to Virginia. It's a lot warmer here, that's for sure. I think we were both nervous and maybe a little on-guard last night when we met. Got to love Mom. She intercepted him like a pro football player and gave him one of her famous hugs. That broke the ice . . . and maybe his back. It also gave me the chance to just watch for a few minutes. He seems nice and so does his thirteen-year-old daughter, Emily, who is a bright and talkative young lady. It was late, so we only talked a bit (surface stuff) and went to bed.

His friends had a family emergency, so Mom and I ended up having to stay here. I hope I don't end up feeling like a trapped animal. As awkward as this is, I can tell he pulled out the stops to make us more comfortable. When he showed us to his room (he's giving up his room—score one point for gallantry), we were met with the subtle wafting of scented candles burning, bouquets of fresh flowers, and dishes filled with assorted hard candies. All the while, classical music was playing softly in the background. What manner of man is this?!

These thoughtful touches were balanced out by two large, framed posters occupying prominent places on the walls that clearly have been here for a while. A single man and his idea of art! I'd forgotten him mentioning John Wayne and Clint Eastwood, but there they were in all their rugged cowboy glory. I think it's safe to say Duane's machismo remains intact. As does my opinion of him (so far).

Duane's Journal
February 15, 2001

I don't know what I expected. I supposed that we'd meet, our eyes would glaze over in unison, and we'd skip off to rainbow land together. So far, that has not happened.

On Selena's second night here, when everyone had gone to bed, we sat alone together on the couch in silence. After a whole day together, she wasn't giving any signal that she was as enamored with me as she had been when there was lots of real estate between us. It appeared to me that she may be regretting having come here. So, in the most generous way I could, I gave her an out. I told her that it was okay if she had a change of heart and we could endure this visit and part ways as friends. It was so quiet and I kept looking into her eyes for clues. I was a little worried about how I would respond to being rejected, thinking, *What if I cry? Oh my gosh! What if I cry?!*

The anticipation of her answer was at least ten times greater than the emotional beating I endured as I waited to see her at the airport. It was so quiet. While I was calm on the outside, inside I was screaming, "Say something!"

She didn't say anything.

Now I waited, not for an answer, but for the moment that I should surely dissolve into dust. It occurred to me just then that the longer she took to respond, the worse the news would be—why would it take a long time to deliver good news?

As I looked at her beautiful face in the dim light, I was treated to the sweetest smile I have ever seen. She smiled and looked into my eyes, then cozied in close to me. We sat like that for a long time, and I have never been so happy.

She still didn't say anything.

Selena's Journal
February 17, 2001

I know Duane would've liked to cancel our plans today (as we have had our first disagreement—oh joy), but Mom insisted "You two need to spend some time alone." Not wanting to risk upsetting her and the kids, we reluctantly followed through with our canoe trip on the river. Neither of us was feeling "the love," though.

Before we knew it, there we were. By ourselves. On the river. In a canoe. For four hours! Oh, and if that wasn't pitiful enough, we kept paddling in circles. Apparently, we are not as in sync as we originally thought. Being in the canoe *not* working together, equally determined our paddling prowess was superior, was miserable to say the least. We felt comfortable enough with each other, however, to argue like adolescents about who should listen to whom. If it weren't for the strong, slow current of the New River, we wouldn't have made any progress at all.

It turns out that being trapped in a canoe on a deep and potentially dangerous river requires a more evolved level of communication, and after the initial hour of tortured give and take, we declared a truce of sorts and actually relaxed enough to enjoy the beautiful weather and the sights along the way. We saw about a dozen turtles sitting on a log, sunning themselves. As soon as we got close to them, they all slid into the water and disappeared. And there I was without my camera!

Before we neared our meeting place a few miles downriver, I pulled out a copy of *The Princess Bride* I'd tucked in my bag last night. While Duane paddled, I read some of my favorite passages to him. By the time we got back on land, we liked each other again.

Though realizing that Duane is a formidable opponent in the battle of wits is new and uncomfortable. He doesn't know it, but he's forcing me to look at myself honestly, and I'm unpleasantly surprised by what I see. I think I got more than I bargained for.

Duane's Journal
February 17, 2001

Joy and fear! Contentment and aggravation! This relationship has it all so far. Selena and I have a little joke between us that we have no choice but to make it work now. At this point, if we call it quits, Mom gets custody of me and Emily will leave our little family to go live in Canada with Selena.

A few weeks ago, I was feeling rather proud of myself for coming up with the brilliant idea of bringing Selena's mother for this visit—to keep everything "above board." I can't begin to express how grateful I am for that little nugget of inspiration. It has meant far more than just legitimizing our first meeting. Margaret has been the voice of reason, the peacekeeper, and the source of hopeful, positive thinking during this little visit.

While Selena and I have a lot in common and much to talk about, we have glaring differences too. She's quiet; I'm an extreme extrovert. She's a country girl; I'm a city-slicker. She's thoughtful and deliberate; I'm flyin' by the seat of my pants spontaneous. She's Venus; I'm Mars, and that boy-girl thing can't be overlooked. On top of everything else (and I never would have thought it would be a factor), she's Canadian. Turns out Canada's like this whole other country . . .

One activity that I had planned for just the two of us was a canoe trip down the New River. The idea would've died on the vine if Mom had not insisted that we go as planned. She shot down every objection we had. We had no choice, so off to the river we went.

It started off much the way I expected. We didn't speak to one other much and our lack of harmony was apparent to anyone who witnessed the spinning canoe going down the river. It crossed my mind more than once that this spinning canoe was a glaring metaphor.

I suppose that what brought us together from the start of this whole thing is what saved us on the river. Neither of us can resist nor deny what's funny—and what's funny to both of us is two people insisting that they each know better how to navigate a canoe down the river as it continues to rotate out of control.

So it did get better. We started to cooperate and move that canoe in a much more respectful manner. We started talking nicer to each other and really enjoying the canoe trip. Selena had brought *The Princess Bride* and began reading it to me. I can't remember the last time someone read to me, but I liked it. We enjoyed nature, a good book, and each other's company for the remainder of the trip. We met up with Mom and the kids at Radford University. When we were coming up the bank holding hands, I could see Mom smiling at us—she definitely knows what she's doing.

Duane's Journal
February 21, 2001

Well, we took Selena and her mom to the airport this morning and hung around until they boarded and the plane actually went down the runway. As the plane disappeared out of sight, we began walking back through the airport, making our way to our car.

The noise in the terminal and my kids talking began to fade into the background as I was indulging in the sweet feelings of the past ten days. Going to Parent's Night together and hearing Emily sing "Part of Your World," our infamous canoe trip, traveling to Savannah and to the beach at Tybee Island, and (last but not least) being able to sit together as a couple in church. As I was thinking of Selena and the time we spent together, my thoughts almost involuntarily went even further back. It was as though a movie was playing in my head.

I saw myself sitting without my wife in church and I remembered how it felt. As it played on, there were clips of temple trips, family outings, events with the kids. I could see myself, not always unhappy, but definitely incomplete. I reviewed the mistakes I had made when I began dating and how I came to understand the necessity of marrying in the faith.

Then I saw the times, over and over again, when I'd come home from work. After our evening routine and the kids had gone to bed, I would sit down at the computer. I could see that I lacked faith and my hope was waning as I would plead with my Father in Heaven, "Let tonight be the night." I would then answer my messages and look at profiles, communicating with all the potential Mrs. Duanes', and then retire for the night. Night after night.

As the movie in my head continued and the Selena chapter began to play, I heard a voice clearly in my head. It was Dr. Dennison's voice: "One day you will stand with the Lord and you will look out over a multitude of worthy sisters. You will interview them one by one, and you will find that one who will go with you and be sealed to you as your wife in the temple of God."

I believe it's happening, just like he said it would.

About the Authors

Duane and Selena Pannell first "met" online while living in Virginia and Alberta, Canada, respectively. After a complicated long-distance relationship spanning four years, they married and have a son together.

Their first book is born of a separation in their lives when Selena was in Alberta for several months in 2013 with her dying father. Duane was going through their old correspondence because he is a "mushy man" and thought this was a story worth telling. After some coaxing, he convinced Selena and, with a little help from Google Docs, they began their collaboration on *3,000 Miles to Eternity*.

They've just completed a three-year mission in the LDS Addiction Recovery Program, where they served as group leaders and led two twelve-step meetings a week in Vernal, Utah. Duane is putting the final touches on a manuscript addressing addiction recovery while Selena homeschools their son and teaches archery in her spare time.